Indian Music

Indian Music.

BY

BHAVANRAV A. PINGLE.

GYAN

Published by

Gyan Publishing House
5, Ansari Road
Daryaganj, New Delhi-110002
Phone: 011-47034999, 9811692060
E-mail: books@gyanbooks.com

Distribution Network
gyanbooks.com
India, USA, Canada, UK, Australia, France

ISBN: 978-81-212-8334-2 (PB)
First Published, 1894

2nd Impression 2023

Printed at: Gyan Press, Delhi.

INDIAN MUSIC
Author: BHAVANRAV A. PINGLE

Indian Music.

BY

BHAVÁNRÁV A. PINGLE.

SECOND EDITION.

Bombay:
PRINTED AT THE
EDUCATION SOCIETY'S PRESS, BYCULLA.

1898.

TO

HIS HIGHNESS

BALASINGJISAHEB,

THAKORSAHEB OF WADHWAN,

WHOSE KINDNESS TO THE AUTHOR HAS ALREADY BEEN ACKNOWLEDGED IN THE PREFACE TO THE FIRST EDITION OF THE PRESENT WORK, AND FURTHER CONTACT WITH WHOM SINCE THEN HAS CONVINCED HIM THAT THE THAKORSAHEB, POSSESSED WITH A KIND AND GENEROUS HEART, IS QUIETLY DOING MORE GOOD THAN IS GENERALLY KNOWN, BOTH AS A FIRM AND INDEPENDENT RULER AND A LIBERAL PATRON OF ART AND LITERATURE, FOR WHICH HIS HIGHNESS HAS ALWAYS DISPLAYED A CULTIVATED AND REFINED TASTE.

AS A SMALL RETURN FOR THE THAKORSAHEB'S FURTHER KINDNESS, WHICH HAS ENABLED THE AUTHOR TO APPEAR AGAIN BEFORE THE PUBLIC AS AN ADVCOATE OF INDIAN MUSIC EXPLAINED IN THE ENGLISH LANGUAGE,

THIS VOLUME

IS,

WITH THE KIND PERMISSION OF HIS HIGHNESS,

Gratefully Dedicated

BY

THE AUTHOR.

PREFACE TO THE FIRST EDITION.

The present work neither pretends to give, nor aims at giving, a complete description of Indian music or demonstration of the phenomena of Sound or of the history and laws of Music. Those who wish to study these subjects thoroughly, whether from their scientific or artistic aspect, must have recourse to special works and special study.

To show briefly the broad outlines of Indian Music as an art, and to test them by the light of Western science, has been the aim and scope of this work, which, it is hoped, will be of some interest to the Public.

If there be anything in this work acceptable to the general reader, it is exclusively due to my drawing on thewritings on the *Phenomena of Sound* by Herbert Spencer, Charles Darwin, and a few other English authors, which I have been studying for some time. If there be anything in it interesting or instructive to the admirer of music, it is wholly due to the charms of Indian music.

My best acknowledgments are due to those who have not only cared to make me more or less happy according to their means, but have liberally allowed me to prosecute my study without taking any compensating work from me, and I, therefore, take this opportunity of publicly expressing my sense of gratefulness to Sheikhsáheb Shri Husenmiásáheb, Chief of Mangrol; His Highness Sir Vakhatsingjisáheb, K.C.I.E., Rájásáheb of Lunawada; Kumár Shri Harbhamji-sáheb of Morvi, M.A., LL.M. (Cantab.), Barrister-at-Law; His Highness Bálsingjisáheb, Thákorsáheb of Wadhwan; and Khánshri Sámatkhánjisáheb, Chief of Gidad.

I cannot close this preface without an expression of thanks to my friends Dr. Narotamdás Indraji Vishnav, M.B., B.S. (Durham), Mr. Anantrái Nánálál Buch, B.A., LL.B. (Bombay), and Mr. Kalianrái Jethá Bakshi of Rajkot, for having helped me in the tedious task of going through the proofs of this work.

The nomenclature used throughout this work is not pure Sanskrit, but is the popular one among Indian musicians, and, therefore, no strict rule of spelling is observed.

BH. A. PINGLE.

Rajkot, Kathiawar,

June, 1894.

PREFACE TO THE SECOND EDITION.

THE idea of this work was first conceived by me many years ago, at a time when I had just finished my perusal of the volumes of the *Asiatic Researches*, in which the modes of Hindu Music were, for the first time, presented to the English-reading public through the exertions of Sir William Jones in 1784 A. C.

My object in submitting this little work to the public is to rectify the prevailing erroneous impressions as to the matter-of-fact particulars concerning Indian Music which are hazarded by some authors and their critics, as well as to present the general outlines of it under what I think and believe to be a just and a more comprehensive view. My knowledge of the English language, however, was not equal to the execution of any literary undertaking like this, nor was it until within the last few years of patient study of it that I was able to regularly devote to the work that continuous and exclusive labour, without which, though much may be done to illustrate detached points, no entire or complicated subject like Indian Music can ever be set forth in a way to attract public notice.

Had any learned treatise on Indian Music in all its branches appeared before or after the publication of my first edition of this work, I should probably not have ventured again on so arduous an undertaking. My object in submitting the first edition, as a discussion on Indian Music, of which the present one is only an extension, which owing to more reasons than one I had held over till now, was to invite public attention to this subject. The first edition of my work, in spite of its many faults—such as bad printing, bad arrangement of the subject-matter and of sequence of thought and argument—faults from which my present edition is, I am afraid, not altogether free, has received a warm reception from many educated persons and princes in India.

Darbársáheb Shri Vájsurválá of Bagasará, Kathiawar, a worthy *alumnus* of the Rajkumar College, Rajkot, has himself translated it into Gujarati and has submitted it for revision to Raosáheb Ganpatrám Anuprám Trawádi, Principal of the Male Training College, Rajkot, one of the few recognized translators of English works into the vernacular. I take this opportunity of publicly expressing my grateful thanks to the Darbársáheb for the time and leisure he has spent in preparing my humble work for the Gujarati-reading public. This translation would have been published; but now that my present edition has preceded it, it is deemed necessary that a translation of this edition and not of the first should be presented to the public.

The ablest scholars in other departments of learning can

hardly be said to be competent to expound or judge of the merits or demerits of Indian Music, unless and until they make a special study of it and are supplied with a certain basis of matters of fact, pure and distinguishable from mere fiction, and unless they secure the aid of Indian artists both knowing the art and willing to disclose it. So far as Indian Music in all its bearings is concerned, it is now-a-days a rare phenomenon to meet with an artist who is capable of placing his art in its proper light, even in a limited way, before the public. Under these circumstances this humble work, I hope, will be at least acceptable, if not instructive, to the lovers music, considering that it is submitted by one who has devote many long years to collect as much information on the subject as is at present procurable.

Since the days of Sir William Jones, H. T. Colebrooke, and others, the study of Sanskrit has been prosecuted in Europe with remarkable success, the stock of information and written works, comparatively scanty, handed down from the ancient Hindus, have been collected and illustrated in diverse ways; and if our Manuscripts cannot be multiplied, we at least have numerous interpretations in Europe to catch, repeat, amplify and explain their half inaudible voice in India. Many of the best Sanskrit and Páli works on religon and philosophy have been translate into the English, German and French languages by eminen scholars, so that the present European literary public have been enabled to form some idea of the new light thrown upon many subjects of Indian antiquities by the inestimable aid of modern European civilization, the degree and perhaps the kind of which the world never saw before. The sages, the law-givers, the grammarians and the poets of ancient India have been almost all rendered both more intelligible and more instructive than they were to a student in the beginning of the present century; and the general picture of the ancient Indians may now be conceived with a degree of fidelity which, considering our imperfect materials, it is curious to contemplate and it is incumbent on each and every student in India to gratefully thank those European scholars, who have devoted their lives to the study of Indian subjects in all their diversity with ability and impartiality.

To depict Indian Music as illustrative of the mind of the ancient Hindus of Paurânic, Buddhistic, Sûtra and Bráhmaṇa Upanishada periods, as well as of the Indian Mahomedans a few centuries in the past, is the task which I undertake an the present work, not without painful consciousness of how much the deed falls short of the will; and a yet more painful conviction that full success on the historical and theoretical sides of it is rendered impossible by an obstacle which no human ability can now remedy—the insufficiency, if not the disappearance, of original evidence and the super-abundance of myths; for, in spite of the valuable exposition of certain able European scholars, our stock of information regarding the ancient art of music still remains lamentably inadequate to the demand of the enlightened public of the present century—"the wondrous age," as the late Earl of Beaconsfield, K.G., puts to "of change and progress." We possess only what has scaped the wrecks of several vicissitudes, to which Indian Thought and things have been subjected since the times of Cyrus (about 546 B. C.), Darius (521 B. C.), Xerxés (485 B. C.), and Alexander (326 B. C.) downwards to the times of the British supremacy in India. We are thus compelled to judge the whole Indian Music, eminently multiform as it must ave been, from a few scattered and detached compositions, Excellent, indeed, in themselves, but unmistakeably bearing ie stamp of Mahomedan influence.

Under all the circumstances stated above I was cautiously slow in venturing to appear before the public as an advocate of Indian Music. I have regularly spent these twenty-five years under very trying circumstances in patiently and resolutely studying it, and overcoming many a difficulty in connection with it. I have regularly studied the instrumental music with the help of certain great musicians of the last generation, and also learnt the principles of Indian Music in all its branches. I have also consulted many learned Pandits on the historical and literal side of it.

Before concluding this preface I gratefully acknowledge once more, that, if there be anything in this work interesting or instructive to the general reader, it is wholly and solely due to my indenting on the writings of European authors whose names appear in several places of this work, and of which I have given a separate list. If there be anything in it interesting or instructive to the lover of music, it is exclusively due to the inherent and intrinsic charm of Indian Music itself. I have only expressed and explained the general details of Indian Music in the English language but certainly have not borrowed a single detail from European Music and palmed it off as of Indian origin. I have also refrained from trying in this work to screw up the possible and probable into the certain and infallible, to suppress counterbalancing considerations and to substitute a pleasing romance in place of half-known perplexing realities. My object in this work is to set forth all which can be ascertained, together with such conjectures and inferences as can reasonably be deduced from it, and nothing more.

In importing into this work the theories and problems of Western philosophy and science concerning emotions or feelings, my object has been to show my countrymen that the

Europeans have treated the subject of music most exhaustively in all its aspects. In doing this, I have given more quotations than are generally found in a work of this kind, but my inability to deal with the subject-matter and my anxiety to support whatever I have said in the succeeding pages on historical and scientific authority is my only excuse to the gentle reader. In conclusion it is my humble request that the public will indulgently over-look the defects of language and arrangement, and devote their attention to the substance of my humble brochure.

The nomenclature used in this book is not pure Sanskrit, but the one in common use among the present musicians. The orthography of the musical and oriental terms is the one generally adopted by Oriental scholars for the transliteration of Oriental alphabet in translating the *Sacred Books of the East*, but no very strict rule of spelling has been observed.

I take this opportunity to express my thanks to Mr. Geo. F. D'Penha, Head Reader, Education Society's Press, Bombay, for his valuable help to me in correcting the proofs and in adjusting the tunes in Chapter V. He is, I am convinced, singularly competent for all his work.

While the last chapter of this book was in the Press, I received the painful news of the death of my "guide, philosopher and friend," Mr. Sitánáth Gopináth Ajinkya, B.A., LL.B., Vakil, High Court, Bombay, and late Subordinate Judge, Bhadgam, Khandesh. I shall be wanting in my duty to the deceased gentleman were I to omit to mention in this preface that, had it not been for his moral and intellectual suasion, these pages would not have seen the light of day. He was one of those quiet and unostentatious men, who are *the* back-bone of the Native community of India.

Though he had not the voice, he had the heart and an exquisitely fine ear for music. From my boyhood he took me under his fostering care, moulded and shaped my character, and gave an impetus to my young musical ideas. He subsequently watched my career day after day, and readily gave me advice and instructions whenever needed. I am also deeply indebted to him for his going through these pages while they were in the Press. It is a matter of regret that this worthy gentleman did not live to see how my humble services to the cause of Indian Music were received by a critical and I trust appreciating public.

THE AUTHOR.

Wadhwan, Kathiawar,

9th October 1898.

LIST OF
EUROPEAN AUTHORS AND THEIR WORKS,
EXCLUSIVE OF THE SANSKRIT, PERSIAN AND HINDI AUTHORITIES, QUOTED IN THE PRESENT EDITION OF "INDIAN MUSIC."

AUFRECHT, THEODOR ... Catalogus Catalogorum.

BAGEHOT, WALTER ... Physic and Politics, seventh Edition.

BAIN, PROFESSOR A. ... The Emotions and the Will, third Edition.

DITTO ... Education as a Science, sixth Edition.

BALLENTINE, J. R. ... Sánkhya Aphorisms of Kapila.

BEAL, SAMUEL ... ... A Life of Budha, 1883.

BIRDWOOD, SIR G. C. M. Industrial Arts of India, 1880.

BLASERNA, PROFESSOR PIETRO. Theory of Sound in its relation to Music, third Edition.

BROWN, PROFESSOR THOMAS. Lectures on the Philosophy of the Human Mind, twenty-first Edition.

BUCKLE, HENRY THOMAS. History of Civilization in England, new Edition, 1894.

BÜLHER, PROFESSOR GEORGE. Apastamba, Gautama, Vasishṭa and Baudhyáyaṇa, 1879.

DITTO ... The Laws of Manu, 1886.

CARPENTER, DOCTOR W. A. Animal Physiology.

COLEBROOKE, H. T. ... Miscellaneous Essays, second Edition.

DITTO ... Essays on the Religion and Philosophy of the Hindus, 1858.

DARWIN, CHARLES ... Descent of Man, second Edition.

DITTO ... The Expression of the Emotions, 1873.

DAVIDS RHYS, T. W. ... Budhist Sûttas, 1881.

DITTO ... The Questions of King Milinda, 1890.

DAY, CAPTAIN C. R. ... Notes on Indian Music, 1894.

DESHCANEL, A. P. ... Natural Philosophy, sixth Edition, translated and edited by J. D. Everett.

DRAPER, DOCTOR J. W.... A Conflict between Religion and Science, 1885.

DRUMMOND, HENRY .. Ascent of Man, 1894.

DUFF, GRANT JAMES ... History of the Marathas, 1864.

EGGLING, JULIUS ... The Shatpata Bráhamaṇa, 1882.

ELPHINSTONE, MOUNT-STUART. History of India, 1874.

FIELD, DOCTOR G. P. ... Diseases of the Ear, third Edition, 1882.

FOWKE, FRANCIS... ... Asiatic Researches.

FERGUSSON, SIR JAMES... History of Indian and Eastern Architecture, 1876.

GANOT ... ... Physics, Translated and Edited by E. Atkinson, Twelfth Edition, 1886.

GROTE, GEORGE ... ... History of Greece, a new Edition.

GUILLEMIN, AMÉDÉE ... The Forces of Nature, translated from the French by Lady Norman Lockyer and Edited by Sir Norman Lockyer, third Edition, 1877.

GUIZOT, F. ... ... The History of Civilization, translated by William Hazlitt, 1887.

HEREN, A. H. L. ... Indian Antiquities and Literature.

DITTO ... Asiatic Nations, 1847.

DITTO ... Historical Researches in Ancient Greece, 1854.

HEINEMANN, GASTOR VUILLIER. A History of Dancing.

HELMHOLTZ, VON HERMANN. Popular Lectures on Scientific subjects, translated by E. Atkinson, First series, 1893.

HENRY, C. S. ... ... Epitome of the History of Philosophy, 1865.

HUGHES, THOMAS PATRIC. A Dictionary of Islam, 1885.

HUNTER, SIR W. W. ... A Brief History of the Indian People, 1883.

DITTO .. Imperial Gazetteer, second Edition, 1886.

DITTO ... Narrative of Journey from Agra to Ouzen.

HUXLEY, PROFESSOR T. H. Man's Place in Nature, 1863.
DITTO ... Physiology.
ANONYMOUS ... ... India, Pictorial, Descriptive and Historical, 1843.
JACOBI, HERMAN... ... Jain Sûtras. The Akáranga Sûtras, The Kulpa Sûtras, 1884.
JOLLY, JULIUS ... ... Nárada-Brihaspati, 1889.
JONES, SIR W. ... ... The Works in Six Volumes.
DITTO ... Asiatic Researches.
KERN, PROFESSOR H. ... Saddharma-Púṇḍarîka, 1884.
KUNTE, M. M. ... ... The Vicissitudes of the Aryan Civilization in India, 1880.
LEWES, G. H. ... ... History of Philosophy, 1871.
LOCKE, JOHN GENT. ... Human Understanding, Fortieth Edition, 1877.
MALCOLM, SIR JOHN ... Zinat-ut-Tavárikh.
MALLESON, COLONEL G. B. Rulers of India—Akbar, 1891.
MAX MÜLLER, SIR F. ... A History of Ancient Sanskrit Literature, 1860.
DITTO ... Chips from a German Workshop, second Edition, 1868.
DITTO ... Introduction to the Science of Religion, 1873.
DITTO ... Lectures on the Origin and Growth of Religion, 1878-1882.
DITTO ... Rig-Véda Sanhita, 1869.
DITTO ... Selected Essays on Language, Mythology and Religion, 1881.
DITTO ... The Dhammapada, 1881.
DITTO ... The Science of Language, 1885.
DITTO ... Upanishads, 1879.
DITTO ... Védic Hymns, 1891.
DITTO ... India, What it can Teach Us, 1883.
MILL, J. S. ... ... Three Essays on Religion, Second Edition.
MOORE, THOMAS... ... Lalla Rookh, New Edition, 1868.
NORDAU, MAX ... ... Degeneration, 1895.

OLDENBERG, DOCTOR HERMANN.	Buddha: His Life, Doctrine and Order, 1882.
DITTO ..	The Grihya-Sûtras, 1892.
....	Orchestral Association Gazette, 1898.
PALMER, E. H.	The Al Qur'ân, 1880.
PANDITA, S. P.	Vikramorvasiám, Second Edition.
SCHLEGEL, A. W. ...	Dramatic Art and Literature, translated by J. B. Black, 1861 Edition.
SCHLEGEL, VON F. ...	Philosophy of History, translated by James Burton Robertson, Seventh Edition.
SCHMIDT, PROFESSOR OSCAR.	Doctrine of Descent and Darwinism, 1884.
SPENCER, HERBERT ...	First Principles, Fifth Edition.
DITTO ...	Principles of Ethics, 1892.
DITTO ...	Principles of Psychology, Third Edition.
DITTO ...	Essays, Scientific, Political and Speculative, 1883.
TATYA TOOKARAM, TH. S.	The Twelve Principal Upanishads, 1891.
TELANG, K. T.	Anugîtá, Sacred Books of the East, Vol. VIII.
DITTO	Bhagavada-Gîtà.
THEOSOPHICAL SOCIETY ...	The Theosophic Gleaners, 1894, September and November.
THOMPSON, W. F. ...	Akhlâk-i-Jalâli.
TOD, LIEUT.-COL. JAMES. ...	Annals and Antiquities of the Rajasthana, Second Edition.
TYNDAL, PROFESSOR JOHN.	Sound, Fourth Edition.
VIDYÁSÁGAR, PANDIT J. ...	Sidhánt-Kaumudi, Second Edition.
VIGNOLI, TITO	Myth and Science, Third Edition, 1885.
WHEELER, J. T.... ...	History of India, 1867.
WHITNEY, PROFESSOR W. D.	The Life and Growth of Language, Fifth Edition.
WILLIAM, SIR MONIER.	A Sanskrit-English Dictionary.
WILSON PROFESSOR H. H.	Theatres of the Hindus, Third Edition.
WOOD, S. G.	Illustrated Natural History.

ERRATA.

Page	Line	For	Read
3	20	The above inference of Professor Max Müller may be supported by	He also supports this inference by
7	21	date	data
7	28	leave	leaves
7	30	190	362
22	28	110	153
29	25	stag	stages
31	20	ndia	India
33	24	*Saered*	*Sacred*
33	27	Sûtrass	Sûtras
34	28	*Hindas*	*Hindus*
35	28	filtered	fettered
36	26	Colebrook	Colebrooke
37	28	Budhus	Buddhas
44	29	cresents	crescent
45	8	Te	The
45	24	princes	princess
45	24	Wisha	Ushá
45	29	H. S.	H. T.
45	35	asrial	aerial
54	27	र	रं
58	30	46	465
63	9	Dhsupada	Dhrupada
74	8	to Mr. N. Lockyer, F. R. S.	to the science acousti cs
First Table	14	Lalata	Lalitâ
,,	15	Lalitá	Soheni
"	33	Soheni	Lalata
90	25	Bibhátsa	Bibhása
93	11	Bibhátsa	Bibhása
94	9	Bibhatsa	Bibhása
104	3	ilasak Bhán.	Biláskkháni
108	16	s	is
119	16	a warming	warming
119	16	effect	effects
120	1	determine	determines
121	28	September	November
134	28	565	465 [*India*, p. 505
138	30	of India	of *Aryan Civilisation in*
138	30	fanatical	wild
140	28	s	is
144	11	Katit	Katiṭ
145	30	kne	knew
153	24	Savrita	Svarita

ERRATA—*continued.*

Page	Line	For	Read
196	18	it	they
218	25	58	56
240	18	latter	later
242	23	six	five
248	25	Williams	William
250	10	tawrine	taurine
251	16	and *Puráṇa*	*Puráṇa*
259	25	स्वरा ;	स्वरा
264	9	*Pratisákhya*	*Prátiśákhya*
264	16	*Pratisákhya*	*Prátiśákhya*
264	17	*Pratisákhya*	*Prátiśákhya*
266	10	eight	in order that
266	11	Italian	Italians
277	26	Schll's	Schlegel's
307	2	o	of
313	20	I	It
314	30	Gaston	Gastor
328	10	or that	or
329	16	स्वरा.	स्वरा :
339	28	feet	feel

CONTENTS.

INDIAN MUSIC.

CHAPTER I.

THE HISTORY OF INDIAN MUSIC AND THE THEORY OF MUSIC IN GENERAL.

Music is said to be of divine origin. However that may be, it cannot be denied that music has in all ages and climes exercised a peculiar fascination over the minds of men. Whether as a science or an art it has more or less engaged the attention of most civilized people. In India especially it has flourished from primordial times, so that India is even believed to be the land of its birth and origin. Be that as it may, we are at present concerned with Indian music as such, and of that we will mainly speak in the following pages.

Speaking then of Indian music, it would be presumption on one's part to decide positively whether the singers of former times were more accomplished than those of the present day without first examining such traditions and records as are available on the subject.

In painting, carving, sculpture, architecture,[1] and

[1] Sir James Fergusson in his introduction to the *History of Indian and Eastern Architecture*, (p. 6,) says :—"* * In addition, however, to these scientific advantages it will undoubtedly be conceded by those who are familiar with the subject that for certain qualities the Indian buildings are unrivalled. They display an exuberance of fancy, a lavishness of labour, and an elaboration of detail to be found nowhere else." The same may not inaptly be said of Indian music in its pristine purity.

in the composition and execution of music, many persons would have us believe that we of the present day have, owing to our contact with Western civilizing influences, progressed. A judgment on the former arts may be formed by comparing the old works in those arts with the new ones, but any opinion on the merits or demerits of ancient music can only be based on an examination of it as now available in the specimens of the art and traditions connected therewith, which have come down to us from time immemorial. It is a fact beyond doubt, that the Ancient Hindu music and musical works, and traditions in regard to them, underwent alterations and modifications through the many vicissitudes to which India has singularly been subjected. Our judgment on the worth of Indian music, whether favourable or unfavourable, will, therefore, be based on a study of the said music, its works and traditions with the said alterations and modifications. Owing to the general reverence for old writings which are received almost as divinely inspired in India, it is difficult to find any persons or authors who have examined and studied the old works on the subject on their own intrinsic merit, but it shall be our attempt to do so in this work.

The Indian musicians, in spite of the absence of material encouragement in recent times, have preserved and protected the ancient plant of music from its total annihilation, and have given us a legacy which, though imperfect, will, if properly utilised, be found to be of considerable assistance to us in coming to a right conclusion.

It is a well-known fact that the art of writing, though known to Indians for centuries,[1] was hardly resorted to by them as a means to perpetuate their learning. Their mode of transmitting knowledge was by means of verses[2] committed to memory[3] under per-

---

[1] Nearchos, who had accompanied Alexander the Great (about 325 B. C.) tells us that in the Panjab the writing was on well-beaten and smooth cloth. Wheeler's *India*, Vol. III., p 200.

Professor Heeren in his *Asiatic Nations*, Vol. II., p. 202, says: " ** Further, Sanskrit literature is not only very rich, but also in a certain sense extremely ancient. Everything concurs to establish the fact that Alphabetical writing was known in India from the earliest time**."

Professor Max Muller reasonably proves that at the time of Panini the art of writing was unknown in India. He bases his inference on the absence of any mention by the great grammarian, of pen, ink, and paper. The learned Philologist says that there are no words in Panini's Sutras for writing materials.

The above inference of Professor Max Muller may be supported by the fact that no mention is made of any writing materials in the Grihya-Sûtras although they mention every act of man from birth to death: in them mention is also made of his *oral studies*, but nowhere of *written studies*. This was the case with the early Greeks before 660 B. C. George Grote's *History of Greece*, Vol. II., p. 83.

[2] H. T. Buckle in his *His. of Civi. in En.*, Vol. I., pp. 132, 133, says: "The Hindu works on grammar, on law, on history, on medicine, on mathematics, on geography, and on metaphysics, are nearly poems, and are put together according to regular system of versification."

[3] Professor M. Muller says:—"Writing was unknown in India before the fourth century before Christ, and yet we are asked to believe that the Vedic literature—in three well-defined periods, the Mantra, Brahamana, and Sutra periods—goes back to at least a thousand years before our era. Now the Rig-Veda alone, which contains a collection of ten books of hymns, consists of 1,017 (1,028) poems, 10,580 verses, and about 153,826 words. How were these poems composed—for they are composed in very perfect metre—and how after having

sonal tuition and expressing the sense in very condensed and concise language, peculiarly adapted to be fastened on the memory. A faculty of recollection intensely cultivated and the brevity of expression above referred to were the principal means of preserving the accumulated knowledge of ages.

The case with musical literature was not otherwise. Much of it was handed down from generation to generation, through the recollection of the great masters and composers. Moreover, such of our ancient writings on music as are extant are greatly mixed up with foreign and imported matter, which has scarcely any relevancy with music, but which is brought in, as a necessary auxiliary to it, when the art of music was thought to be a gift from the divinity of Anthropomorphites. Under such circumstances the study of these traditions and writings is not attended with inconsiderable difficulty.

Indian traditions abound in instances of musical talent, such as Haradása, Rámadása, Suradása, Tánasena,

---

been composed were they handed down from 1500 before Christ to 1500 after Him, the time to which most of our best Sanskrit MSS. belong? Entirely by memory. The art of teaching had even at that early time [1500 B. C.] been reduced to a perfect system, and at that time certainly there is not the slightest trace of anything, such as a book, or skin, or parchment, a sheet of paper, pen, or ink, being known even by name to the people of India; while every expression connected with what we should call literature, points to a literature (we cannot help using that word) existing in memory only, and being handed down with the most scrupulous care by means of oral tradition." *India, what it can teach us*, pp. 208, 209. This was the case in Greece before the seventh century B. C.

Láda, Kapola, and their predecessors and successors too many to mention here. These artists in their respective times had made music their life-long study, and had been so much absorbed in it that most of them preferred an ascetic life to wordly enjoyments, and thus had become not only men of reverence and genius of their generation, but are even remembered and respected to this day on account of the keenness of sense in their execution and compoeition.

When we examine without bias the various sources of music, such as the hymns from Sáma-Veda,[1] religious ceremonies, devotional prayers, social performances, desultory works on music, and the cultured practice of many a family of musicians in which it has so extensively been spread; and when we bring it in a system-

[1] The Sáma Veda, if heard when recited by sweet voices and studied as a musical piece, shows that almost all the elements of our present music are to be found in their ancient forms, although not well-defined and developed. The Sáma is subsequent to the Rig, and shows a progress in music when compared with the Rig, which has its own metrical system. The Sáma does not deal only with the metres, but also with the tones of which some are explosive, combined, and trilled. The present reciters of Sáma show that what they perform by the right hand and its fingers is a notation which Colebroke tells us was once well established. They have in all from four to six svaras (notes) and a few upasvaras (supplementary notes). When they emit a long sound they measure its duration in time by counting the fingers with the thumb of the right hand. When there is a combination of notes (we have nothing to do here with the letters of the hymn recited) it is shown by drawing a line by the thumb on the last finger. The trill is shown by shaking the index finger, and the explosive is shown by a stroke or percussion of the thumb and the index finger without producing a noise. If the Sáma is recited according to its rule with due regard to its notes the impression cannot be otherwise than musical. It is true that the Sáma is a musical declamation of the ancient Hindus. If our Hindu princes and nobles care and attempt to revive their ancient hymns on the model of chorus singing of Europe, the Sáma will be typical for its religious music.

atized form to tell its own tale, we can safely affirm, without fear of exaggeration, that it had once reached a higher stage of development than it is generally credited with.

The above assertion will be looked down upon by many as absurd, and even be thought paradoxical by right-thinking men, who justly admit that Western education has successfully instilled and widely spread a new force of European growth into Indian thought, which has progressed and is still progressing, under the British supremacy, in refinements, arts, sciences, and in general knowledge.

The validity of the said assertion, however, is not a hypothetical one, but is based on reliable and reasonable sources, which form the subject-matter of this work. It is true, that we have no direct evidence of history in its narrow sense, but this difficulty can be overcome by critically examining the extant and traditional resources which go to form a history.

History, as is said in its earlier stages, was regarded chiefly as a form of poetry,[1] recording the more fabulous and dramatic actions of Kings, Queens, Heroes, Heroines, Sages, Poets, Singers, &c., and was sung as ballads[2] by bards, and was told as legends or stories by story-tellers. History, as comprehended

[1] "What we now read as poetry and legend was once accredited history and the only genuine history which the first Greeks could conceive or relish of their past time." George Grote's *History of Greece*, Vol. I., Preface, p. viii.

[2] See H. T. Buckle's *His. of Civi. in England*, Vol. I., p. 291.

now, teaches us that the historical or great men were the products of their societies. Without certain antecedents and a certain average national character, they could neither have been generated nor could have had the culture which formed them. If their societies were reinfluenced by them to a certain extent, they were both, before and after birth, influenced by their societies. They were the results of all those influences which fostered the ancestral character they inherited and the social institutions to which they belonged, so that such social changes, which were directly attributable to individuals of unusual power, were still indirectly traceable to the social causes which produced these individuals.

Instead of enlarging on the elements of history, let us rather attempt a justification of the proposition predicated by us that Indian music was of higher origin and of nobler development than it is generally considered to be, and that it is dying out for want of support. This we shall now proceed to do by reasonable inferences and deductions from solid date of history in its extended sense.

It is said of Tánasena,[1] the famous singer of the latter part of the 16th century, that this wonderfully

---

[1] Within the enclosure which surrounds this monument (at Gwalior) is a small tomb to the memory of Tánasena, a musician of incomparable skill who flourished at the Court of Akbar. The tomb is overshadowed by a tree (tamarind) concerning which a superstitious notion prevails, that the chewing of its leave will give an extraordinary melody to the voice. *Narrative of a Journey from Agra to Ouzein*, by W. Hunter. Lalurukha, Note 235, p. 190.

skilled and gifted artist sang so melodiously and so irresistibly charmed the feelings of his hearers with his emotional cadences, that the kind and great Akbar, then Emperor, on hearing his performance, styled him a paragon of cadences. The vocalist was not only raised to be one of the Emperor's immediate courtiers, an honour deservedly bestowed on those admitted to be specialists in their respective spheres of vocation, but was paid adulation as a personification of sound. It is a well-known fact that in our day instances seldom occur of similar infatuation—if by infatuation is meant appreciation and admiration—which overpowered Akbar so much. It is lamentable that we have got no immediate means to fathom how many pious, heroic, and noble hearts must have been impressed by different emotions, how many bright eyes must have been made brighter, and how many fair bosoms must have heaved on hearing the dulcet notes and religious pathos of Suradása, Bhikudàsa,[1] Rámadása, Tulsidása, Kabiradàsa and other celebrities of past ages. What known and unknown conquests those artists must have achieved in their times and places? But our present public are more circumspect and are taught to keep their feelings more under command than to give way to hasty expressions of delight in public, and they cannot be blamed for so doing, otherwise the world would

---

[1] The elder brother of Tánasena was famous for reciting the *Máhábhárata* in Rágas. He did not embrace the Mahomedan religion as his younger brother did.

not perhaps be edified thereby. Therefore, the mask worn by the public to screen their emotional expressions may be said to be a necessary evil with which we must remain content, and must bring ourselves to be looked upon as more intellectual than emotional !

H. T. Buckle[1] says :—"The emotions are as much a part of us as the understanding[2] ; they are as truthful ; they are as likely to be right. They obey fixed laws ; they follow an orderly and uniform course ; they run in sequences ; they have their logic and method of inference. Poetry,[3] therefore, is a part of philosophy, simply because the emotions are a part of the mind."

To be dead to any natural expression of emotion is simply impossible from a naturalist's standpoint. If any being is devoid of natural expressions, it necessarily follows that it is dead to the impressions, which act as stimulants, technically called *reflex actions*.

The law of reflex action teaches us, that an impression on the end of an *afferent* (sensory) nerve is conveyed to some ganglionic centre, and is thence usually reflected along an *efferent* (motor) nerve to one or more muscles which it causes to contract ; nervous

1 *History of the Civilization in England*, Vol. III., p. 378.

2 Doctor W. A. Carpenter says :—"With ideas are associated feelings of various kinds, which constitute passions and emotions."—*Animal Physiology*, pp. 349, 350.

3 H. Spencer says :—"Poetry is a form of speech used for the better expression of emotional ideas."

excitation always tends to beget muscular motion ; and when it rises to a certain intensity, it always does beget it. Those external actions, through which we read the feelings of others, show us that under any considerable tension the nervous system, in general, discharges itself on the muscular system, either with or without the guidance of the will. It is manifest that emotions and sensations tend to generate bodily movements which are forcible in proportion as the emotions or sensations are intense.

It is proved that equal stimulants produce unequal effects on differently constituted and circumstanced species of animal including man with his different stages of civilisations or advancement to adaptation. It is moreover proved that, as knowledge progresses, the mode of impressions and expressions, metaphysically called objective and subjective, becomes more complex and economical than simple and violent, in obedience to the law of the least resistance and greatest traction or the resultant of the two, but none the less impressive and expressive in its total effect.

The following paragraphs, though long and many, completely show how the superfluities or original necessities are cast away and the economical or better adapted ones are acquired and accumulated.

It is an open secret that the art of writing is of later origin than that of speaking. It is said that the arts of writing and printing have descended from picture-language. The most primitive form of permanently symbolizing a thing was by depicting it on a wall, that is by representing something like the thing to be imitated. In process of time, as the symbols grew habitual and extensive, the most necessary of them became fixed and thus economized, and passing through the hieroglyphic and idiographic stages, they lost all apparent relations to the things signified, just as the verbal language did.

Verbal language, according to H. Spencer, "consists, at the beginning, of symbols which are alike to the things symbolized as it is practical to make them. The language of signs is a means of conveying ideas by mimicking the actions or peculiarities of the things referred to. Verbal language is also, at the beginning, a mode of suggesting objects or acts, by imitating the sounds, which the objects make or with which the acts are accompanied. It needs but to watch the gesticulations with which the savage accompanies his speech—to see a Bushman or a Kaffir dramatizing before an audience, his mode of catching game, or to note the extreme paucity of words in primitive vocabularies—is to infer that at first attitudes, gestures, and sounds were all combined to produce as good a *likeness* as possible of the things, animals, persons or events described; and that, as the sounds came to be understood by themselves, the gestures fell into disuse, leaving traces, however, in the manners of the more excitable civilized races."

With regard to the origin and development of language, Charles Darwin says:—"After having read on the subject, I cannot doubt that language owes its origin to the imitation and modification of various natural sounds, the voices of other animals, and man's own instinctive cries, aided by signs and gestures. When we treat of sexual selection, we shall see that primeval man, or rather some early progenitor of man, probably first used his voice in producing true musical cadences, that is, in singing as do some of the *Gibbon-apes*[1] at the present day; and we may conclude from a widely spread analogy, that this power would have especially been created during the courtship of the sexes and would have expressed various emotions, such as love, jealousy, tri umph, and would have served as a challenge to rivals. It is, therefore, probable that the imitation of musical cries by articulate sounds may have given rise to words expressive of various complex emotions. The strong ten-

[1] S. G. Wood, M. A., F. L. S., in his *Illustrated Natural History*, pp. 35-37 says:—"Rather more has been noticed of this wonderful creature (Gibbon) and further insight into its habits has been gained by means of a female specimen, which was captured and brought safely to London, where it lived for some-time. * * * To judge of the cry of the female Gibbon, it is quite a musical performance, capable of being set to musical notes, and coming to an abrupt conclusion, by a couple of bars in octaves. The animal achieved the chromatic scale, admirably effecting the descent with a precision and rapidity as those of the limbs. The note on which the creature began was E; and starting from this note, she began a series of chromatics, first ascending to the above octave, and then descending in the same way, but always sounding the lower E, almost simultaneously with the upper note, whatever that note might be."

dency in our nearest allies, the monkeys, microcephalous, idiots, and in the barbarous races of mankind, to imitate whatever they hear, deserves notice as bearing on the subject of imitation. Since monkeys certainly understand much that is said to them by man, and, when wild, utter signal cries of danger to their fellows; and since fowls give distinct warning of danger on the ground, or in the sky from hawks, may not some unusually wise ape-like animal have imitated the growl of a beast of prey, and thus told his fellow-monkeys the nature of the expected danger? This must have been a first step in the formation of a language. As the voice was used more and more, the vocal organs would have been strengthened and perfected through the principle of the inherited effects of use—and this would have re-acted on the power of speech. But the relation between the continued use of language and the development of the brain has, no doubt, been far more important. The mental powers in some early progenitor of man must have been more highly developed than in any existing ape before even the most imperfect form of speech could have come into use; but we may confidently believe that the continued use and advancement of this power would have reacted on the mind itself, by enabling and encouraging it to carry on long trains of thought, which no more can be carried without the aid of words, whether spoken or silent, than a long calculation without the use of figures or algebra. It appears, also, that even an ordinary train of thought almost requires, or is greatly facilitated by, some form of language. A long succession of vivid and connected ideas may pass through the mind, without the aid of any form of language, as we may infer from the movements of dogs during their dreams. We have also seen that animals are able to reason, to a certain extent, manifestly without the aid of language. The intimate connection between the brain, as it is developed in us, and the faculty of speech, is well shown by those various cases of brain diseases in which speech is especially affected. There is no more improbability in the continued use of the mental and vocal organs leading to inherited change in their structures and functions, than in the case of hand-writing, which depends partly on the form of the hand and partly on the disposition of the mind, and hand-writing is certainly inherited."

"Several writers have lately insisted that the use of language implies the power of forming general concepts, and that as no animals are supposed to possess this power an impassable barrier is formed between them and man. With respect to animals, I have already endeavoured to show that they have that power, at least in a rude and incipient degree. As far as infants from ten to eleven months old are concerned, it seems to me incredible that they should be able to connect certain sounds with certain general ideas, unless such ideas were already formed in their minds. The same remarks may be extended to the more intelligent animals. A dog forms a general conception of cats or speech, and knows the corresponding words as well as a philosopher. And the capacity to understand is as good a proof of vocal intelligence, though in an inferior degree, as the capacity to speech."

"Why the organs now used for speech should have been originally perfected for this purpose rather than any other organs, it is not difficult to see. Ants have considerable powers of intercommunication by means of their antennæ. We might have used our fingers as efficient instruments, for a person with practice can report to a deaf man every word of a speech, rapidly delivered at public meeting; but the loss of our hands whilst thus employed would have been a serious inconvenience. As all the higher mammals possess vocal organs, constructed on the same general plan as ours, and used as a means of communication, it was obviously probable that these same organs would still be further developed if the power of communication had to be improved; and this has been effected by the aid of adjoining and well adapted parts, namely, the tongue and lips."

"The fact of the higher apes not using their vocal organs for speech, no doubt, depends on their intelligence not having been sufficiently advanced. The possession by them of organs, which with long continued practice, might have been used for speech, although not thus used. is paralleled by the case of many birds which possess organs fitted for singing, though they never sing. Thus the nightingale and crow have vocal organs similarly constituted, these being used by the former for diversified song, and by the latter only for croaking."

Professor W. D. Whitney[1] says:—"Man is, to be sure, an imitative animal, as we may fairly say, but not in an instinctive or mechanical way. He is imitative because he has the capacity to notice and appreciate what he sees in other animals or in Nature, and to reproduce it in imitative show, if anything is to be gained thereby—whether amusement or artistic pleasure or communication. He is an imitator just as he is an artist; the latter is only the higher development of the former.* * The scope of the imitative principle is by no means restricted to the sounds which occur in Nature, although these are the most obvious and easiest subjects of significative reproduction."

Professor Huxley[2] says:— "Brutes, though from the absence of language (as understood from a theologist's point of view), can have no trains of thoughts, but only trains of feelings, yet have a consciousness which, more or less, distinctly foreshadows our own."

Tito Vignoli, in his philosophical treatment of *Myth and Science*, says:—"Nor will it be disputed that we find in animals implicit memory, judgment, and reasoning, the inductions and deductions from one special fact to another, the passions, the physiological

[1] *Life and Growth of Language.*
[2] *Man's Place in Nature.*

language of gestures, expressive of internal emotions, and even, in the case of gregarious animals, the combined action to effect certain purposes ; so that, as far as their higher orders are concerned, animals may be regarded as a simple and undeveloped form of man, while man, by his later psychological and organic evolution, has become a developed and complex animal."

According to modern researches, the voice is a transformation or equivalent of the respiratory movements. The respiratory mechanism with its adjuncts, in addition to its respiratory function, becomes of service in the case of man, animals, birds, and some insects, as a means of expressing emotion. The respiratory column of air, moreover, in its exit from the chest, is frequently made use of, in a mechanical way, to expel bodies from the upper passages. Hence arise a number of peculiarly modified and more or less complicated respiratory movements, such as sighing, coughing, laughing, &c., to secure special ends, which are not distinctly respiratory. But as we have to confine our remarks solely to vocal sound, we of necessity should not enlarge on the movements of the organ of respiration. The vocal organ is nothing more than a wind instrument. A blast of air, driven by a more or less prolonged expiratory movement, throws into vibrations two elastic membranes, the *Chordæ Vocales*. These impart their vibrations to the column of air above them, and so give rise to the sound we call voice.

The emission of sound by the organ of voice in many kinds of animals, including man, is efficient in the highest degree as a means of expression. When the sensorium is strongly excited, the muscles of the body are generally thrown into violent action, and as a consequence loud sounds are uttered, however silent the animal generally may be.

The phenomenon of sound, which is most interesting and instructive to us, is produced by the organ of voice in man, under different sensations and emotions. The vocal sound, as an indispensable interpreter of our thoughts and feelings, and the peculiar sounds and noises of animals, which express their wants and emotions, pleasurable and painful, are caused by the reflex action.

Charles Darwin philosophically says[1]: "Through man's power of intellect, articulate language has been evolved, and on this his wonderful advancement mainly depended. A physiological analysis of the faculty of language shows that even the smallest proficiency in it might require more brain-power than the greatest proficiency in any other direction. This faculty has justly been considered as one of the chief distinctions between man and other lower animals. But man is not the only animal that can make use of language to express what is passing in his mind, and can understand more or less what is expressed by another : a kind of monkey, when

---

[1] *Descent of Man*, pp. 8 to 92.

excited, utters at least six distinct sounds, which excite, in others of its kind, similar emotions. The movements of the features and gestures of monkeys are understood by us, and they partly understand ours."

"It is a more remarkable fact that the dog, since being domesticated, has learnt to bark in at least four or five distinct tones. Although barking is a new art, no doubt the wild parent species of the dog expressed their feelings by cries of various kinds. With the domesticated dog, we have the bark of eagerness, as in the chase; that of anger, as when growling; the yelp or howl of despair, as when shut up; the baying at night; the bark of joy, as when starting on a walk with his master; and the very distinctive one of demand or supplication on wishing for a door or window to be opened. How the barking of the dog, which serves to express various emotions and desires, and which is so remarkable from having been acquired since the animal was domesticated, and from being inherited in different degrees by different breeds, was first learnt, we do not know; but may we not suspect that imitation has had something to do with its acquisition (to meet new conditions or environments), owing to dogs having long lived in strict association with so loquacious an animal as man?"

"Language is an art. It differs, however, widely from all ordinary arts, for man has an instinctive tendency to brew or bake. Moreover, no philologist supposes that any language has been *deliberately* invented. It has been evolved and unconsciously developed by many steps. The sounds uttered by birds offer, in several respects, the nearest analogy, for all the members of the same species utter the same instinctive cries expressive of their emotions; and all the kinds which sing exert their power instinctively; but the actual song and even call-notes are learnt from their parents or foster-parents. These sounds are no more innate than language is in man. The first attempt to sing may be compared to the imperfect endeavour in a child to babble. The young males continue practising for ten or eleven months. Their first essays show hardly a rudiment of the future song; but as they grow older, they sing their song. Nestlings which have learnt the song of a distinct species, as with the canary-birds educated in Tyrol, teach and transmit their new song to their offsprings. The slight material differences of song in the same species inhabiting different districts may be appositely compared to provincial dialects; and the songs of allied, though distinct, species may be compared with the languages of distinct races of man."

"The habitual use of articulate language is, however, peculiar to man, but he uses, in common with the lower animals, inarticulate cries to express his meaning, aided by gestures and the movements of the muscles of the face. This especially holds good with the more simple and vivid feelings, which are but little connected with higher intelligence. Our cries of pain, fear, surprise, anger, together with their approximate actions, and the murmur of a mother to her beloved child, are more expressive than any words."

"That which distinguishes man from the lower animals is not the understanding, for every one knows dogs understand many words and sentences. It is not the mere articulation which is our distinguishing character, for parrots and other birds possess this power. Nor is it the mere capacity of connecting definite sounds with definite ideas, for it is certain that some parrots, which have been taught to speak, connect unerringly words with things and persons with events."

The foregoing details by H. Spencer, Ch. Darwin, and others, show that an instinctive tendency to acquire an art is not peculiar to man; the lower animals, however, differ from man solely in his almost infinitely larger power of associating together the most diversified sounds and ideas; and this obviously depends on the higher development of his mental power.

It is absolutely true that even the higher animals, excluding man in higher stage of evolution and civilisation, have no exact idea of the determinate intervals (musical notes) which are the fundamental basis of higher music. It is to be clearly understood that the philosophers and naturalists, on whose writings we have been drawing, never thought of asserting that the present man-like apes, with all their structures and functions, would ever reach man; but they have scientifically proved that there exist common traits, structural and functional, between man and ape, which show that the ancestors or progenitors of both were from a common stock in the remotest period possible. As this subject is not strictly within the limits of this work, we only recommend the reader, for further information, to study Professor T. H. Huxley's *Man's Place in Nature*. The Professor[1] says: " . . . At the same time, no one is more strongly convinced than I am of the vastness of the gulf between civilized man and the brutes; or is more certain that, whether from them or not, he is assuredly not of them; or as it is put by Henry Drummond,[2] 'It is certainly the fact that Man is not descended from any existing ape. The anthropoid apes branched off laterally at a vastly remote period from the nearest human progenitors' . . For an anthropoid ape could as little develop into a man as could a man pass backwards into an anthropoid ape."

It is evident that mere words are dull sounds if they are not accompanied by some force or by different accents, and that the same sounds, if differently modulated, produce different ideas. These modifications of voice, produced by feelings, are the means by the aid of which the like feelings in others can be engendered. Add to this voice, expressions and gestures of face, which give life to the otherwise dead sounds in which the intellect utters its

[1] T. H. Huxley's *Man's Place in Nature*, p. 110.
[2] Henry Drummond's *Ascent of Man*, p. 10, 1894.

ideas and which enable the hearers, not only to understand the state of mind they accompany, but to participate in it. All speech is composed nominally of two elements, but in reality they are so inseparably interwoven that we cannot draw a line where the words end and the tones, in which they are uttered, begin. But we can say that the words are the signs of ideas and the tones are those of feelings. It is true that certain articulations express the thought, while certain vocal sounds convey more or less the feeling of pain or pleasure which the thought gives; or, in other words, the word or concept is predicative, while the tone or accent in which it is uttered is demonstrative. The one is the co-relative of the other. In the absence of word, no concept[1] is possible; and in the absence of accent, no demonstration is possible.[2]

Prof. Muller says[3]:—"Formerly the accent might have been considered as something late, artificial, and purely grammatical: but the science of language has

[1] Professor Max Muller, *Chips from a German Workshop*, Vol. IV., p. 463, says:—"The conceptional thought is impossible without language * * * Professor Carriere Munchen says: 'Language is meant first for forming, afterwards for communicating, thought.' Word-making, he says, with great truth, 'is the first philosophy—the first poetry of mankind;' we can have sensations, desires, intentions, but we cannot think, in the proper sense of the word, without language."

[2] Professor Oscar Schmidt, in his *Doctrine of Descent and Darwinism*, says: "The greater number of authorities, on linguistic grounds, comparative and philosophical, have been forced to the conclusion that, from an irrational primordial state, manlike beings became human; while with language, the work of many years, reason made its appearance. Stenthal says 'As language arises mind originates.'"

[3] *Chips from a German Workshop*, Vol. IV., p. 223.

shown that it is as old as language itself, and it has rightly called it the very soul of words."

He also says :—"We may speak in singing, and sing in speaking ; we may speak in whispering, and whisper in speaking ; we may even sing in whispering, and whisper in singing ; in fact, we seldom speak without either singing or whispering certain portions of our words."

Using the phrase "vocal expression" in an extended sense as covering all modifications of vocal sounds, we may say that vocal expression is a means for the conveyance of thoughts and feelings. This double function of even spoken language is dimly recognized, but in practice we invariably find that more weight is attached to the tones than to the words, and the former are more relied upon than the latter.

Tito Vignoli says:—"When chanted speech was formulated in a fixed order by means of rhythm and the modulations of the voice, it became verse, and the melody itself, as the simple expression of the song which had been cast into verse, or even into an articulate chant, was naturally evolved from it. An artistic education is not needed in order to experience the pleasure of rhythmic order in the succession of sound, for a predisposition of the nervous system will suffice. Savages and children, and even animals, are sensible of rhythm, which is the order and symmetry of sensations. The dance, as Beauquier justly observes, is the practical form of rhythmic motion and the gesture of music. The motion impressed by sound on the internal organism tends to manifest itself in external gesture, and in fact, the rhythm of the music is repeated in dancing in the limbs and in the whole body of the dancer. Vico, Strabo and others[1] have asserted that primitive men spoke in song, and there is great truth in the remark. Since gesture and pantomime only help out the meaning of imperfect speech, which was at first poor in the number of words and their relative forms, and this is still the case among some people, so song, vocal modulation, and the rhythmic expression of speech seem to stimulate emotion. Thus speech, gesture, and song, in the larger sense of the word, had their origin together."

The tones of speaking, of reciting, and of singing severally exemplify one general principle—that the tones of excited feelings are more sonorous than those of common conversation, because muscular action is directly proportional to mental excitement. Expressiveness of speaking, of reciting, and of singing, is a question of tones, for these three phases of vocal sounds, under which all vocal phenomena are explained, are interchangeable by the admission or dismissal of the variety and duration of tones.

Music, which is said to be the most powerful of all arts, has been evolved from its most primitive function in a great number of animals, including man with his

[1] *Science and Myths*, p. 295.

different stages of development—to charm and call the opposite sex; and that in man's advanced stage of civilization it has been evolved to emotionally express the most complex sentiments, which intellectual or articulate language and poetry could not express. To add more to the vocal charms, science began to invent many musical instruments, or supplementary senses which, in animals, are confined to bodily movements, intensely performed during the pairing season on the earth, in the water and the air.

Professor A. Bain[1] says :—" . . The third and last power of music is derived from *expression* or the reflex of the human emotions. Music imitates the tones of the human voice, which are the most flexible and expressive signs of human feeling, and is capable of representing emotional strength or intensity."

Dr. Seemann[2] most thoughtfully says :—" We can concentrate greater intensity of feeling in a single musical note than in pages of writing."

In human nature feeling and intellect, though apparently different, are undoubtedly inseparable because there could be no feeling without intellect and intellect without feeling. Every student of philosophy or *unification* of knowledge knows that no thought is possible without things thought of; moreover, we may treat intellect and feeling objectively, and infer that no thought or intellect is possible without emotion

---

[1] *Emotions and Will*, p. 236.

[2] *Descent of Man*, p. 571—Ch. Darwin.

or feeling of pain or pleasure which is its attribute, and that complexity of thought or intellect involves complexity of emotion or feeling, and that complexity of impressions involves complexity of expressions.

It is a truism that the highest intellectual manifestations imply a good balance of the highest feeling; but it is also true that the highest intellect is possible only with the highest feeling. They are so inseparably interwoven that we cannot draw a sharp line of *demarcation* where intellect or thought begins, and emotion or feeling proper to that intellect or thought ends, or *vice versâ.*

The tissue of every thought or feeling resolves itself into affections of consciousness. What we call affections of consciousness are subjective states of objective forces.

I have treated the above subject at some length to rectify the erroneous notion of many of my countrymen who believe that the highest intellect means the absence, total or partial, of emotion or feeling; and that, when music, even in its higher stage of development, means emotion or feeling, it must either be abandoned or discouraged. It can be said with confidence that as higher intellect is a product of civilization, so is also higher emotion the product of the same agency.

Apart from the above considerations, which belong more to natural sciences and philosophical speculations than to music proper, let us consider what was the state of the Indian society in which those wonderful singers, of whom we have spoken before, lived, and what is its present state. From all that can be gathered, it seems, that in former times there were a few fine voices in existence in each generation, as is the case now. But in our day there appears to be an amount of affectation, which, if dilated upon, would, at once, seal the fate of many who pass as artists of no mean calibre. Besides, it is a question whether people in the present age are so capable of appreciating music as they were in former times, and whether we have got the same opportunities and facilities to indulge in it. Is it too much to say that music as an art is not at all understood except by a very few, who are probably prejudiced in favour of an artist or two whom they delight to pet and flatter? Are not our educated men quite indifferent to music, partly for its objectionable surroundings and partly for their want of taste for it? Nobody cares for its revival and encouragement, because the well-to-do are not generally alive to its charms, and those who like it and practise it as a vocation are hardly above their immediate wants in the struggle for life owing to changed circumstances. Lastly, what steps have been taken to solicit the State patronage towards learning music as such? To suppose that music will be resuscitated and systematized without the necessary support[1] from the State, is too idle a dream to be realized. Under the

[1] Professor A. Bain, in his *Education as a Science*, p. 97, says:—"In the exercises suited to infants, Time and Rhythm are largely employed. Of all the fine arts, the most available, universal, and influential is Music. This is, perhaps, the most unexceptionable, as well as the cheapest, of human pleasures.

present educational policy of Government, and even from the report of the last Education Commission, there is no hope of any movement in the direction of State help. Government are quite in the dark about the true value of Indian music. They paid neither attention nor rendered help to it which they did to Indian literature, prose and verse. Unless music forms a part of the curriculum in schools and colleges, as do the classical and vernacular languages and even athletics, and unless some enterprising[1] European scholars of music devote themselves to its regeneration, there will neither be its revival nor will it be brought to such a system as would meet the wants of modern society. The most elementary way to teach music is to make the pupils recite their poems to the accompaniment of the harmonium or such other instruments, and thus to cultivate a taste in youths to produce a musical voice, and to appreciate it. It is really a pity to hear the rude and rustic tones in which poetry is recited in our educational institutions without the least regard to concordance. Our Indians never make any progress independently of the ruling power. Men, who have closely studied the problems of Indian administra-

---

It has been seized upon with avidity by the human race in all times; so much so that we wonder how life could ever have been passed without it. In earlier stag , it was united with Poetry, and the poetical element was of equal, if not of greater, power than the musical accompaniment."

[1] Lieut.-Col. J. Tod (*Rajasthan*, Vol. I., p. 466) says :—"An account of the state of musical science, amongst the Hindus of early ages, and a comparison between it and that of Europe, is yet (A. D. 1806 to 1817) a desideratum in oriental literature." Sir W. Jones, Professor H. H. Wilson, Sir W. W. Hunter, and a few others are also of opinion that Indian music deserves to be inquired into by European scholars."

tion, say that the Indians are so unpatriotic as not to be able to do anything substantial without State assistance because they have been subjected from time immemorial to a despotic Government—a Government by whom everything is done for the people and nothing by them.

It will not be out of place here to mention, that even the Mahomedans patronized Hindu music to the best of their means, notwithstanding their religion[1] was averse[2] to music in any form.[3] It is a fact that the Mahomedans took a liking for music when their religious fervour was sufficiently tempered by the intermixture of new conversions, by their intermarriages and contact with the Hindus, and by acclimatization, and also when they began to look upon India as their adopted home. It is true that the Mahomedans had marred and checked every progress of Hindu

---

[1] In the sacred books of the Mahomedans no mention of music in any form is made, except at page 166 (*Sacred Books of the East*, Vols. IV. and IX.), where it is said:—" * * nor to their people shall they return ; but the trumpet shall be blown, and behold from their graves into their Lord shall they slip out."

[2] " Music is generally held by Mahomedans to be contrary to the teachings of the Prophet ; for Náfi relates that when he was walking with Ibn'Umar on a road they heard the music of a pipe, and that Ibn'Umar put his fingers into his ears and went on another road. Náfi then asked Ibn'Umar why he did so, and he said : 'I was with the Prophet, and when we heard the noise of a musical pipe, he put his fingers into his ears, and this happened when I was a child." *Musiát*, Book XXII., Ch. IX., Pt. 3; *A Dictionary of Islam*, by Thomas Patrick Hughes, B. D., M. R. A. S., 1885.

[3] " From attending a single party or listening to a single couplet (poetry) of this description the mind may contract vice from which it can only be freed by long perseverance in irksome expedients and diversified remedy," p. 156, *Practical Philosophy of the Mahomedan People*. Translation of the *Akhlák-i-Jalálí*, by W. F. Thompson, Esquire, of the Bengal Civil Service.

thought and things in the beginning of their conquests and consolidation of their power and authority, as they did in other parts of their conquests. But eventually they have not only adopted Hindu music as an ennobling art, but resorted to it with certain alterations as an additional force to their Marshiás[1] and Sojas,[2] which are composed and sung to the sacred memory of their Imàms, Hasen and Husen. It is exceedingly probable that the love with which Hindu music inspired the Mahomedans was considerably due to the intolerance of their religion for natural expressions of emotion. They had brought with them their arts and poetry for which they were celebrated, but no music. As a matter of course, their patronage and intercourse were so powerful and forcible that they changed the feature of original music, and wonderfully separated it from its parent stock. This fact can be verified by comparing the Sanskrit music (which is very rare in its original purity) of Southern ndia with the one prevailing in Northern India, which now form the two principal schools of Indian music. Both are based upon the same original musical stock, *i.e.*,

---

[1] It is a remarkable fact that the easiest and most common mode of reciting Marshias or wailing songs of the Mohorams has been adopted since some few years back, in vernacular schools, Kirtana and in Nataka to recite poems conveying diverse emotions or feelings.

[2] Sojas are old and really musical as they are set to various Rágas and only sung by the professional Mahomedan musicians during the Mohorams. In these performances no instrumental music is resorted to by them, while Marshias are recited without regard to musical notes, and it is a custom to have new ones for every year if available. Anis' and Dabir's are the best of Marshiás in the Urdu language.

Aryan, and the differences between them are only on the surface and due to the cultivation of the same in the North and South by the Mahomedans and the Dravidians respectively. This is confirmed by the fact that the two schools of music do not so materially differ from each other as do the Aryan and Dravidian families of languages. It is opportune to say that our present music is an offshoot of the ancient Sanskrit music. Our present poetry of music is mainly in the Brija Bháshá. The oldest poems set to music (Chijás), that have come down to us, are in the Brija Bháshá, and the present nomenclature of music is Sanskrit, though in a corrupt form. Five words in six, perhaps, of the Brija Bháshá are derived from Sanskrit: so the two languages are allied. For further information about the alliance of the Brija Bháshá with music, see *Asiatic Researches*, Vol. I., p. 340.

It is said, that the ancients must have heard an amount of sweet and plaintive voices, because no ceremony, either religious or social, was performed without music. Music was thought to be a necessary part, not only of secular enjoyments and of religious devotion,[1] but of bloody warfares and funeral ceremo-

[1] "Therefore, let a priest who is going to perform the sacrificial work of Sáma singer, desire that his voice may have a good tone, and let him perform the sacrifice with a voice that is in good tone." *Brihadáranyaka-Upanishada*, Adhyáya 3, Bra. 27; *Sacred Books of the East*, Vol. XV., p. 83. This clearly shows that the ancient Hindus were very scrupulous about the music of their Sáma-Veda and religious prayers.

nies.[1] Music is said to have been performed by a number of devotees by day and by night. Temples and halls are said to have been thronged by numerous musicians and bards. It is said that music was so much developed and spread that different melodies were fixed for different parts of the country and of the day and night and even for different seasons. Every village of importance had a bard or minstrel of its own who entertained his village patrons by extolling the deeds and personalities of great men and women, or by singing moral poems composed by great sages. Those sages were revered who were more stoic than epicurean. It is believed that the art of music was the principal enjoyment of the ancient Aryas, because they had a limited number of arts and sciences to attend to.

It is said that there were many musicians in possession of lands free from State imposition. This method of patronizing music was of great antiquity. Rávana[2] of the *Rámáyana*, according to tradition, had given a large province to his musicians, and he was himself proficient in music. There is still a musical instrument, which is now played by the beggars in Guzarat and other parts of India, called Rávanhatá. Almost all the kings,

---

[1] Ashvaghosha (*Sacred Books of the East*, Vol. XIX, p. 322) in his life of Budha, says:—"They placed the dead body of Tathágata; * * then using every kind of dance and music." This custom seems to be very ancient as we find it in *Grihyasútras*. It was also in practice among the past historical nations. In Europe there are a few musical compositions designated as Dead March.

[2] Grant Duff's *History of the Marathas*, Vol. I., p. 18.

who governed Ancient Indians, were more or less patrons or artists of music, and they were given special instructions[1] in it. Even Royal ladies were not prohibited from acquiring the arts of singing, dancing, and gesticulation.

In short, looking at the historically fabulous number of musicians who were employed in religious,[2] political and social[3] institutions, and looking at the method of their music, we are forced to admit that the ancients had a considerable taste for music. Arts like commodities are improved only by their corresponding demands. It is said that, as a relic of former times, we have many religious and itinerant singers who are spread all over the country, and that they show in a wonderful degree the sweetness and plaintiveness of voice which is attributed to its hereditary transmission and its further development.

It is true that the songsters of whom we have just spoken are generally minstrels who sing either to the Ektárà (one-stringed lyre), Morli (wind instrument made of gourd), or to the Kinri (crude form of Sarangi

---

1 "Chand remarks of his hero, the Chohan, that he was master of the art, both vocal and instrumental. * * The sacred music was a part of early education with the sons of kings."—Tod's *Rajasthan*, Vol. I., p. 558.

2 It appears from the literature of India that in the palaces of kings there was a chamber or hall known as the Sangita-shálá, the music saloon, in which dancing and singing were practised and sometimes exhibited. *Theatre of the Hindus*, Vol. I., Preface ix., Vol. VI., Third Ed.—H. H. Wilson.

3 The Princes of ancient India not only received instructions in music, but they also composed musical poems or hymns. Colebrooke's *Essays*, p. 10.

or fiddle) heroic or religious narratives versified by themselves and set to music of their own composition, and thus they unite in themselves the separate offices in advanced societies of poet, composer, and instrumentalist.

We have selected the above case as a typical one of the lowest form of music, to show that the progress from simple to complex was considerably displayed in the multiplied differentiations which each of them underwent in Aryan societies. Instead of dwelling here on the many forms of dancing, poetry, and music, which must have come into use in the course of Aryan civilization, and instead of occupying space in dilating upon the progress of poetry[1] of the various forms of metre, of

---

[1] M. Yate (Sanskrit alliteration in *Asiatic Researches*, Vol. XX., p. 159) says :—" No other people (excepting the Hindus) have ever presented an equal variety of poetic compositions. The various metres of Greece and Rome have filled Europe with astonishment; but what are these compared with the extensive range of Sanskrit metres under its three classes of poetical writing ?"

H. T. Buckle (*His. Ci. En.*, Vol. I., p. 133) says :—" The Sanskrit can boast of metres more numerous and more complicated than have ever been possessed by any of the European languages."

Heerene (*Indian Ant. and Lit.*, Vol. II., p. 109) says :—" Poetry, in all its various forms, whether lyric, epic, or dramatic, appears to have been the peculiar appanage of Sanskrit, as is sufficiently evinced by the many excellent poets of either class, who, for so many ages, have made it the vehicle of their compositions. It also admits the employment of rhyme, without, however, being filtered by its restrictions, nor is it unacquainted with alliteration, while it seems to have appropriated all the most delicate species of metre for which the Indian ear is susceptible."

The composition of Aryan verse and metre as shown by the researches made by Westphal and others into the metrical system of the Vedic Aryans, from the Turanians and the Greeks, implies a common origin of the fact that their metres are the same. The demonstration is complete, if we compare the iambic

rhyme, and of their general culture, let us confine our attention to the immediate subject in hand.

To return to our subject, we say that we do not find a single class of Indians, however crude its social institutions may be, dead and insensible to music of its own. Some of the airs, which are sung by certain classes, are pleasant if musically performed. It was a common practice, in former times, to teach the youths their lessons in tones of music. This practice was considerably due to the oral[2] transmission and verse-literature. Every Hindu of high caste was taught, more or less, to praise and pray to his divinity by certain intonations called Vratta, Chhanda, Prabandh, Gita, &c. The Vrattas and Gitas, which have come down to us, are really pleasant if musically expressed, and these give us an idea of the poetical singing of the ancient Hindus. This class of singing has not at all been influenced by the Mohomedan intercourse on account of its religous bearing.

Those who have studied the above subject pronounce that this class of singing has not been what we call singing; but nearly allied to it, and, as such, is much less

---

metre of Archilochus with that of the Vedic hymns. There are in both these series of iambuses—the diametre, the calaileptic, trimetre, and acataleptic.

In short, the orientalists, such as Max Müller, Schlegel, H. H. Wilson, Colebrook, and many others, who have studied the subject of Indian metres, pronounce that the Hindu metres are highly developed and show a great deal of beautiful style; and that the Hindus had poetry in its three principal branches, *viz.*, lyric, epic and dramatic.

[2] The poetical form—rhythm and metre impresses the ear, and is an aid to memory.—Professor A. Bain.

remote from common speech than singing is, for poetical singing is, in all respects, intermediate between speech and song. Its average effects are neither so loud nor so low as those of song. Its tones are less sonorous in *timbre* than those of song. Commonly it travels to a smaller extent from the middle notes, and it uses notes neither so high nor so low in pitch. Those intervals habitual to it are neither so wide nor so varied. Its rate of variation is not rapid; and, at the same time, its primary *rhythm* is less decided. It has none of the secondary *rhythm*, which is one of the marked characteristics of song; and last, but not least, its average duration of notes is neither so long nor so short as that of song.

The Hindus were such devoted admirers of music that they worshipped it not only as an off-shoot[1] of one of the four sacred Vedas,[2] but they composed their *Sáma-Veda* to be chanted or sung. Ascetic or stoically abstemious Budhists[3] and Jains, too, were not indifferent to the charms of music. Even now, it is generally believed by the Hindus that the royal way

[1] Gándharva Veda is upa Veda or supplementary Veda.

[2] The conception of the Maruts as singers was most familiar to the Vedic Rishis. *Rig Veda Sanhita*, Vol. I., p. 78.—Max Müller.

[3] I-tsing, the Chinese priest, says:—"The hymns used in the Budhist church during his visit to India (671 to 695 A. D.) were composed and arranged by Ashvaghosha. This Ashvaghosha, who was afterwards revered as one of the Budhus, was a musician and poet. He travelled in India about the first century A. D. with a body of musicians and was the means of converting many persons of distinction by his skill." *Sacred Books of the East*, Vol. XIX., Introduction, xvxvi.; *Chips from a German Workshop*, Vol. I., p. 217; *India, What can it teach Us?* p. 211.—Professor Max Müller.

to win over the deity is to say its praise and prayer in music. Every religious act is performed either in singing, in bodily movements, or in muttering and in gesticulation. We cannot pass over without remarking the fact that, even in the most advanced nations of the world, the praise and prayer are generally accompanied by music. This class of music, which is called devotional music, is used like an all-absorbing, engrossing and concentrating agency or force—to completely divest oneself of all the affairs of all-powerful and ever-felt secularism, and to impress on him or on her nothing but vague (though believed to be grand and solemn) influence of Him or the Unknowable. In the Chinese annals it is said, "music hath the power of making heavens descend upon earth." People, who are religiously inclined, call music a divine[1] art.

It will not be grudged to quote here Herbert Spencer's most thoughtful exposition of the vocal sounds. He says: "The vocal phenomena have a physiological basis. They are so many manifestations of the general law that feeling is a stimulus to muscular action—a law confirmed throughout the whole economy—not of man only—but of every sensitive creature—a law, therefore, which lies deep in the nature of animal organization. The ex-

[1] Tito Vignoli (*Myth and Science*) says:—"The ordinary modes of expression respecting music, which are in use not only among uneducated people, but among those who are educated and civilized, display the earlier and innate belief in the mythical representations of this art. The expression may be often heard: What divine music! What angelic harmony! This song is really seraphic! and the like."

pressiveness of those modifications of voice is therefore innate. Each of us, from babyhood upwards, has been spontaneously making them when under the various sensations and emotions by which they are produced. Having been conscious of each feeling at the same time, we heard ourselves make the consequent sound, we have acquired an established association of ideas between such sound and the feeling which caused it. When the like sound is made by another, we ascribe the like feeling to him; and by a further consequence we not only ascribe to him that feeling but have a certain degree of it aroused in ourselves: for to become conscious of the feeling which another is experiencing is to have that feeling awakened in us, which is the same thing as experiencing the feeling. Thus these various modifications of voice become not only a language, through which we understand the emotions of others, but also the means of exciting our sympathy with such emotions."

The illustrious Charles Darwin says:[1] "Music and impassioned speech become *intelligible* to a certain extent, if we may assume that musical tones and rhythm were used by our half-human ancestors during the course of courtship, when animals of all kinds are excited not only by the love, but by the strong passion of jealousy, rivalry, and triumph. From the deeply laid principle of inherited associations, music in this case would be likely to call forth vaguely and

---

[1] *Descent of Man*, pp. 572, 573.

indefinitely the strong emotions of a long-past-age. We have every reason to suppose that articulate speech is one of the latest, as it certainly is one of the highest, of the arts acquired by man, and, as the instinctive power of producing musical notes and rhythms is developed low down in the animal series, it would altogether be opposed to the principle of evolution, if we were to admit that man's musical capacity has been developed from the tones used in passioned speech. We can thus understand how it is that music, dancing, song, and poetry are such ancient arts. We may go further than this, and believe that musical sounds afforded one of the bases for the development of language. As the males of several quadrumanous animals have their vocal organs much more developed than in the females, and as a female Gibbon, one of the anthropomorphous apes, pours forth a whole octave of musical sounds and may be said to sing, it appears probable that the progenitors of man, either the males or females, or both sexes, before acquiring the power of expressing their mutual love in articulate language, endeavoured to charm each other with musical notes and rhythms. So little is known about the use of voice by quadrumana during the season of love, that we have no means of judging whether the habit of singing was first acquired by our male or female ancestors. Women are generally thought to possess sweeter voice than men, and, as far as this serves as any guide, we may infer that they first acquired musical power in order to attract the other sex. But, if so, this must have occurred long ago, before our ancestors had become sufficiently human to treat and value the women merely as useful slaves.

"The impassioned orator, or bard, or musician, when he with his voiced tones and cadences excites the strongest emotion in his hearers, little suspects that he uses the same means by which his half-human ancestors long ago aroused each other's ardent passions during their courtship and rivalry.

"Naturalists are much divided with respect to the object of the singing of birds.[1] Montagu and a few others maintained that the males of song-birds and of many others do not in general search for the female, but, on the contrary, their business in the spring is to perch on some conspicuous spot, breathing out their full and amorous notes, which, by instinct, the female knows, and repairs to the spot to choose her mate. Mr. Jenner Weir informs me that 'this is certainly the case with the nightingale.' Beepsteen, who kept birds during his whole life, asserts that 'the female canary always chooses the best singer, and that in a state of nature the female finch selects that male out of a hundred, whose notes please her most.' There can be no doubt that birds closely attend to each other's song. Mr. Weir has told me of the case of a bull-finch which had been taught to pipe a German waltz, and he was a good performer. When this bird was

[1] *Descent of Man*, pp. 368-370.

first introduced into a room where other birds were kept, and when he began to sing, all the others, consisting of about twenty linnets and canaries, ranged themselves on the nearest side of their cages, and listened with the greatest interest to the new performer. Many naturalists believe that the singing of birds is almost exclusively the effect of "rivalry" and "emulation," and not for the sake of charming their mates. This was the opinion of Daines Burrington and White of Selborne, both of whom especially attended to this subject. Burrington, however, admits that 'superiority in song gives to birds an amazing ascendancy over others,' as is well known to bird-catchers. It is certain that there is an intense degree of rivalry between the males in their singing. Bird-fanciers match their birds to see which will sing longest. I was told by Mr. Yarrell that a first-rate bird sometimes sings till he drops down almost dead, or, according to Beepsteen, quite dead from rupturing a vessel in the lungs. Whatever the case may be, male birds, as I hear from Mr. Weir, often die suddenly during the season of song. That the habit of singing is sometimes quite independent of love is clear for a sterile hybrid canary-bird has been described as singing whilst viewing itself in a mirror, and then dashing at its own image ; it likewise attacked with fury a female canary when put into the same cage."

The above facts, which are so philosophically expounded, show that we do like the sounds which habitually accompany agreeable and pleasurable feelings, and dislike those sounds which invariably accompany disagreeable and painful feelings. Music adopts all the sounds which we like, and intensifies them more and more when it ascends to its higher and higher forms, and becomes music or language of emotion simply in virtue of thus intensifying them. Music is rationally supposed to have influenced man in making those involved cadences in common conversation by which he conveys his complex thoughts and feelings.

Again, music, in every stage of development, is an embodiment of all the sounds which men make when they are under pleasurable sensations and emotions. In ordinary speech and poetry they are used as instruments to express pleasure and humor, and do not last long, and their intensity is of no great magnitude. In music these instruments are lengthened and determined. In painful sensations and emotions the voice is never steady, but makes abnormal leaps from one sound to another with the greatest possible irregularity; while in music it preserves a certain regularity of duration and pitch. Hence music, in its higher form, deals more with the determinate intervals (musical notes) than do poetry and speech.

To return to the subject in hand we say that we have but a very small portion of the ancient music.

A large quantity of classic music must ever remain sealed to us, because we neither possess the means to collect and decipher many manuscript works[1] on music which are secreted in different quarters like a sacred and invaluable trust, nor are we conversant with the knowledge of old musical works and notations,[2] nor have we any standard work and notation of the modern origin in force. These difficulties are partly due to the proverbial selfishness of Indian musicians who do not like to part with the secret of their art, and partly to the want of taste in the public at large. If we attempt to write on Indian music as a science, independently of European researches and resources, we have but very scanty means at our command to produce even a small treatise. Such a treatise cannot stand the critical test of a devout student of music and convince an impartial judge that the modern treatment of it is as thoughtful and original as it was in the

---

[1] In Theodor Aufrecht's *Catalogus Catalogorum*, an Alphabetical Register, we find the names of about forty-four manuscripts on music by different Hindus of different times; and some of them are supposed to have been copied from ancient literature. We shall give the names along with other names of the works in the chapter on the History of Musical Scale.

[2] Sir W. Jones says :—"* * By substituting long vowels, the *time* of each note is doubled, and other marks are used for a further elongation of them; the octaves above and below the mean scale, the connection and acceleration of notes, the graces of execution or manners of fingering the instrument, are expressed very clearly by small circles and ellipses, by little chains, by curves, by straight lines, horizontal or perpendicular, and by crescents, all in various positions: the close of a strain is distinguished by a lotus-flower; but the time and measure are determined by the prosody of the verse and by the comparative length of each syllable, with which every note or assemblage of notes respectively corresponds * *." *Asiatic Researches*, Vol. III., p. 69.

times when Nárada, Bharata,[1] Shiva,[2] Hanumana and Kanáda[3] (the recognised author of the doctrine of Vaisheshik or atomic theory) flourished. Kanâda was right in saying that sound was propagated by undulations that sent wave after wave in all directions from a central point. Some of the maxims, which we find in some of these authors are presented in an unorganized

---

[1] H. H. Wilson (*Theatre of the Hindus*, Vol. I., p. xx., 3rd Ed.) says:—"Te attribution of dramatic performances to Bharata is, no doubt, founded upon his having been one of the earliest writers. by whom the art was reduced to a system. His Sûtras (aphorisms) are constantly cited by commentators of different plays, and suggest the doctrines which are taught by later authors but, as far as has been ascertained, the work of Bharata has no existence in an entire shape, and it may be sometimes doubted whether the rules attributed to him are not fabricated for the occasion."

[2] (*Ibid.*) "The invention of the dramatic entertainments is usually ascribed by Hindu writers to a Muni or inspired sage, named *Bharata.* * * * The dramatic representations first invented consisted of three kinds: Náṭya Nritya, and Nritta. Siva added to these two other styles (Nritya and Nritta) of performance, the *Tandava* and *Lasya* * *. The *Tandava* and *Lasya*, which appear to be grafts upon the original system, are merely styles of dancing; the former so named from Tandava, one of Sivá's attendants, whom the god (Siva) instructed in it, whilst the *Lasya*, it is said, was taught by Párvatí to the princes *Wisha*, who instructed the Gopis of Dwarka, the residence of her husband, in the art; by them it was communicated to the women of Sauráshṭra, and from them it passed to the females of various regions." There is a common belief among the present musicians of India that there were in former times four different schools of music, namely, Shiva, Hanumat, Bhárati, and Márgi.

[3] H. S. Colebrooke (*Essays. Re. Phe. Hus.*, p. 154) says:—"According to Kanáda five elements are produced from the five elementary particles or rudiments:—(1st) A diffused ethereal fluid (Akásha) occupying space: it has the property of audibleness being the vehicle of sound, derived from the sonorous rudiment or ethereal atom. (2nd) Air, which is endowed with the properties of audibleness and tangibility, being sensible to hearing and touch, derived from the tangible rudiment of aerial atom." In this description we find the ancient Hindus had discovered that the vehicles of sound were solid, liquid, and gaseous bodies; and that the cause of its production was either purcussion or friction or both. But the language used is certainly not so explicit. English equivalents used by Colebrooke are conjunction (percussion) and disjunction (friction); the former is illustrated by the cymbals, drum, and stick, and the latter by the rustling of leaves.

form, or they stand isolated dogmas or empirical generalizations, which are neither so clearly comprehended nor so much respected as they would be, were they reduced to some intelligible form.

When we look, without bias, at the researches of Kanáda and others we are forced to admit that the ancients had made a considerable progress in music, not only as an art, but as a science in the remotest period of their civilization. It is deplorable that the data, which must have been adopted by Kanáda and others to propound their theory of sound, should permanently be lost and nothing left of them, except the simple generalizations of their researches, to show and prove specifically what were the means which had caused a theory of sound probable at such a remote time of antiquity.

Professor H. H Wilson[1] says :—"It is impossible to conceive a language so beautifully musical, or so magnificently grand, as that which contains many of the verses of Bhavabhuti and Kálidása."

F. Schlegel[2] says:—"In its grammatical structure the language of India is absolutely similar to the Greek and Latin, even to the minutest particulars. But the grammatical forms of the Sanskrit are far richer and more varied than those of the Latin tongue, and more regular and systematic than those of Greek."

---

[1] *Theatre of the Hindus*, Vol. I., Diction XIII.

[2] *Philosophy of History*, p. 191.

Professor Max Muller says:—"The orthography of Sanskrit is the most complete and the language inflectionable."

When the Sanskrit language has thus been admitted on all hands to be one of the most inflective and grammatically finished languages of the civilized world, it seems inexplicable why the language of emotion which is not only its co-existent but parent-stock—should be discarded and condemned as barbarous. It cannot be said to be a sane proposition that Hindus were civilized only in expressing their intellect or thought but they were barbarous in expressing their feeling or emotion. These two elements of vocal expressions are inseparable, and are the necessary outcome of civilized life.

Sir W. Jones and Col. Tod[1] say:—"Amongst Hindus of early ages music appears to have attained a theoretical precision at a period when even Greece was little removed from barbarism."

We assert without fear of contradiction, that the ancient music and works on it, which have come down to us, if properly fathomed to the bottom, abound in artistic, scientific, and philosophical speculations. It is a fact that the old works have scarcely been brought forward in a connected form; we are obliged to collect their tenets more from a number of scattered fragments which are dispersed through works on mythology, theology and literature, than from a treatise exclusively devoted

[1] Tod's *Rajasthan*, Vol. I., p. 466.

to the subject. When mythology and theology are duly eliminated it seems simply absurd to deny that the ancient Hindus had made a considerable progress in music as an art as well as a science. Their inventions and researches of the musical scale, their treatment of the Gamut, their distinction between sound and noise, their composition of so many Vratas, Gitas, &c., and their selection of so many Rágas and Tálas are too thoughtful to be trifled with.

In concluding this chapter, which treats partly of the history of Indian music and considerably of the origin and development of music in general—though in not a very connected form—it must be stated that a higher form of music is not possible in the absence of a complete musical scale. We have now to see whether the Hindus of the ancient times had a complete scale. This we intend to do in Chapter II. by giving a comparative ratio of the European and Hindu theories of Gamut, not with the object of refuting the European theory which is admitted to be correct, but to prove that the ancient Hindus had invented a Gamut perfect in practice as the European one.

It should be borne in mind that, however the ratios may theoretically differ in the European and Hindu theories of Gamut, or Gráma, practically that is not the case. That which is discordant to the one is also discordant to the other. The difference lies only in composing the Notes which form a musical piece, but not in the *Notes themselves.*

CHAPTER II.

THE THEORY AND PRACTICE OF MUSICAL SOUNDS.

The name of "Gamut" (Gráma or Saptaka) is given to a series of seven sounds which succeed each other, proceeding from the grave to the acute, or *vice versâ*. The grave and acute sounds are the two extreme notes having the following character, namely, the highest sound is produced by double the number of the vibrations of the lowest. The most acute note being the eighth of the series, the two extreme notes are the octave of each other: one being the lower octave, the other the higher one. If we now start from the eighth note, considered as the starting-point of a series of notes similar to the first, and if we take care to strike a new series of notes having between them the same degree of pitch as the first, it will be noticed that the impression left on the ear by their succession has the greatest analogy with that which results from hearing the notes of the first scale. A melody, thus formed of a succession of notes taken from the first series, preserves the same character if it is sung or played with the help of notes of the same order taken in the second series. It would be the same if we formed in a similar manner one or more Gamuts, higher or lower.

A musical scale of the above kind, formed of consecutive Gamuts, is unlimited, or at least has no other limits than those of our power of perceiving sounds.

We may remark that the note from which we start to form a Gamut is arbitrary,[1] because there is a vast number of similar musical scales placed by Nature at the disposal of musicians.

In Europe the seven sounds are called C, D, E, F, G, A, and B. These letters are repeated for each octave, with the terms sharps and flats for the intermediate notes. The same sounds are also called by other names, which are derived from the first syllable of each line of a Latin hymn written by Paulus Diaconus.[2]

The European and Hindu schemes of Gamut (Saptaka), if expressed mathematically, would stand thus :—

	1	2	3	4	5	6	7	8
European—	Ut or Do.	Re.	Mi.	Fa.	Sol.	La.	Si.	Do_2.
	24	27	30	32	36	40	45	48
	1	2	3	4	5	6	7	8
Hindu[3]——	Sá.	Ri.	Ga.	Ma.	Pa.	Dha.	Ni.	$Sá_2$.
	22	26	29	31	35	39	42	44

[1] In Europe, for practical purposes, they have conventionally adopted a fixed point of departure.

[2] Ut quam laxis
Resonare fibris
Mira gestorum,
Famuli tuorum
Solvi Polluti
Labii reatum
Sancte Johannes.

The Italians substituted *Do* for *Ut* for the first note of the Gamut, in the seventeenth century (A. D.) *The Forces of Nature.* Amédéé Guillemin. Edited by Lockyer, pp. 187. Third Ed.

[3] "Sa, ri, ga, ma, pa, dha, ni."

"Three of the above syllables are, by a singular coincidence exactly the same, though not all in the same place, with three of those invented by David Mostare, as a substitute for the troublesome Gamut used in his time, and which he arranges thus: Bo, ce, di, ga, lo, ma, ni." Sir W. Jones, *As. Res.*, Vol. III., pp. 68, 69.

These notes are distinguished by the relative number of vibrations each makes in a second. So that whatever note we might conventionally select as a true Sá. (C) having a certain number of vibrations per second, the relation of all the other notes to it could be expressed mathematically, and this is exactly what is done in the above schemes.

The ratio of one sound to another is the determining cause of consonance and dissonance, or, in other words, a musical scale is the melodious relationship of the number of vibrations (per second) of the notes of which it (musical scale) is formed. Here in connection with the Gamut it may be mentioned that in the Hindu system these ratios are styled "Shrutis" which literally mean what is heard or perceived. In the older Sanskrit works their number is stated to be 22, thus:— चतुर्भिर्जायते षड्जो मध्यम : पंचमस्तथा । द्वाभ्यां द्वाभ्यां गनी ज्ञेयौ रिधौ च त्र्यात्मकौ तथा ॥१॥ In some of the modern writers their number is variously stated as 16 or 27, thus :—

Sá.	Ri.	Ga.	Ma.	Pa.	Dha.	Ni
1	3	3	2	1	3	3 =16
1	5	5	5	1	5	5 =27

But there appears to be no scientific basis for these, and therefore the less we speak of them the better.

Sá, Ri, Ga, Ma, Pa, Dha, and Ni, are the initial syllables of the names by which the seven sounds of the Indian Saptaka (Gamut) are called, and these letters are repeated for each octave with the terms "Komala"

(Flat) and "Tivra" (Sharp) for the intermediate notes. These names of the notes seem to be as arbitrary as those adopted in Europe, though attempts have been made by early Hindus to justify them. The names are thus:—(1st) Khashṭaja or Kharaja or Shaḍja, (2nd) Rikhaba or Rishaba, (3rd) Gandhára, (4th) Madhyama, (5th) Panchama, (6th) Dhaivata, and (7th) Nikháda or Nisháda.

Practically speaking, all the tones (which are given in the above schemes), in spite of their respective differences in the ratio of the number of vibrations per second which correspond to each of them, are classed as Shudh-Svaras (whole tones) and Komal-Svaras (half-tones or semi-tones). The Saptaka, like its European analogue the Diatonic scale, consists of seven notes, of which five are whole tones, *viz.*, (2nd) Ri., (3rd) Ga., (5th) Pa., (6th) Dha., and (7th) Ni.; and two are semi-tones, *viz.*, (4th) Ma., and (8th) the duplex of the first Sá. Excepting the 4th and the 8th or the first, which are already Komala (flat) or semi-tones, we can reduce or flatten the remaining five tones to ten semi-tones, and thus get in all twelve notes (as in the scale) called chromatic as distinguished from the Diatonic.

The above classification is in complete accord with that adopted in Europe. But the peculiarity of the Indian's is that, though the Panchama (Sol. or G), which when reduced to a half-tone ought to be named Komala-Panchama consistently with the nomenclature adopted in the case of the other 4 Komala notes, is nevertheless called by them Tivra or Kaḍi Madhyama (Fsh.) instead. There are reasons given for this departure from the general rule in the old works, but they are simply puerile.

The names[1] of the 12 notes are :—

(1) Shaḍja (C), (2) Komala-Rikhaba (C Sh.), (3) Rikhaba (D), (4) Komala-Gandhára (D Sh.), (5) Gandhára (E), (6) Madhyama (F), (7) Tivra Madhyama or Kaḍi Madhyama (F Sh.), (8) Panchama (G), (9) Komla-Dhaivata (G Sh.), (10) Dhaivata (A), (11) Komala-Nikháda (A Sh.), (12) Nikháda (B), and (13) Shaḍja (C′, repetition of the first in the second octave).

It would be well to observe here that in the old Sanskrit works on music the notes of the Diatonic scale are called अविकृत and those of the chromatic scale विकृत. "शुद्धा: स्वरा: सप्त विकृता द्वादशाप्यमी ।"

Physiologically speaking, the ordinary human ear is capable of appreciating tones having 33 to 4,000 vibrations per second, *i. e.*, from the lowest bass (C, 33 vibrations) to the highest treble (C^5, 4,224 vibrations of the Piano) ; tones above and below these, even when audible, can hardly be distinguished from each other.

According to the Indian idea of music, the compass of the human voice (generally of a matured male) is

[1] Francis Fowke, in describing the "Biná," says:—"It is very observable that the semitones change their names on the same semitones as in the European scale." *Asiatic Researches*, Vol. I., pp. 250-254, Popular Ed., No. V.

three scales (Saptakas)—one (Ánudátt) below the register (Svaritt) and one (Udátt) above it. This is also the general arrangement of their instruments. Indians were not satisfied with the 12 notes (chromatic scale), and so increased the number of notes under the name of Murchhanás (musically ¼ part of a tone). The number of these Murchhanás is 21, but it ought to be 12 only. These Murchhanás are distributed over all the Rágas with the greatest advantage. The Indian scale with the aforesaid addition stands thus—5 tones, 2 semi-tones of the diatonic scale or 12 notes of the chromatic scale and 12 Murchhanás. We shall allude to the latter presently.

Indian music is popularly divided into Rágas[1] and Ráginis or Bháryás, *i. e.*, female Rágas. They are not however, as is popularly supposed, two distinct modes, of musical composition. For looking to their formation, a Rága is as much a Rágini as a Rágini is a Rága. This distinction, therefore, into a Rága and a Rágini, is a distinction without a difference. The Ráginis are said to be female Rágas simply because their names end in ई ("*I*"), a feminine termination.

Practically speaking, the real division is between Rágas or Ráginis and Jilhá or Dhun. The characteristic distinction between a Rága or Rágini and Jilhá or Dhun is that the former has a fixed number of notes (no

---

[1] 'रञ्जयतीति रागः' इति भरतः Bharata defines a राग (Rága) as a musical composition that pleases.

accidentals[1]), a regulated arrangement of traversing the notes upwards and downwards, and above all a number of Murchhanás ($\frac{1}{4}$ part of a tone). Again, the former has, in addition to tones and semitones which are the only constituents of the latter, the principle of Árohana (ascent, or going from the grave to the acute) and Avarohana (descent, or going from the acute to the grave), of Murchhaná, of Gamaka or Ghrashṭaka (literally that which slips, *i. e.*, musically a connecting of two or more notes), of Menḍa or Minḍa, which is also musically a joining of two or more notes but practically effected in a slightly different way on certain musical instruments, as will be explained hereafter; while the latter is free from all these restrictions, that is, it has only tones and semitones, but never a Murchhaná, and very rarely Ghrashṭaka or Minḍa; and no fixed arrangement of Árohana and Avarohana. This distinction, however, is not strictly observed nowadays, as practised musicians often embellish a Jilhá with some of the characteristics of a Rága at random.

Gamaka, or Ghrashṭaka, or Menḍa (now called Minḍa) is a way of sliding from a note to another or others at a stretch; it is not jumping, but is an exceedingly attractive mode of connecting two or more notes. The Minḍa or Ghrashṭaka is an impossibility on the Organ, Piano, Harmonium, Concertina, and such other instruments, so long as they exist in their present form.

---

[1] Notes which do not enter into the original composition of a Raga.

Although we admire the real excellence of European instruments, we are reluctantly constrained to say that, however slow or fast one may attempt to traverse from any one note to any other on these instruments, the impression left on the ear is always of jumping and not that of imperceptibly connecting two notes. To give an idea of Miṇḍa or Ghasiṭa (a corruption of Ghrashṭaka), we give below diagrams to show how it is produced.

(1st) SIMPLE JUMPING IN THE DIATONIC SCALE :—

1 2 3 4 5 6 7 8
Sá. Ri. Ga. Ma. Pa. Dha. Ni. Sá.

(2nd) SIMPLE JUMPING IN THE CHROMATIC SCALE:—

1 2 3 4 5 6 7 8
Sá. K.-Ri. Ri. K.-Ga. Ga. Ma. T.-Ma. Pa.
9 10 11 12 13
K.-Dha. Dha. K.-Ni. Ni. Sá.

(3rd) TRAVERSING BY MIṆḌA[1] OR GHASIṬA IN THE DIATONIC SCALE :—

1 2 3 4 5 6 7 8
Sá.—Ri.—Ga.—Ma.—Pa.—Dha.—Ni.—Sá.

(4th) TRAVERSING BY MIṆḌA OR GHASIṬA IN THE CHROMATIC SCALE :—

1 2 3 4 5 6 7
Sá.—K.-Ri.—Ri.—K.-Ga.—Ga.—Ma.—T.-Ma.—
8 9 10 11 12 13
Pa.—K.-Dha.—Dha.—K.-Ni.—Ni.—Sá.

[1] Whenever we want to show a Miṇḍa or Ghasiṭa we shall do it by a dash connecting two or more notes together.

There is no fixed method of producing a Miṇḍa or Ghasiṭa of a particular note from a particular note, but the production depends on the capability of the voice and instruments and on the construction of Rágas. We shall refer to this subject in its proper place. It may be noted that the Miṇḍa or Ghasiṭa may be produced in Árohana (ascent) or Avarohana (descent). The dashes in the third and the fourth diagrams given above, connecting one note with another, show the Miṇḍa or Ghasiṭa. Many persons believe that, in traversing by a Miṇḍa or a Ghasiṭa from one note to another or others, the intermediate note or notes must needs be touched, whether we will or no, but practically that is not the case. Suppose we ascend by a Miṇḍa or Ghasiṭa from Sá. (C) to Ma. (F), we can touch Ma. (F) from Sá. (C) without producing the intermediate notes, *viz.*, K-Ri. (C-Sh.), Ri. (D), K.-Ga. (D-Sh.) and Ga. (E). The same remark is applicable to a Miṇḍa or a Ghasiṭa in descent. This fact can easily be verified on the fretted string-instruments called Biná, Satára, &c.

The Ghasiṭa is a peculiar way of sliding from a point to a point or points on the unfretted string-instruments. It is a substitute for the Miṇḍa, and we shall speak of it presently.

Miṇḍa and Ghasiṭa have been so much favoured and practised by Indian artists that they have constructed special instruments for them, such as the

Biná,[1] Rabába,[2] Sursingára (not extant), Saroda, Satára,[3] Sárangi (Indian fiddle), etc., etc. Credulous people fancy that in playing the Biná all the ten fingers are used, but in fact only six are used, 3 of the right hand and 3 of the left. The usual musical limit of touching the notes from a fret of the Biná or Satára by a Minḍa is five notes, for instance from Sá. (C) to Pa. (G). This limit considerably varies when the artist moves from steel-wire to brass-wire: this is due to the differences of densities, the relative dimensions, and tensions of the respective metals. On the Rabába, Saroda, Sárangi and such other instruments, or on instruments having no frets, the limit of a Ghasiṭa is not fixed, because it can be produced by slipping the finger over the wire from any one point to any other point, and not by stretching or drawing aside the wire at a point, as is done in the case of a Minḍa. The characteristic distinction between a Minḍa and a Ghasiṭa, is that the former connects the notes by the tension of a wire, while the latter joins them by reducing the length of a wire. Many artists prefer a Minḍa to a Ghasiṭa, but, musically speaking, the question seems to be more a matter of taste than of any intrinsic value. Moreover, certain instruments are fit only for the Minḍa and certain others for the Ghasiṭa. The instruments, which are used for the Minda are the long,

[1] See *Asiatic Researches*, Vol. I., pp. 250-254, Popular Ed., No. V.

[2] Persian name.

[3] Satára may be identical with the primitive Santára of Souráshṭra or the Greek *Cithara* of Strabo. Tod's *Rajasthan*, Vol. I., p. 46.

fretted ones (excepting the Táusa) which are not played by means of a bow, while those which are used for the Ghasiṭa, are the short, unfretted ones with strings (not always metallic), which are generally played by means of a bow. Under the former class comes the Satára, and under the latter the Sárangi. It may be remarked *en passant* that the Ghasiṭa can be produced on the Biná and Satára, despite their frets; but the impression made on the ear is not the same as that produced by the Minḍa.

The male voice is better adapted to the Minḍa or Ghasiṭa than the female voice; this is due to the relative shortness of the female vocal chords. It is true that the voice is capable of producing a sequence of connected or joined notes, but whether this is done by the Ghasiṭa or the Minḍa we are not in a position to decide.

Since we want to speak at some length on the Minḍa and the Ghasiṭa, we may here briefly refer to the phenomenon of vocal sound.

Voices, like sounds, differ from one another in respect of three qualities, *viz.*, (1) Loudness. This depends on the strength of the expiratory blast. (2) Pitch. This depends on the length and tension of the vocal chords. Their length may be regarded as constant, or varying only with age. It consequently determines the range only of the voice, and not the particular note given out at any time. The shrill voice of the child is determined by the shortness of the chords in infancy, and the voices of a soprano, tenor, and baritone are all dependent on the respective lengths of their vocal chords. Their tension is, on the contrary, variable; and the chief problem connected with the voice refers to variations in the tension of the vocal chords. (3) Quality or *Timbre.* This depends on the number and character of the over-tones accompanying any fundamental note sounded, and is determined by a variety of circumstances, the chief among which is the physical quality of the chords.

According to Prof. Max Müller, "the average length of the vocal chords in man is $18\frac{1}{2}$ m. m. when relaxed, and $23\frac{1}{2}$ m. m. when stretched; in woman, $12\frac{2}{3}$ m. m. when relaxed, and $15\frac{2}{3}$ m. m. when stretched:" thus giving a difference of about one-third between the two sexes, which accounts for the different pitch of the male and female voice, or, as Ch. Darwin[1] says, "Man's vocal chords are about one-third longer than in woman or in boys." Sir Duncan Gibbs says: "The voice and the form of the larynx differ in different races of mankind; but with the Tartars, Chinese, etc., the voice of the male is said not to differ so much from that of the female, as in most other races."

Music with Minḍa requires more exertion than without it, and such music is also slow. The same may be said of the Ghasiṭa. An excellence in Minḍa or Ghasiṭa is measured by the greater number of notes connected in a given time.

---

[1] *Descent of Man*, p. 566.

It is exceedingly probable that the Minḍa or Ghasiṭa is developed to express energy, resolution, and decision. The action of the vocal muscles, which produces the Minḍa or Ghasiṭa, is analogous to the muscular action which produces the energetic, resolute, and decisive movements of the body, indicating these states of mind. The Minḍa or Ghasiṭa is so impressive and touching, that it is superfluous to say that emotions are equally, if not better, expressed by connecting[1] one note with another or others,

---

[1] In connection with this subject it may be observed that in compound letters and diphthongs the process of pronunciation, and even that of writing (Hindu), is of joining (Minḍa) them. The same may be said of syllables. Among the letters the R and L are classed as trills, the primordial origin of Murki. There are certain dialects, *e. g.*, the Chinese, in which no development of the compound and trilled letters has taken place. Those dialects wanting in these advanced materials of a highly organized language may adopt them later on, if practicable, but certainly need not condemn them. The English (only in pronounciation) and Sanskrit languages are very rich in compound letters. In compounding two or more letters and in diphthongs we find the crudest form of the Minḍa or Ghasiṭa and of Murki or trill, or of both at times. This form of sounding notes is, to a certain extent, practised by certain animals and birds. It may be remarked in passing that in certain words, such as *strike*, *sprout*, *shrill*, etc., etc., the process of combination is of three or four different kinds of letters.

When we, in our common speech, use the combinations of different letters having different intensity, pitch, and quality, why should we not adopt the same principle in music, which is after all not altogether a different thing, but is an extended form of speech to express emotion or feeling? We wonder what makes the European Savants, such as Prof. P. Blaserna (for whose writings we have the greatest respect and admiration, and from which we must confess we have derived much instruction and aid in our survey of Indian music) and many others to condemn wholesale the principle of joining two or more notes in music. This is the fundamental difference between the European and Hindu music. Thus we find that Prof. P. Blaserna (*Theory of Sound in its Relation to Music*, pp. 110 and 111, 3rd ed.) says:—" If the history of music be examined with attention, even if all the evidence possible concerning the music of barbarous nations be collected, this constant phenomenon will

as by simple jumping from one note to another or others.

The Murchhanás are so charmingly distributed over different Rágas, that if these are taken away from them they (the Rágas) considerably lose in their effectiveness. A Murchhaná is always touched by a Minḍa or Ghasiṭa, but not otherwise. Those who are practised in the Indian Rágas can easily understand why the Rága Darbári-Kánaḍá is reduced to Sinda-Bhairavi (a Jilhá) by eliminating only the Murchhanás. A mere taking away of the Murchhanás changes the Rága Sáháná-Kánaḍá into Káfi (a Jilhá), the Rága Jogi and Asávari into Bhairavi (a Jilhá), etc.

It is really a very difficult, if not almost an impossible, task to deal with the above facts without entering deeply into the primary and secondary composition of Rágas. The scope of this treatise will not admit of this being done at great length. We shall, however, briefly treat of this subject in its proper place.

---

be found, that music proceeds by notes clearly separated from one another. Among the immense number of notes adopted for musical purposes, there are only a few that go to make up the various musical systems. A style of music in which it would be necessary to pass from one note to another through all the intermediate notes, would become almost intolerable. It is true that our singers, and violin and violincello players, sometimes make use of this style with success. But the slide (Ghasiṭa) from one note to another is only tolerated when it is used sparsely; and it always remains doubtful whether it would not be better to forbear from it entirely. Music proceeds, then, by musical *intervals*, precisely as a man walks with separate, firm, and decided steps." Be it as it may, we have, we hope, satisfactorily shown (p. 57) that two notes may, and can, be (as they practically are in Indian music) joined without producing the intermediate note or notes.

There are certain fixed modes of rendering the Rágas or Ráginis and Jilhás or Dhuns, in vocal as well as instrumental music. There are a variety of these modes which have acquired distinctive names. The principal among these are the Alápa or Joḍa and Dhrupada, Ṭappá and Khyála, Trivaṭa, Taráná and Chatranga, Ṭhumri and Gajala, Sargams, Padas and Bhajanas, and others too numerous to mention.

The difference between the Joḍa and Dhsupada is that the former has no poetic words in its composition and is less restricted by a Tála (measure of time), while the latter is composed in poetic words and is entirely restricted by a Tála, and it has less Minḍa or Ghasiṭa. The Joḍa can be sung or played only in Bilambapada (slow-going measure or *largo*) and Madhya (middle-moderate measure or *andante*) but not in Druta (fast measure or *presto*); while the Dhrupada can pass through all these three stages. The Joḍa cannot be sung or played very fast, because it is simply impracticable to connect notes with rapidity which the Druta (fast) measure presupposes. For instance—

Minḍa—	1	3	5	5	6	8	8	10	12
	Sá,—	Ri.—	Ga.,	Ga.-	Ma.-	Pa.,	Pa.	Dha.—	Ni.
Jumping-	1	3	5	5	6	8	8	10	12
	Sá,	Ri,	Ga.,	Ga.	Ma.	Pa.,	Pa.	Dha.	Ni.

Instead of words, mere syllables—Noma, Toma, or the letters Ṭ, Ḍ, T, Th, D, N, R, L, etc., are employed in singing the Joḍa.

The Joḍa music is a later or advanced form of the Dhrupaḍa, as the Dhrupaḍa is a later form of the original Padas or Bhajanas (prayer or praise). The Joḍa music is really charming for its fullness in Minḍa or Ghasiṭa and for its Murchhanás, in spite of the absence of poetic words and technicalities of the Tála (time). But now-a-days this class of music is very rare, being found to a limited extent only in the instrumental music, such as the Biná[1] (Indian lyre), Saroda, Satára, etc.

Those string-instruments, which are not handled by means of a bow, are played very fast without the Minḍa or Ghasiṭa, by means either of the Javá[2] or the Mijráfa or Nakhi.[3] With the Javá and Nakhi, it takes but a minimum of time to give a stroke out and in, to a tensed string of the aforesaid instruments. This facility of giving the strokes swiftly has enabled the instrumentalists to compose their own tunes, called Zálás and Gatis, which are a specialty in instrumental music. The former are played in Joḍa with Madhya (moderate time) with an accompaniment on the Chikárá or the last wire of the Saroda, Biná and Satára; the latter are played in Rágas as well as in Jilhás. The Gatis are nicely formed, though they are composed in only four technical syllables Dá,—

---

[1] G. C. M. Birdwood (*Industrial Arts of India*, p. 233) says:—"Indian musical instruments have remained unchangeable for the last two thousand years. * * * * and the Viná (Biná, so called for its finger board, is made of bamboo or Bánsa) is of equal antiquity."

[2] A triangular piece of bone or ivory used in playing on the Rabába and Saroda.

[3] A triangular ring of wire used in playing on the Biná and Satára.

Ḍá, Diḍ, and Ḍid or Ḍadá. The stroke which is given in, is named Dá, and that given out is called Ḍá. When the in and out strokes are rapidly given, so as to produce in the same time a combined sound which Dá or Ḍá takes, the combination is called Diḍ; and this process of giving the strokes in and out, if reversed, goes by the name of Ḍid or Ḍadá. There are hundreds of Gatis in the Saroda and Satára music, which are really artistic on account of their Minḍa, Ghasiṭa, Murchhaná and Murki—an advanced form of the trill.

The Murki[1] (a collective name of Giṭakaḍi, Sása or Ása) is less valued and regarded by Indian musicians than the Minḍa and Ghasiṭa, and is considered inferior to them. Musically speaking, the Murki is equally, if not more, attractive with the Minḍa and Ghasiṭa. The reason of this inferiority of Murki seems to be that it is of later formation, and the female voice is better adapted to it than the male voice. This is due to the relative shortness of the female vocal chords. The difference in the adaptations of the Minḍa or Ghasiṭa and Murki to the male and female voices respectively, is a subject which admits of a generalization:—*All things being equal, the longer and the thicker the sonorous body, the better the Minḍa*

[1] How the Murki is to be produced may be seen on fretted instruments by keeping the index finger of the left hand stationary on a fret without sounding the wire by the right hand finger and then the next finger or middle one of the same hand should sound the wire. If the rapidity of the middle finger is great in giving the strokes it constitutes Murki. On the Satára the Murki is produced by two fingers, while on the Sárangi by three. The same may be said of Ása which is the lowest form of Murki. One stroke of the finger or fingers denotes Ása; two strokes comprise Giṭakaḍi, and more than two produce Murki.

or Ghasiṭa: all things being equal, the shorter and the thinner the sonorous body, the better the Murki.

To render the above proposition more clear, we must define the intensity or loudness and the pitch of sound in the language of Acoustics. The intensity of sound is determined by the amplitude of the vibrations: the greater the disturbance of the air or other medium, the intenser the sound. The pitch of sound is ascertained by the wave-length of the vibrations: the shorter the wave-length the higher the pitch, *i. e.*, it has the larger number of consecutive vibrations which fall upon the ear in a second.

All things being equal, the longer the wave-length of the sonorous vibrations, the better the Minḍa or Ghasiṭa: all things being equal, the shorter the wave-length of the sonorous vibrations, the better the Murki.

The above proposition can easily be verified by changing the length and thickness of the wire of a string-instrument. Even the change of thickness will give us an idea of it. It is probable that the Murki is expressive of gentler and less active feelings, and that is so because it implies the smaller muscular vivacity, due to a lower energy. The Murki has wonderfully progressed in recent times, owing to its employment in the composition called Ṭappá. Indian artists have considerably lessened the rigidity of the Tála in order to encourage the Murki. Music with the Murki is slower than with the Minḍa or the Ghasiṭa. Excellence in the Murki is measured by the rapidity of strokes on two or more notes in a given time. When this motion is moderate it is called Giṭakaḍi, and when it is the lowest it is called Sása or Ása.

Whenever we have to show a Murki (trill) we shall do it by putting one or more asterisks between two or more notes. When there is only one asterisk it shows the *Sása* or *Ása*; when there are only two asterisks they show the Giṭakaḍi; and three or more asterisks denote the Murki.[1] The Giṭakaḍi is only an intermediate mode between the *Asa* and *Murki.*

The difference between Ṭappá[2] and Khyála (a later form of Dhrupada[3]) is that in the former there are

---

[1] From a practical point of view the Murki is neither a pure jumping (the number of its strokes is not fixed), nor is it a pure combination, but it is a mixture of the two. In producing a Murki on the Satára, Sárangi, etc., the one or the first note must not die out absolutely before the second or third is produced. In playing the Murki on the frets of a Satára only three fingers are used The index finger is kept stationary, and the other two touch the two notes one after the other in rapidly intermittent succession. In producing the Minḍa and Ghasiṭa, the connection of two or more notes is continuous, and comparatively forcible; while in the Murki it is not so. On the Piano, Harmonium and such other instruments, two or more sounds are not blended together, but they give the impression of distinct and separate notes in rapid succession. This can be verified by producing a Sása, the lowest form of Murki, on the fretted instrument and on the Pianos or Harmonium.

[2] Col. Tod (*Rajasthan*, Vol. II., p. 612) says:—"There is a plaintive simplicity in this music, which denotes originality, and, even without a knowledge of the language, conveys a sentiment to the most fastidious, when in the impassioned manner which some of these sirens possess, while the Maráthá delights in the dissonant *droopud* (Dhrupada), which requires rapidity of utterance, and quite surpasses Rajput repose in his *tuppa.*"

[3] When there is any dispute about the form or the skeleton notes of a Rága the Indian artists, instead of referring to Sanskrit works on music, always

more Murkis than Minḍas or Ghasiṭas, and it is generally composed in Jilhás; while the latter is always sung in Rágas, and it has more Ghasiṭas or Minḍas than Murkis. The above distinction is not strictly observed now-a-days, for any kind of Chija (musical piece) is sung in Rágas as well as in Jilhás.

Musical compositions which go by the name of Tirvaṭa-Tarání and Chataranga are thus distinguished:—The former is composed only of the drum technicalities, and the latter is a combination of poetry and the drum technicalities. This kind of singing is performed very swiftly, and Tála (time) seems to be the principal item of it, though it is sung in Rágas as well as in Jilhás. In the singing of Sargams, the initial letters of the notes to be touched are set to music in Rágas and Jilhás, instead of the poetic words of a song; this mode of singing seems to be ancient.

The Pada or Bhajana (musical prayer songs or psalms or love-songs of Krishna), Ṭhumri (love-song), Gazal, etc., etc., are very common, yet exceedingly musical. They are adapted more to Nritya (dancing) and Háva-Bháva or Artha (pantomime) than to classical music. There are many songs of this description which are really charming for their poetry and music.

cite the Dhrupada as an authority for deciding the skeleton notes of a Rága. Such Dhrupadas generally differ but very little from the old works and practice. In the absence of Sanskrit knowledge, they use Duhás, a form of poetry, which describe the number and names of the notes of a Rága. The Rágas are so composed that each one has its peculiar *sargams*, *i. e.*, skeleton or fixed order of the successive notes of a Saptaka (Gamut) comprising it.

The shaking of the body is one of the necessary incidents of certain passions, or perhaps all passions, when pushed to an extreme. It is a matter of common experience that we have the trembling of anger, of fear, of hope, of joy ; and that the vocal muscles being implicated with the rest of the body, the voice too becomes tremulous. This trembling (Kampa[1]) of voice is not only taken advantage of by the Indian musicians, but its opposite—the principle of steadiness (Sthiratá or Ṭhairná)—is marvellously attained by them.

Tána or Strain consists in producing a larger number of notes, but in a shorter time (relatively to the general time of the piece of music in which it is interspersed). It is made use of in singing or playing a piece of music with a view to embellish it and to make it more effective. It is produced either by the process of simple jumping from note to note, or by the Minḍa, Ghasiṭa or the Murki severally or conjointly. It may be added that a Tána combining in it all these varieties is rare, and would require for its artistic execution a high command over the voice or instrument. The Tána is a property common to the Khyála, Ṭappá, Ṭhumri, Pada, etc., etc.

Tána or variability of pitch is a characteristic of emotional speech. Instead of attempting a metaphysical discussion of this subject, we must content ourselves

---

1 Whenever we want to show a note as shaking we shall give its number in *Italics*, thus :—*1*, *13*, *25*.

with the knowledge that the muscular excitement is shown not only in the strength of contraction, but also in the rapidity with which different muscular adjustments succeed each other.

The principle of the Arohana (ascent) and the Ávarohana (descent) is so strict that the slightest change alters a particular kind of Rága into a different Rága, as the case may be. Instead of treating this principle at length, suffice it to say that while speech is comparatively monotonous, singing makes use of wider intervals. The speaking-voice seldom wanders over more than three (in some cases four) notes, above or below its medium, and that too by small steps, but the singing-voice not only wanders over higher and lower notes of its register, but goes from one note to another by larger intervals.

We shall now speak of the principle of unison, or the musical sympathy that exists between any two sounds or notes of equal pitch. Every true musician knows that the faculty of a musical ear is the first essential to a mastery of music as an art. In the progressive study of the Saptaka or Gamut, the first step is to acquire the art to discern the least defect in the unison of notes and in the consonance between an initial note and its octave. The next step is to perceive the subtle sympathy between Sa. (C) and Pa. (G); and the third is ordinarily to perceive that between Sa. and Ga. (E). Really speaking, the first note and its octave are not separate notes, but the latter reinforces some of the harmonics of the former.

The wonderful sympathy of Sá. (C) with Ga. (E) and Pa. (G), which is called in Acoustics simple ratio or Harmony, is well known not only to Physicists, but practically to Indian musicians also, who, by their keen perception of it, acquire the requisite skill to attune a musical scale with the greatest possible precision and to test its accuracy. The simple but sure method they employ is as follows :—

First they adjust Sá. (C), Ga. (E), and Pa. (G) (the perfect major chord), which adjustment is the first and essential step in Indian music ; and then the remaining four notes, Ri. (D), Ma. (F), Dha. (A), and Ni. (B), are tested thus :— Ri. (D) is tested with Dha. (A), Ma. (F) with Sá (C), and Ga. (E) with Ni. (B).

The sympathy between Ri. (D) and Dha. (A), Ma. (F) and Sá. (C), Ga. (E) and Ni. (B), artistically speaking, is the same which exists between Sá. (C) and Pa. (G).

The above method teaches us that the 12 notes (of the Chromatic scale) stand in sympathy or relation with each other in the following way :—

	1....................		8	1....................		5
1	Sa. (C)	with	Pa. (G)	Sa. (C)	with	Ga. (E)
2	K.-Ri.	„	K.-Dha.	K.-Ri.	„	Ma.
3	Ri.	„	Dha.	Ri.	„	T.-Ma.

	1		8	1		5
4	K.-Ga. (C)	with	K.-Ni. (G)	K.-Ga. (C)	with	Pa. (E)
5	Ga.	„	Ni.	Ga.	„	K.-Dha.
6	Ma.	„	Sá.	Ma.	„	Dha.
7	T.-Ma.	„	K.-Ri.	T.-Ma.	„	K. Ni.
8	Pa.	„	Ri.	Pa.	„	Ni.
9	K.-Dha.	„	K.-Ga.	K.-Dha.	„	Sa.
10	Dha.	„	Ga.	Dha.	„	K.-Ri.
11	K.-Ni.	„	Ma.	K.-Ni.	„	Ri.
12	Ni.	„	T.-Ma.	Ni.	„	K.-Ga.
13	Sa. (Ć)	„	Pa. (Ǵ)	Sa. (Ć)	„	Ga. (É)

The above method is well known to Mahomedan artists, who designate it by the term Sur-Bevrá or Bevḍá.

The above description is a practical illustration of the *nodes* and *ventral segments* of the science of Acoustics,[1] or of the perfect major chord as it is called by some scientists.

We shall be doing scanty justice to the present topic if we omit to say a few words here about the variety, intensity and velocity of sound, and about noise.

---

[1] "The division into segments is often distinctly *visible* when the string of a sonometer is strongly bowed, and its existence can be verified, when less evident, by putting paper riders on different parts of the string. These (* *) will be thrown off by the vibrations of the string, unless they are placed at the nodal points, in which case they will retain their seats. If two strings tuned to unison are stretched on the same sonometer, the vibration of the one induces similar vibrations in the other; and the experiment of the riders may be verified, in a very instructive way, by bowing one string and placing the riders on the other. This is an instance of a general principle of great importance—that a vibrating body communicates its vibrations to other bodies which are capable of vibrating in unison with it. *Natural Philosophy* by A. P. Deschanel, translated and edited by J. D. Everett, Sixth Edition, pp. 912 and 913.

The variety of sound depends on the forms and nature of the sonorous body, and on the way in which the sound is conveyed to our ears. The intensity of sound varies according to the density of the medium which propagates it. The velocity of sound is uniform at every portion of the distance traversed, and it is the same with sharp and dull sounds. Neither the line, nor the precision of a piece of music, is altered, whatever may be its distance from the listener; only when the distance increases, all the sounds are lessened in the same degree.

Noise frequently proceeds from a confused mixture of different sounds, which the ear can scarcely distinguish from one another; or, in other words, noise is nothing but a sound, the vibrations of which do not last long enough to enable the listener to appreciate the relative pitch.

"Doctor W. B. Carpenter[1] says:—" It has been stated that the sensation of hearing is produced by the successive undulations or vibrations communicated to the ear from the sonorous body, either by the air, or by liquid or solid medium. This is the case with all *continuous* sounds or *tones*, but single momentary sounds, such as those produced by the discharge of a pistol, the blow of a hammer, * * or the tick of a clock, make their impression on the ear by a single shock. All continuous tones are, in fact, caused by a

[1] *Animal Physiology*, p. 410.

succession of such shocks communicated to the ear with sufficient rapidity for the interval between them not to be distinguished."

Prof. Max Muller says :—" Noise is produced by irregular impulses imparted to the air, and tone is produced by regular periodical (isochronous) vibrations of elastic air."

According to Mr. N. Lockyer, F. R. S., when two melodious sounds follow each other at a sufficiently short interval, the sensations are fused into one. When two sounds, not quite in tune, are struck together, the clashing together of their mutual vibrations gives rise to an alternating rise and fall of the sound, known in Acoustics as "beats." When the beats follow each other, as rapidly as 132 in a second, they cease to be recognized, that is to say, the sensations which they cause become fused. Before they disappear, they give a peculiar disagreeable roughness to the sound. The pleasure, which is given by musical sounds, depends largely on the absence of this incomplete fusion of the sensations.

Professor A. Bain[1] says :—" Since a sweet note is already a harmony, the influence of the recognized musical concords is not something absolutely new, but an extension of the same harmonizing process.* * The simple musical ratios ($\frac{2}{1}$ $\frac{3}{2}$ $\frac{4}{3}$, etc.) express the best chords, and, as the ratios are further removed

[1] *Emotions and Will*, p. 234.

from simplicity, the harmonious effect gives place to discord, which is at last painful."

In Lock's *Human Understanding*, p. 156, it is said "every articulate word is a different modification of sound, by which we see that, from the sense of hearing such modifications, the mind may be furnished with distinct ideas to almost an infinite number. Sounds, also, besides the distinct cries of birds and beasts, are modified by diversity of notes of different lengths put together."

Mr. Clark, in the *American Naturalist*, says :— "A musical sound is never simple but complex ; it consists of one fundamental sound and of other harmonious sounds at close intervals ; the first and the most perceptible intervals are the 8th, 5th, 4th, and 3rd major. Each of the simple sounds—sounds, which, taken together, constitute the whole sound—causes the vibration of a special group of fibres in the auditory nerve. This fact, often repeated, generates a kind of organic predisposition which is confirmed by heredity. If from any cause one of these groups is set in motion, the other groups will have a tendency to vibrate. Therefore, if a singing animal, weary of always repeating the same note, wishes to vary its height, it will naturally choose one of the harmonic sounds of the first. The ultimate origin of the law of melody in organized beings is therefore only the simultaneous harmony, realized in sounds of inorganic nature. This theory is confirmed by the analysis which has often been made of the song of some birds; the intervals employed by these are generally the same as those on which human melody is founded, the 8th, 5th, 4th, and 3rd major. * *"

Professor P. Blaserna says:—"In the music of all nations two unfailing characters are found, rhythmic movement and procedure by determinate intervals. The first appertains also to the speech and other acts of man, as walking, swimming, dancing, etc.; the second belongs exclusively to music."

"A musical sound is always a compound sound, its vibrations are more or less complicated, and it by itself constitutes a true harmony. * * It follows that in combining two, three, or more musical sounds in order to form a chord, it is not enough that the fundamental notes should bear simple ratios to each other, but it is also necessary that the harmonics should obey this law."

"All nations have selected notes * * * have collected them together * * * and have thus created one or more *musical scales.* By a musical scale is meant the collection of all the notes, comprised between the fundamental note and its octave. * *

"It seems strange that a few notes put together in a musical scale should be able to acquire a true importance in the study of music. If it were a question of an assemblage of notes made haphazard or capriciously, the matter would be of no importance ; but the musical scale is always the product of the musical activity of many centuries. It was not established before music, but is developed with it. A very prefect form of music must have a perfect scale ; an imperfect and primitive form of music, on the other hand, will have a scale of little value. The study of the musical scale gives one of the most important and concise means of judging of the musical state of a nation. * * "

If we accept (as what scientific observer will not) these conclusions of Professor Pietro Blaserna, that a perfect form of music is correlative or co-existent with a perfect musical scale, and that a nation's musical scale, in its turn, connotes or implies that nation's musical state, then, indeed, it cannot but be acknowledged by every impartial student of music that Indian music had from a very ancient time attained a very high degree of perfection ; possessing as it does not only a complete scale of 12 notes (an improvement by-the-bye over the original Diatonic scale), but the further addition to it by the ancient Hindus of the 12 Murchhanás or quarter tones, calling them *Tivratara* (*i. e.*, sharper or double) and *atikomala* (*i. e.*, very flat) which is still the desideratum of European music—a desideratum which the learned and accomplished professors of it like P. Blaserna, Helmholtz and others, have endeavoured to supply by advocating the introduction of (an octave of) twenty-four keys or notes, which, if effected, would, in their opinion, be a decided improvement in the present music of the West.

Instead of showing the utility of the Murchhaná ($\frac{1}{4}$ part of a tone) in higher music, we simply quote the following paragraphs.

Professor Helmholtz, in suggesting some reforms in the temperate[1] scale, says:—"By starting from somewhat different considerations, it is possible to provide for everything in a very satisfactory manner, with twenty-four notes per octave."

---

[1] "*Tempered Gamut.*—A great variety of keys are employed in music, and it is a practical impossibility, at all events in the case of instruments like the piano and organ, which have only a definite set of notes, to maintain these ratios strictly for the whole range of possible key-notes. Compromise of some kind becomes necessary, and different systems of compromise are called different *temperaments* or different *modes of temperament.* The temperament which is most in favour in the present day is the simplest possible, and is called *equal temperament*, because it favours no key above another, but makes the tempered gamut exactly the same for all. It ignores the difference between major and minor tones, and makes the limma exactly half of either. The interval from Do to Do_2 is thus divided into 5 tones and 2 semitones, a tone being $\frac{1}{6}$ of an octave, and a semitone $\frac{1}{12}$ of an octave. The ratio of frequencies corresponding to a tone will therefore be the sixth root of 2, and for a semitone it will be the 12th root of 2.

"The difference between the natural and the tempered gamut for the key of C is shown by the following table, which gives the number of complete vibrations per second for each note of the middle octave of an ordinary piano:—

Tempered Gamut.		Natural Gamut.
C	258·7	258·7
D	290·3	291·0
E	325·9	323·4
F	345·3	344·9
G	387·6	388·0
A	435·0	431·1
B	488·2	485·0
C	517·3	517·3

Natural Philosophy, by A. Private Deschanel, Translated and edited by J. D. Everett, Sixth Edition, pp. 899 and 900.

Professor P. Blaserna says :—"Certain notes adopted by the Greeks at a period of decline—as, for example, quarter tones—are decisively rejected by us. It is therefore an error which many commit, to think that music, and especially modern music, has an absolute character and value, and therefore to reject every musical system which does not agree with ours. There is nothing absolute in it but the laws of notes and their combinations, but the application of these laws is rather vague, and there remains a very wide and indeterminate field, which will be traversed in very different ways by different nations at various historical epochs."

* * * "It may be well believed that even twenty-four keys well arranged would not offer insurmountable difficulties of execution, and even if musical complications and arabesques had to be abandoned, true and serious music would only be the gainer."

Whether the scale above referred to was an indigenous or exotic one, forms the subject-matter of a separate chapter entitled "A Short History of the Musical Scale." Before going to this history we shall treat of the Rágas and Tálas to see how this scale with twenty-four notes, of which Professors Blaserna and Helmholtz speak with so much decision and favour, was treated by the ancient Hindus in their practical music.

We give in the next chapter the Rágas and their formation.

CHAPTER III.

THE RAGAS AND THEIR FORMATIONS.

The Rágas given in the tables in this chapter are selected for treatment and analysis in this work, both because most of them are familiar to our musicians, and also because there is very little difference of opinion on their respective Sargams or skeletons. They admit of being explained in the following tables without intricate technicalities. There are several other finished compound Rágas, but a scientific treatment of them is not possible without going into minute details, which is beyond the scope of a treatise like the present. It may, however, be safely asserted that the conclusions arrived at after the analysis of the Rágas given below, will hold good with all the other Rágas, which are now in practice.

It may not be out of place here to state that there is a slight difference of opinion in the Sargams or skeletons of some of the Rágas which are practised by artists of different schools. This difference is considerably due to their oral transmission during so many generations, although they were once committed to writing, and not orally taught, as they are at the present day. At the present day, one rarely hears the Rágas sung or played in their original purity. Heard, however, as coming from real masters of the art, some of the current Rágas exhibit the highest order of musical activity. Some Mahomedan musicians have scrupulously preserved the original purity of the skeletons; but from peculiarly narrow and superstitious notions, these make it a sort of family heritage, confining such high and pure exhibition of the art to members of their own family. In public performances they always mutilate the original notes and mix them up with others, with a view to prevent a sort of musical pilfering of what they regard as their own valued possession.

All Rágas are divided into four divisions—1st, Ohḍava (consisting of 5 notes); 2nd, Khoḍava or Shoḍava (consisting of 6 notes); 3rd, Sampurna (consisting of 7 notes); and 4th, Sankirna (literally, mixed). These last consist of seven or more notes, and the arrangement of their ascent and descent is not the same as in the first three divisions, and, therefore, we shall call them Mishra, or compound Rágas.

In order to understand the following three tables, it must be remembered that the Saptaka (Diatonic scale) consists of 5 tones and 2 semitones, or 12 notes (Chromatic scale), the 13th being simply a repetition of the first in the second octave; and that the Indians call the 7th note, which is a semitone and ought consistently to be named Komala-Panchama (G Fl.),

Tivra-Madhyama or Kaḍi-Madhyama (F Sh.), *vide* pp. 52 and 53.

The arrangement adopted in the following tables is a simple one, and needs no lengthy explanation. The Rágas are not arranged in their alphabetical order, but they are given under the four heads Oḍhava, Khoḍava, Sampurna, and Sankirna, with the numbers and names of the notes which go to form them. In the first three classes, which are given in the first table, the order of ascent and descent of notes is the same. The Sankirna Rágas are given in the 2nd and 3rd tables. Some of the Rágas in the 2nd table contain more than seven notes, but the distinction in principle between the two sub-divisions is that in those given in the second table the notes used for descent are different from those for ascent; while those in the 3rd table have a peculiar feature which is, that both the ascent and descent of notes is not continuous along the line, but is an interrupted one, *i. e.*, the formation is by ascending or descending notes over a part of the scale, and then there is a reversion to a lower or higher note before taking up the rest of the ascending or descending scale: *e. g.*, in Hámira (No. 2 in Table III.) the ascent is continuous up to the 8th note as S, R, G, T-M, P; but before taking up the next higher note, the 11th, there is a reversion from P to G, from where the ascent is again continued as G, M, K-N, N, S. Similarly, in the descent for the same Rága, the descending notes go along the line up to R, and then comes the reversion to the higher note P from where the descent is again continued as P, T-M, G, R, S.

The initial letters, which are used in the following tables, and in the subsequent part of this work are:—(1) S for Shaḍja, (2) K-R for Komala-Rikhaba, (3) R for Rikhaba, (4) K-G for Komala-Gandhára, (5) G for Gandhára, (6) M for Madhyama, (7) T-M for Tivra-Madhyama, (8) P for Panchama, (9) K-Dh for Komala-Dhaivata, (10) Dh for Dhaivata, (11) K-N for Komala-Nikháda, (12) N for Nikháda, and (13) S for Shaḍja, which is the repetition of the first in the second octave (Áshṭaka), and from where the descent (Avarohana) begins.

Since we have concisely described the artistic meaning of the word Rága in the last chapter, we need not interest ourselves, at this stage of the work, with its origin, growth or history, supposing it were possible to give such origin or history. The most we can say concerning the word is, that, though strictly speaking, any combination of notes may be termed a Rága (from Ranj, to please), yet in practice it has been used for a very long time to connote particular combinations of certain musical notes expressed in particular ways, briefly alluded to in Chap. II. as Ghasiṭa, Minḍa and Murchhanás, with stated orders of ascent and descent. This subject will be dealt with again, after the study of the skeletons of the different Rágas.

Before giving the following tables, it is necessary to assure the reader that the author has spared neither pains nor time to adjust the tables consistently and with due regard to the theoretical aspect of the question as found in old and standard works of authority on the subject, as also to the practice of the art in its best form and highest order. In the absence of a rigid unanimity on the skeleton notes of certain Rágas the author has followed the majority of the best artists and authoritative works available. As regards the names of the Rágas classified in the several divisions as Oḍhava, Khoḍava, Sampurna and Sankirna, the author has principally relied upon the writings of Sir W. Jones,[1] who has evidently taken great care and pains to find out the names of the Rágas and the number of their respective notes.

[1] Sir W. Jones (*Asiatic Researches*, Vol. III. pp. 76-81) in one place observes: "It is impossible that I should have erred much, if at all, in the preceding table, because the regularity of the Sanskrit metre has (p. 79) in general enabled me to correct the manuscript; but I have some doubt as to *Velávali*, of which Pa is declared to be the *Ansa* or tonic, though it is said in the same line, that both Pa and Ri may be omitted: I, therefore, have supposed Pa to be the true reading, both Mirjákhana and the (Sangita) Náráyana exhibiting that note as the leader of the mode (Rága). The notes printed in *Italic* letters are variously *changed* by temperament or by shakes and other graces; but, even if I were able to give you in words a distinct notation of those changes, the account of each *mode* would be insufferably tedious and scarce intelligible without the assistance of a masterly performer on the *Indian lyre*. Accordi-

Between them, the three preceding tables contain not less than 81 Rágas. At first sight they seem quite distinct and separate from one another, but on a closer study of their formation it will be observed that a simpler analysis of them, based on a common chord of notes running through groups of them, is possible. It will thus be seen that, classified on this principle, all the 81 Rágas form themselves into eleven distinct groups as under :—

(1st) Rágas with Komala-Rikhaba (C Sh.), followed by Komala-Gandhára (D Sh.) in ascent, and *vice versá* in descent, would be—Gurjari, Jogi or Jilhá-Bhairavi, Bilásakháni-Toḍi, Toḍi, Asávari (K-G, not in ascent), and Multáni (K-R, not in ascent).

(2nd) Rágas with Komala-Rikhaba (C Sh.), followed by Gandhára (E) in ascent, and *vice versá* in descent, would be—Bibhása, Rámashri or Gunkali, Gounḍáshri, Lalata, Lalitá, Jaita, Puriá or Renaki, Márvá or Dipak, Soheni, Basanta, Kálangḍá-Jilhá, Purvi, Varáṭi or Puriá-Kalyána, Gouḍi (G, not in descent), and Purvi-Hindi.

(3rd) Rágas with Komala-Rikhaba (D Fl.), preceded by Gandhára (E) in descent, would be—Jogiá, Shri, Bhairava or Jilhá-Kálangḍá, Jaitáshri, and Paraja.

(4th) Rágas with Rikhaba (D), followed by Komala-Gandhára (D Sh.) in ascent, and *vice versá* in descent, would b —Náyaki-Kánaḍá or Karnáṭi, Madhura-

Kánaḍá, Darbári-Kánaḍá or Jilhá Sind-Bhairavi, Sáháná-Kánaḍá or Jilhá-Káfi, Dháni-Kánaḍá, Sinda-Kánaḍá or Jilhá-Káfi, and Jejevanti-Kánaḍá or Jilhá-Sindorá.

(5th) Rágas with Rikhaba (D), preceded by Komala-Gandhára (E Fl.) in descent, would be—Jounpuri or Jilhá Sind-Bhairavi, Miáki or Tánsen's Malhára, Palása or Jilhá-Barvá, Dhanáshri or Jilhá-Káfi, Gandhára, Bágeshri-Kánaḍá or Báhár, and Bhimpalás or Jilhá-Sind-Bhairavi.

(6th) Rágas with Rikhaba (D), followed by Gandhára (E) in ascent, and *vice versâ* in descent, would be—Bhupa or Bibhása, Bhupáli, Susthávati, Jangalá, Kalyána, Bilávala or Velávali, Áliá-Bilávala, Yamana-Kalyána, Hámira, and Náta.

(7th) Rágas with Rikhaba (D), preceded by Gandhára (E) in descent, would be—Deshási, Soraṭa or Jilhá Khamácha, Desa, Gounḍa or Malhári, Kakubha, Kámoda or Kámbodi, Bhyágaḍá Bhyága, Shankará-Bharana, Shankará, Kedárá Chháyá, and Gounḍa-Malhára.

(8th) Rágas with Rikhaba (D), followed by Madhyama (F) in ascent, and *vice versâ* in descent, would be—Megha or Sura-Malhára, Bindrábani-Sáranga, Sura-Sáranga, Baḍahansa-Sáranga, Madhumáta-Sáranga, Rámadáshi-Sáranga, and Gouḍa-Sáranga. (The last is a misnomer, as it has but very little similarity with other Sárangas, and in descent R is preceded by P instead of M. In all the varieties of Sáranga, excepting this, G and T-M are not used at all.)

(9th) Rágas without Komala (flat) or Shudha (Diatonic) Rikhaba (D) but with Komala-Gandhára (D Sh.), followed by Madhyama (F) in ascent, and *vice versâ* in descent, would be—Málkosa or Malāva and Koushi.

(10th) Rágas without Komala(flat) or Shudha (Diatonic) Rikhaba (D) but with Gandhára (E), followed by Madhyama (F) in ascent, and *vice versâ* in descent, would be—Bangáli, Tilanga, Madhumádhavi, Deshi, Panchama and Khamácha or Khambáti.

(11th) Rágas without Komala (flat) or Shudha (Diatonic) Rikhaba (D) but with Gandhára (E), folowed by Tivra-Madhyama (F Sh.) in ascent, and *vice versâ* in descent, would be—Máleshri or Málavashri, Hinḍola, and Ṭankiká.

This classification of all the Rágas into eleven groups is, of course, not quite scientific, as it is based only on one common chord of notes, but it is of use as helping one to draw the following conclusions:—

(1st) There is not a single Rága, simple or Shudha (Oḍhava, Khoḍava and Sampurna) or compound (Sankirna), which contains all the 12 notes (Chromatic scale).

(2nd) There is no Rága which has less than six notes from the register or fundamental S (C) to the S (C′) in the second octave inclusive.

(3rd) There is no Rága which has two Rikhabas (Ds), Komala (flat) and Shudha (Diatonic), or two Dhaivatas (As), Komala (flat) and Shudha (Diatonic).

(4th) There is only one Rága which has two Gandháras (Es), Komala (flat) and Shudha (Diatonic) *viz.*, Jejevanti Kánaḍá or Jilhá Sindorá, the 6th in the second table.

(5th) There are some Rágas which have two Panchamas (Gs) or Tivra-Madhyama (F Sh. or G Fl.) and Panchama (G) —9th, 16th, 28th, 29th, 32nd, 36th, 37th, and 42nd in the first table; 4th, 15th, 19th, 21st, 23rd, 25th, and 27th in the second table; and 1st, 2nd, 6th, and 9th in the third table.

(6th) There are some Rágas which have two Nikhádas (Bs), Komala (flat) and Shudha (Diatonic)—43rd, 44th, and 45th in the first table; 5th, 7th, 10th, 13th, 14th, and 27th in the second table; and 2nd and 3rd in the third table.

(7th) Every Rága must have either G (E), M (F), or P (G), and N (B), or K-R (C sharp or D flat), R (D), K-G (D sharp or E flat), and G (E).

As regards conclusion (3rd) given above, it is difficult to conceive the reason why two Rikhabas (Ds) or two Dhaivatas (As) were thought to be incongruous or incompatible for a Rága, when two Gandháras (Es), two Panchamas (Gs), and two Nikhádas (Bs) were considered to be harmonious or artistic for a Rága. The absence of a Rága with two Rikhabas (Ds) or of two Dhaivatas (As) seems to be a mere accident. It cannot be denied that most of the Rágas, which are given in the foregoing tables, are highly melodious. They show a wonderful degree of thought and labour spent in combining the notes to form so many Rágas without allowing them to be confounded one with the other. It must also be admitted that the said Rágas are quite distinct from one another, so far as their respective notes and their orders of ascent and descent are concerned, and that they are highly finished. It is not possible to believe that so many Rágas were the formation of a mere process of permutations and combinations, and in reality they seem to have been gradually evolved during the practice of the art for a long time.

It may be noted that in practice Indian musicians do not simply traverse along the notes of a Rága in a given time from one octave to another or others, but they begin their Rága first in Kharaja (one octave below the register), then they go to the Ástái (corruption of Sthái, *i. e.*, the register octave), thence to Antará (one octave above the register), and finally they end it in S (C or tonic) of the first or register octave: thus covering three octaves[1]: one below (Anudátta) and one above (Udátta), the register (Svarita) octave.

[1] Certain works on music call the register octave by the name of Mandra (lit., high), the octave below the register is called Anu-Mandra, and the one above the register is denominated Tára. In the technicalities of music Mandra would be *bass* and Tára *treble*.

The most ordinary or common kind of singing, which consists of singing Chijas like the Ṭhumaris or Gazals (pieces of poetry set to music), one so often comes across in ordinary performances, is confined to the register (Svarita) octave. This singing contains more words than notes, and the music in a performance of this kind consists at times in what are technically termed Tánas (*i.e.*, strains), which are interspersed between the words of the piece.

It is true that the singing of Chijas in some of the Rágas does not always begin with the register (Svarita) S. or tonic; but this arrangement does not conflict with the principle of Árohana (ascent) and Avarohana (descent). It is all the same whether one begins the first word or words of a Chija from the tonic or from any other note of the Rága, provided the distribution of the subsequent words of that Chija is regulated with strict regard to the principle of Árohana and Avarohana.

A Rága is frequently extended or diffused (Prastára) by repeating (while going from the S to its octave) once or often a combination of the same notes or any of them, and the Rága is not changed or affected in the slightest degree if in so doing the principle of the ascent and descent of notes for that Rága is rigidly adhered to; for instance, in Bhupa or Bibhátsa (2nd in the first table) for which the skeleton notes are—

1	3	5	8	10	13
S	R	G	P	Dh	S,

artists give the Prastára as follows :—

1	3	1	3	5	3	5	8	8	10	13	13	10	8	10	8
S	R	S	R,	G	R	G	P,	P	Dh	S	S,	Dh	P	Dh	P,

10	8	5	8	10	8	5	3	5	3	5	3	1
Dh	P	G	P,	Dh	P	G	R,	G	R	G	R,	S.

In Bindrábani-Sáranga (4th in the first table), for which the skeleton notes are—

1	3	6	8	11	13
S	R	M	P	K-N	S,

they give :—

1	3	6	8	6	3	3	6	8	8	11	13	13	11	8	11
S	R	M	P,	M	R	R	M,	P	P	K-N	S,	S	K-N	P	K-N,

8	6	3	6	3	6	3	1
P	M	R	M,	R	M	R	S.

In Bangáli (7th in the first table), for which the skeleton notes are—

1	5	6	8	11	13
S	G	M	P	K-N	S.

they give :—

1	5	6	8	6	5	6	8	11	8	11	13	13	11	8	6
S	G	M	P,	M	G	M	P,	K-N	P	K-N	S,	S	K-N	P	M,

5	5	6	8	6	8	6	5	1
G	G	M	P,	M	P	M	G,	S.

In Jogi or Jilhá-Bhairavi (30th in the first table), for which the skeleton notes are—

1	2	4	6	8	9	11	13
S	K-R	K-G	M	P	K-Dh	K-N	S;

they give :—

1	2	4	6	6	8	9	8	8	9	11	13	13	11
S	K-R	K-G	M,	M	P	K-Dh	P,	P	K-Dh	K-N	S,	S	K-N

9	8	9	8	6	4	6	4	2	2	1
K-Dh	P,	K-Dh	P	M	K-G,	M	K-G	K-R	K-R,	S.

In Kalyána (42nd in the first table), for which the skeleton notes are—

1	3	5	7	8	10	12	13
S	R	G	T-M	P	Dh	N	S,

they give:—

1	3	5	3	5	7	8	8	10	12	10	12	13	13	12	10
S	R	G	R,	G	T-M	P	P,	Dh	N	Dh	N,	S	S	N	Dh,

8	10	8	7	5	5	3	1
P	Dh	P	T-M,	G	G	R	S.

In Aliá-Bilávala (7th in the second table), for which the skeleton notes are—

1	3	5	6	8	10	11	12	13
S	R	G	M	P	Dh	K-N	N	S (see second table),

they give:—

1	3	5	8	10	11	12	13	13	12	11	10	8	10	11	10
S	R	G	P,	Dh	K-N	N	S,	S	N	K-N	Dh,	P	Dh	K–N	Dh,

10	8	6	5	3	5	8	6	5	5	3	1
Dh	P	M	G,	R	G	P	M,	G	G	R	S.

In Gouḍa-Sáranga (6th in the third table), for which the skeleton notes are—

1	3	6	5	7	8	10	12	13
S	R	M	G	T-M	P	Dh	N	S (see third table),

they give:—

1	3	6	5	5	7	8	8	3	1	1	3	6	5	5	7
S	R	M	G,	G	T-M	P	P,	R	S	S	R,	M	G	G	T-M,

8	8	10	12	10	12	13	13	12	10	8	3	6	5	8	3	1
P	P	Dh	N,	Dh	N	S	S,	N	Dh	P	R,	M	G	P	R,	S.

The above extensions, which are purposely made most simple, and without regard to the restrictions of Tála (time), strictly preserve the principle of ascent and descent, and show a way as to how Rágas can be extended. It is not necessary to adhere to the above formations. Any formations, with due regard to the principle of ascent and descent, would do as well.

In the Prastára, artists also take the liberty (akin to what is called poetical license) of over-leaping a note in the scale, either in the ascent or descent.

The following illustration, in which the arrangement of ascent and descent is only apparently irregular, will render this more clear.

The skeleton notes of Bhupa or Bibhátsa (2nd in the first table) are $\overset{1}{\text{S}}\ \overset{3}{\text{R}}\ \overset{5}{\text{G}}\ \overset{8}{\text{P}}\ \overset{10}{\text{Dh}}\ \overset{13}{\text{S}}$. An artist, however, drops any one or two notes in the actual performance, either in the ascent or descent, thus :—

1	5	5	3	1	1	10	8	5	3	13	10	5	3	8	5	3	1
S	G	G	R	S,	S	Dh	P	G	R,	S	Dh	G	R	P	G	R	S,

over-leaping in the ascent $\overset{3}{\text{R}}$ and again $\overset{3}{\text{R}}\ \overset{8}{\text{G}}\ \overset{5}{\text{P}}$, and in the descent over-leaping $\overset{8}{\text{P}}$, and so on.

It will be seen that the notes jumped over are not altogether dropped, but given to the audience in the subsequent production of the Rága; and thus, with strict regard to the principle of Árohana and Avarohana, a good artist introduces a variety not only in the production of the Rága without marring its original features, but even lending an additional charm and a happy effect to it, which of course, depends upon the artist's command over the various ways of producing the notes like the Minḍa, the Ghasiṭa, or the Murki. This subject will be fully discussed and explained in Chap. V.

An attempt is made below to give a few compositions of some of the Rágas as produced by the Minḍa or the Ghasiṭa, showing how an artistic formation is effected. These compositions are, of course, not set to any Tála (time).

Bhupa or Bibhátsa (2nd in the first table) :—

1 3 5 3 5 8 5 3 5 8 10 13 13 10 8 5 3 5 3 1

S R-G R, G-P-G R, G P-Dh S, S-Dh-P G, R-G-R S.

Darbári-Kánaḍá (38th in the first table) :—

1 3 3 4 3 4 6 8 8 9 11 13 13 11

S R R-K-G, R-K-G-M-P, P-K-Dh-K-N-S, S K-N

9 11 9 8 6 8 8 6 6 4 3 4 3 1

K-Dh-K-N, K-Dh-P M-P, P-M M-K-G, R K-G-R S.

(This Rága, if deprived of its Minḍas or Ghasiṭas, is reduced to a mere Jilhá-Sind-Bhairavi.

Desa (11th in the second table) :—

1 3 6 5 3 3 6 8 8 10 12 13 13 12 10 8 6 5

S R-M-G, R R-M-P, P Dh-N-S, S N Dh P, M G

3 6 6 5 3 1

R-M, M-G R S.

The three compositions of Bhupa or Bibhátsa, Darbári-Kánaḍá, and Desa given above, are, no doubt, difficult to appreciate as given here on paper, but, if produced either vocally or on instruments, will give the reader a fair idea of the musical and artistic effect of the Minḍa or Ghasiṭa.

The subject of artistic execution of the Rágas belongs more properly to the domain of practical music, and is hardly one for theorising or discussion; much less can it be said to form a legitimate subject for this work within its narrow limits. However, a careful study of the above formations, along with the other information contained in these pages (*vide* Chap. V. *post*) and a little practical knowledge of the art, will, it is hoped, go a long way to show how a Rága is set to music, and how it is extended or embellished. As a matter of fact, the artistic execution of a Rága is not complete without its Murchhánas being touched by the Minḍa or the Ghasiṭa.

It is superfluous to say that all Rágas admit of being extended, though in different degrees, on account of the difference in the number of their skeleton notes. This extension is, as stated above, called Prastára.

Artists touch a note or notes in the register (Svarita) octave and the same corresponding note or notes in the octaves below and above (Anudátta and Udátta). The touching in the register octave is called Vádi, and in the other two octaves Samavádi, for instance, in Kalyána (42nd in the first table):—

Samavádi, Anudátta.			Vádi. Svarita.			Samavádi. Udátta.		
1	3	5	1	3	5	1	3	5
S	R	G.	S	R	G.	S	R	G.
7	8	10	7	8	10	7	8	10
T-M	P	Dh.	T-M	P	Dh.	T-M	P	Dh

Instead of touching the corresponding notes of a Rága in the other two octaves, they sometimes touch other notes of the same Rága in the said octaves. This process goes by the name of Anuvádi, for example, in Kalyána (42nd in the first table) :—

Anuvádi.	Vádi.	Anuvádi.
Anudátta.	Svarita.	Udátta.
7 8 10	1 3 5	7 8 10
T-M P Dh.	S R G.	T-M P Dh.

It is not compulsory to touch Vádi first, then Samavádi, and then Anuvádi, but any arrangement, with due regard to the principle of ascent and descent, is permissible. Nor is it necessary to touch an equal number of notes in the Vádi, Samavádi, and Anuvádi, for instance, in Kalyána (42nd in the first table) :—

Anuvádi.	Vádi.	Samavádi.
Anudátta.	Svarita.	Udátta.
7 8 10 12	1 3 5	1 3 5 7 8
T-M P Dh. N.	S R G.	S R G T-M P.

It is needless to say that Vádi, Samavádi, and Anuvádi are not only touched in simple jumping, but, also, in the Minḍa or the Ghasiṭa, and but seldom in the Murki. The insertion of a note or notes in any Rága outside its proper skeleton notes is termed Vivádi, and is, therefore, condemned as an unmusical composition.

There is some controversy as to the meaning of the words Vádi, Samavádi, and Anuvádi, but it is difficult to understand any meaning of the words as based upon the relative arrangement of notes; and it is submitted that the only consistent meaning which can be attached to the words is that given above as implying a change of octaves.

The old orthodox superstition amongst Hindus was that music consisted of the three Grámas, Shaḍja, Madhyama, and Panchama, called respectively Nandyá-Varta,[1] Subhadra,[2] and Jimúta.[3]

It is not easy to comprehend what was exactly meant by this notion, and it would be a profitless task to speculate about the origin or meaning of the popular belief. However, if we are to attach any practical meaning to the word "Gráma," the word was not intended to convey any other idea than that of a "Gamut," and so the three "Grámas" seem to be intended for the three octaves mentioned above; and their location in this and a higher or lower world seems in this as in many other instances due to the influence of religion upon music.

It has been stated above that the introduction of the Vivádi in a Rága is considered unmusical. It would be difficult to assign any theoretical grounds why

[1] Nandi, a bull, is an emblem of the earth.

[2] Very good or higher.

[3] Cloud, hence celestial.

such a composition of notes should be termed unmusical. There are certainly none intrinsically in the composition itself, but there can be no doubt that, to the practised ear, nothing is more charming than to listen to the different Rágas, carefully preserved as regards the purity of their original skeleton notes and sung or performed with rigid adherence to the distinctive principle of ascent and descent. This principle, along with others, admirably preserves the individual Rágas, and prevents their being confounded one with the other.

The confusion of Rágas invariably generates (in the practised ear) an impression as of a chaotic group of notes, however skilful and regular in time the notes may be. There is no doubt that, with the progress in music, the number of Rágas must necessarily increase, but it is also true that the new Rágas, in order to deserve the dignity of the name, must have, like those now in vogue, their distinctive signs. The number of Rágas in recent times has not only not been increased, but rather, if anything, decreased. The increase, if any, has partly been on the side of Chijas (poetry set to music) in Rágas, and principally on the side of Chijas in Jilhás or Dhuns.

Before dismissing this subject, it may be said that one of the most artistic characteristics of Indian Rágas is the Murchhaná, *i. e.*, quarter tone.

It has been said before [in the second chapter] that the 12 Murchhanás are distributed over all the Rágas, and that they (the Murchhanás) are touched only in the Minḍa or the Ghasiṭa. Now, let us add that each Rága consists of two Murchhanás, the first being called "Graha" (lit., place) and the second "Nyása" (lit., distance or interval), and that there is no Murchhaná proper in a Jilhá or Dhun. This number of Murchhanás in a Rága has been admirably increased in later times, not only in the compound Rágas, but also in the simple Rágas of Komala-Svaras (semitones), and the effect has been simply charming.

Artistically speaking, the simple production of the notes of a Rága, in a given time, does not give one a complete idea of that Rága, unless its proper Murchhanás are added to the notes of which they (Murchhanás) form parts. The Murchhaná is touched first, or next to the note of which it forms a part, but never separately. No stand (pause) is made on a Murchhaná, which is never produced without a Minḍa or a Ghasiṭa. If this arrangement is not strictly observed, the Murchhaná will be a discordant and violently shaky *note*, which it is not, and ought not to be. Speaking from an artistic point of view, the Murchhaná is a quarter part of a tone, and it is always produced in a Minḍa or Ghasiṭa along with the note of which it forms a part, and its number is limited in each Rága. There are many Rágas of which the Murchhanás are the characteristic and distinguishing marks. An omission of the distinctive signs is the destruction of the Rágas so characterized: this is the reason which confounds the Jogi or Asávari with the Jilhá-Bhairavi (30th in the first table and 1st in the second table), the Darbári-Kánaḍá with the Jilhá-Sinda-Bhairavi (38th in the first table), the Sáháná-Kánaḍá with the Jilhá-Káfi (39th in the first table), the Sinda-Kánaḍá with the Jilhá-Káfi (5th in the second table), the Jejevanti-Kánaḍá with the Jilhá-Sindorá (6th in the second table), the Jounpuri with the Jilhá-Sind-Bhairavi (8th in the second table), the Soraṭa with the Jilhá-Khamácha (10th in the second table), the Palása with the Jilhá-Barvá (16th in the second table), the Dhanáshri with the Jilhá-Káfi (17th in the second table), the Bhairava with the Jilhá-Kálangḍá (20th in the second table and 35th in the first table), and the Bhimpalása with the Jilhá-Sind-Bhairavi (8th in the third table).

The fact of the above confusion amply proves, as we have said before, that the Rágas, if deprived of their Murchhanás and of their principle of ascent and descent, result in Dhuns (not complete) or Jilhás of those Rágas: this is the reason why the Jilhá or Dhun is recognized only as an incomplete Rága, giving only as it were a shade of it and not the whole distinctive feature. It is hardly necessary to say that even the touching of the notes of a Rága with a Minḍa or Ghasiṭa, without touching or producing its Murchhanás, results only in the Dhun of that Rága. When the production of notes of a Rága is devoid of a Minḍa or Ghasiṭa, it results in a simple Jilhá or jumping. It is not to be understood that, in so saying, we imply any disparagement of the process of simple jumping of the notes, which has of course its own charms. We have used the word "jumping" simply as appropriately distinguishing the process from the Minḍa or the Ghasiṭa which connotes a connection between, or the co-mingling of the notes. Even in the complete production of a Rága, each and every note of it is not encumbered with a Minḍa or Ghasiṭa and a Murchhaná, unless, of course, an artist only wishes to show that he has achieved an unusually dexterous feat, and does not care for the sweetness and melody of the music he gives. If the trill shake, and other variations adorn and embellish the notes, it must be admitted that the Minḍa or Ghasiṭa and the Murchhaná at least do the same if not more.

To render the above facts clear, we give below the 12 Murchhanás with the 12 notes (Chromatic scale) on which they (Murchhanás) depend. The Murchhanás are the chief, if not the only, item of Indian Rágas, and they are also called Tivratara (double sharp or sharper) or Ati-Komala (very flat). Each Murchhaná being considered as quarter of a tone, their total number must necessarily be in exact proportion to the number of half-notes (Chromatic scale); and this is the reason why the author considers that number to be twelve and not twenty-one as some persons assert. There is another minuter, but none the less perceptible, division of the Murchhaná, but as it comes under the principle of shaking, we need not treat it separately. In shaking a note, however skilfully, the result is always either to raise or to lower a note, but generally the former. The artistic effect of the shaking of a note cannot be called discordant or violent.

Instead of giving a table to show the 12 notes (Chromatic) on which the 12 Murchhanás (quarter part of a tone) depend, it will suffice to state that the first Murchhaná is between S (C) and K-R (C Sh.), the second stands between K-R (C Sh.) and R (D), the third between R (D) and K-G (D Sh.), the fourth between K-G (D Sh.) and G (E), and so on. According to this arrangement, the first Murchhaná is between S (C) and K-R (C Sh.), and the 12th between N (B) and S (C). Whenever it is desired to show a Murchhaná in this work it will be done or expressed by inserting "¼" after the note to which it belongs.

The above description shows that, to produce a Murchhaná in a Miṇḍa or Ghasiṭa, one must touch the note on which it depends. If one wants to produce, for instance, the first Murchhaná, one can do it only in two ways—first, by touching the note S (C) and then the Murchhaná, or touching first the K-R (C Sh. or D Fl.) from the S (C) and then the Murchhaná. It is hardly necessary here to remind the reader that to touch the S (C) by a Miṇḍa or Ghasiṭa, he must go first to N (B) or to K-N (B Fl. or A Sh.), to Dh (A) or to K-Dh (A Fl. or G Sh.), as the case may be, for he must know that there are Rágas from which the three notes—N (B), K-N (B Fl. or A Sh.), and Dh (A)—are excluded, as in the cases of Bibhása (1st in the first table) and Rámashri or Gunkali (12th in the first table).

What does an artist do when he wants to touch the first Murchhaná, which is a Murchhaná of Purvi and such other Rágas ? He first touches the note S (C) from N (B) or from any other note, as it suits his convenience, then the Murchhaná, and thence the K-R (D Fl.), and finally he reverts to the S (tonic) ; or he goes first to the K-R (C Sh.) from S (C) and then touches the Murchhaná, before reverting to the S (C).

In showing the second Murchhaná, which is a Murchhaná of Bibhása and such other Rágas, the performer gives the Murchhaná first, and then the K-R (D Fl.), or the reverse. The third Murchhaná is a Murchhaná of Sárangas and such other Rágas. We give below the Rágas according to the order of the number of the Murchhaná appropriate to them for their first Murchhaná, and denoting the second Murchhaná appropriate to them by a figure given after the name of each.

Rágas with the first Murchhaná are:—Gounḍáshri 8th, Jaita 8th, Puriá or Renki 7th, Márvá or Dipaka 7th, Purvi 8th, Varáṭi or Puriá-Kalyána 8th, Gouḍi 7th, Shri 8th, Jaitáshri 8th, and Purvi-Hindi 8th.

Rágas with the second Murchhaná are :—Bibhása 9th, Gurjari 9th, Rámashri or Gunkalith, Lalata 9th, Lalitá 10th, Jogi 9th, ilasakBháni Toḍi 9th, Toḍi 9th, Soheni 9th, Basanta 10th, Asávari 9th, Jogiá 9th, Bhairava 9th, and Paraja 10th.

Rágas with the third Murchhaná are :—Bhupa or Bibhása 10th, Megha or Sura-Malhára 10th, Bindrábani-Sáranga 11th, Sura-Sáranga 12th, Baḍhansa-Sáranga 10th, Madhumáta-Sáranga 12th, Bilávala or Velávali 10th, Rámadáshi-Sáranga 10th, Aliá-Bilávala 10th, Deshási 10th, Soraṭa 10th, Desa 10th, Gounḍa or Malhári 10th, Miáki or Tánasen's Malhára[1] 10th, Kakubha 10th, Gounḍa-Malhára 10th, and Gouḍa-Sáranga 10th.

Rágas with the fourth Murchhaná are :—Málakosa or Málava 11th, Koushi 11th, Náyaki-Kánaḍá or Karnáṭi 11th, Madhura-Kánaḍá 12th, Darbári-Kánaḍá 11th, Sáhána-Kánaḍá 11th, Dháni-Kánaḍá 12th, Sinda-Kánaḍá 11th, Jejevanti-Kánaḍá 11th, Jounpuri 11th, Palása 11th, Dhanáshri 11th, Gandhára 12th, Multáni 12th, Bágeshri-Kánaḍá or Báhára 11th, and Bhimpalása 11th.

Rágas with the fifth Murchhaná are :—Bangáli 11th, Tilanga 12th, Máleshri or Málavashri 12th, Hinḍola 12th, Bhupáli 12th, Susthávati 12th, Madhu-

[1] Tánasen's Malhára is wonderfully finished for its Murchhanás. It has the Murchhanás of Megha or Sura-Malhára, of Kánaḍás and of other Rágas. Whoever hears this Rága, in its true form, cannot fail to have an idea as to the wonderful gifts of the celebrated singer for composing Rágas.

mádhavi 11th, Deshi 12th, Ṭankiká 12th, Panchama 12th, Jangalá 12th, Kalyána 12th, Khamácha or Khambáti 11th, Bhyága 12th, Shankará 12th, Shankará-Bharana 12th, Yamana-Kalyána 12th, Hámira 12th, Náṭa 12th, and Chháyá 12th.

Rágas with the sixth Murchhaná are :—Kámoda or Kámbodi 12th, Bhyagaḍá 12th and Kedára 12th.

It is needless to dilate upon the distribution of the 12 Murchhanás. Suffice it to say, that with the progress of the Minḍa or Ghasiṭa, the touching of the Murchhanás is marvellously developed. The number of the Murchhanás is increased even in a simple Rága. This increase of Murchhanás in a Rága is in proportion with the number of the Komala-Svaras (semitones) which that Rága requires.

We give below a common formation, without Tála (time), of Kalyána (42nd in the first table), to show how the two Murchhanás of it are covered. It is hardly necessary to repeat that the Murchhaná is a quarter part of a tone, and it is produced only in a Minḍa or a Ghasiṭa, and no stand (pause) is made on it.

1 3 5 3 5 3 5 7 8 8 10
S R G, R—G-¼—R—G—T-M—P, P Dh,
10 12 10 12 13 13 12 10 10 8
Dh—N-¼—Dh—N—S S, N—Dh Dh—P,
7 5 5 3 1
T-M G, G—R—S.

The above formation, which is an ordinary piece for an artistic singer or player of Joḍa-music, may not be well reproduced either by the voice or on instruments by a novice without long practice. Therefore, the subject of Murchhanás is not further discussed here, but the reader will find the same referred to again in Chap. V. However, in concluding this subject, we may repeat that, with the progress in the Minḍa or Ghasiṭa, the number of Murchhanás is increased in a Rága of Komala-Svaras (semitones) ; for instance, in Kalyána (42nd in the first table) there is room for a third Murchhaná between Tivra-Madhyama (F Sh. or G Fl.) and Panchama (G), and the number of the third Murchhaná would be seven. In an artistic performance of a Rága, the artist does not show a Murchhaná only once, but, at a stretch, he shows the Murchhaná along with the note on which it depends, more than once, and the effect, thus produced, is simply beautiful. When a Minḍa or Ghasiṭa does not show a Murchhaná, it goes by the name of Khaḍi, and when it shows one, it is called Suda.[1]

This would, perhaps, be a proper place to observe that each Rága has certain notes as its Pradhána or Pramukha (principal) on which a comparatively longer stand is made. This subject is peculiar to the practice of the art, and, therefore, a word or two about it will not be out of place.

---

[1] Suda probably is a corruption of Shudha (pure) or Sandhi (joining).

Those who are well versed in the Rágas give a preponderance to certain notes, which are considered to be the principal notes of that Rága, the remaining notes being considered as subordinate to them. The object of selecting particular notes on which to make a prolonged stand seems to be that when several Rágas blend with one another considerably there must be as many distinctive marks as possible, and the "Pradhána" notes appear to be some of them. For general guidance, it may be added that such principal or Pradhána notes of a Rága would be generally the notes on which the Murchhanás of that Rága depend.

We consider it necessary, here, to say a few words about the so-called six Rágas (males) and thirty Ráginis (spouses or female Rágas) which are referred tó by the old and new writers on music. In various Sanskrit works on music, the number of Rágas is given as from five to ten. In the *Máhábhárata* and other ancient works, such as *Brihadáranyaka*, *Kaushitaki*, and other *Upanishadas*, the expressions "five kinds" and "ten kinds" of music probably refer to the Rágas or melodies.

It is exceedingly probable that this arrangement of classifying certain combinations of musical notes into six Rágas was borrowed from the *Vedángas*,[1] which are

---

[1] Apastamba, ii., 4, 8, says :— "शिक्षा कल्पो व्याकरणं निरुक्तं छंदो ज्योतिषं The study of these six *Vedángas* was necessary either for the reading, the understanding or the proper sacrificial employment of the Veda. Professor Max Muller's *History of Ancient Sanskrit Literature*, p. 111.

also six in number. The number six appears to have a peculiar sanctity in the Vedic and Pauránic literature. The number of Hindu shástras[1] is six; his duties[2] during the day are supposed to be six (*shaṭkarma*). Six is also the number of the senses.[3]

It appears that to harmonise with this number—which was the number of the best and most sacred things and attributes—the number of the principal Rágas was hit upon as being six, and the total number of Rágas and Ráginis together only a multiple of the same sacred number, *i. e.*, thirty-six, which again is the recognized number of their Kalás (arts), tribes[4] or families, passions,[5] Tálas (Time), etc.

Even in the Buddhistic literature we find the number thirty-six as the number of the passions. There s a verse in the *Dhammapada*,[6] which runs thus :—" He whose thirst running towards pleasure is exceeding

---

[1] Orthodox systems of the Hindu philosophy.

[2] See Manu, Apastambha, and other law-givers.

[3] According to orthodox Hindus, the mind, instead of denoting a group or aggregate of perceptions and sensations, is a separate organ or sense by itself. In European classification, the senses are five, and are considered to be the transformations of the primordial, tactual or gravitative perception. The Sánkhya doctrine of Hindu philosophy similarly teaches that the five intellectual senses are a mere modification of the sense of touch.

[4] Tod's *Rájasthan*.

[5] The Rasas or passions are eight according to Bharata. According to some authorities they are nine. They are: Shringára, love; Háshya, mirth; Karuná, tenderness; Raudra, fury; Vira, hero m; Bhayánaka, terror; Bibhatsha, disgust; and Adbhuta, wonder. The ninth is Shánta or tranquility.—H. H. Wilson's *Theatres of the Hindus*, Vol. I., p. lviii., Third Ed.

[6] Max Muller's *Dhammapada*, p. 80, Chap. XXIV., verse 339.

strong in the thirty-six channels (passions), the waves will carry away that misguided man * * *"

All this only serves to illustrate the influence of religion upon music. In the earlier ages of almost every nation the identity of the two is, of course, almost unbroken. In this country, at a time when music—in fact, all learning—was the monopoly of the Brahmanical order, it was inevitable that its progress should mainly follow religious lines. This may be the probable reason why the Rágas came to be considered as being six in number.

Every reader of the ancient literature of India must have remarked the strong allegorical tendency of the early Hindus to personify the forces of Nature; and, therefore, it is no matter for surprise that certain combinations of musical notes came to be termed Rágas (passions) and others as their females (Ráginis), and yet others, above the number of thirty-six, as their issue. This tendency towards personification, which is observed here, vitiated, in early Greek literature the otherwise considerable progress in literature, and arts. To show what false notions have been created by this personification of inanimate things we draw upon Prof. Max Muller,[1] who says:—"To say that the Pitris or Manes appear as stars to mortal eyes, is another assertion that requires considerable limitation, and is apt to convey

[1] *Chips from a German Workshop*, Vol. II., pp. 205 and 206.

as false an idea of the primitive faith of the Vedic Rishis, as when we read that the Ápas (waters) are cloud-maidens, brides of the gods, or navigators of the celestial sea (Návyah), and that the Apasarás are damsels destined to delight the souls of the heroes, the *houris,* in fact, of the Vedic paradise. The germs of some of these ideas may, perhaps, be discovered in the hymns of the Veda, but to speak thus broadly of a Vedic paradise, of *houris,* and cloud-maidens, is to convey, as far as we can judge from texts and translations hitherto published, an utterly false idea of the simple religion of the Vedic poets."

It may be observed in passing that the tendency of personifying inanimate objects is, more or less, according to the most thoughtful treatise on Myth and Science by Tito Vignoli, prevalent, not only among the human race, civilized or barbarous, but even in the animal kingdom. Tito Vignoli rationally proves and concludes that as *knowledge progresses* this tendency decreases, and its opposite *ratiocination* (science) *increases.*

The six Rágas and thirty Ráginis with their names, as found in the most authoritative works on music collated by the industry of Sir W. Jones[1] are as given below :—

(1) Bhairava—Varáṭi, Madhumádhavi, Bhairavi, Saindhavi (this is not a Rága as it has four notes only), and Bangáli.

[1] *Asiatic Researches,* Vol. III., pp. 77-79.

(2) Málava—Toḍi, Gouḍi, Gounḍáshri, Susthávati and Kukubha (not mentioned by Soma, author of the *Sangita-vibodha*), and Sangita-Náráyaṇa.

(3) Shrirága—Málavashri, Márvi, Dhanyáshi, Vasanti, and Asáveri.

(4) Hinḍola—Rámashri, Deshashi, Lelitá, Velávali, and Paṭamanjari (omitted).

(5) Dipaka (omitted)—Deshi, Kámbodi, Neṭṭá, Kedári and Karnáṭi.

(6) Megha—Taccá (a mixed mode and not in our tables), Mellári, Gurjari, Bhupáli (Bhupa of our table), and Desháshri.

From the names and the number of notes of the above six Rágas, as given in our tables, it will be seen that out of the six, two—Bhairava and Shri—are mixed (Sankirṇa), one—Dipaka—is Khoḍhava (consisting of six notes), and the Málava, Hinḍola and Megha are Oḍhava (having five notes, the least number of musical notes to constitute a Rága).

A careful perusal of the skeleton notes of the above Rágas and Ráginis, of which there are most if not all in the tables in this work with somewhat altered names, will convince the reader that the above classification, in most cases, is crude and unmethodic. To prove this let the reader compare a particular Rága with its Ráginis. Such comparison will convince an impartial mind that the above classification, as a whole, is based neither on any system nor on any considerations of melody in the proper sense of the word.

If the above classification has no affinity of melody between a Rága and its Ráginis for its groundwork, has it any with the names of the Rágas and their respective Ráginis? The answer, it is apprehended, must be in the negative.

It is impossible to find any rational cause why Bhairava should have been linked with Sindha, Varáṭi (a country through which the Pándavás had travelled during their journey), Saindhavi (Sindha or Sindhu) and with Bengali; Málava with Toḍi (a tribe) and Gauḍa or Gonḍáshri (a country); Shri with Vasanta (spring or a metre); Hinḍola with Deshási; Dipaka with Karnáṭi and Deshi; and Megha with Gurjari (modern Guzrat).

A careful perusal of the names of the several Rágas in the tables in this work distinctly suggests that they have been named either after the names of the authors or of the parts of the country where any particular composition of notes was first brought into vogue and practice.

The Pingala,[1] the science of poetry, gives the names of Rasas (passions), which are the names of our Rágas,

[1] See Colebrooke's *Essays*, Vol. II., pp. 152-164, and other works on Pingala or Prosody.

such as Sáranga, Vasanta, Souráshṭriká, Kámodi, Koushṭubha, Jaita, etc.

It is at present difficult to say whether the names of the Rágas were borrowed from the names of the Chhandas (metres) or *vice versá*, but it is certain that melodies now called Rágas were given distinct names in ancient Vedic songs, distinct from hymns, such as Rathantara,[1] Brihata, Vairupa, Vairága and Shakvara-raivata.

Soraṭha or Sourashṭra, Gurjari or Guzrat, Márvi or Márváḍa, Khambáti or Cambay, Gonḍa or Bengal, Berári or Berars, Karnáṭi or Kánaḍá, etc., are clearly named after countries, while Sáranga and Hámira (author of the Rása of this name) owe their names to the authors. There are some such as Vasanta and Megha which appear to be named after the seasons. The Purvi seems to be named after the Purva or the East.

It would not be a very difficult task to find out the original Aryan or Sanskrit names of the Rágas, which were at one time called after particular parts of the country or particular individuals, in spite of their present corrupted and Mahomadenized names; but we cannot spare any larger space for the subject, as no practical purpose is likely to be served by so doing, it being properly a subject for antiquarian research. The subject may, therefore, be closed with an earnest request to lovers of music not to treat the Rágas from a mythological belief, but to appreciate their relative value from a scien-

[1] *Maitráyan-Brahman-Upanishad*, seventh Prapathak.

tific point of view; to discard and eschew any formations they find inartistic and unmelodious, notwithstanding their great names or high antiquity; and to collate all the new Rágas which Mahomedan musicians of several centuries have composed. These new Rágas and Jilhás or Dhuns are not confined to any particular locality from which one can easily secure them. To get at them is a work almost impracticable in the present state of Indian music. The majority of our present musicians are artists ranging below mediocrity, and those few who are still in possession of certain really precious Rágas and Jilhás or Dhuns, cannot be made to part with their treasure unless and until they are offered some irresistible inducement to do so. The present musicians, as a class, are satisfied with the execution, within moderate bounds, of the most superficial music, and never take the pains to enrich the art by further cultivation. Again, there are others who, though highly gifted, grudge to satisfy the yearnings of a seeker after real music, and do not in the least encourage his attempt to write a book. Such musicians give us no information about their art, and if we wish to recover the old rules of music we must do it by making the best of stray hints or chance stories. It is the common belief of the Hindus that Mahomedan musicians, as a class, excepting Tánasena, who was at first a Hindu Brahmin, have only contaminated the purity and the sacredness of the Rágas, but such a notion must be at once emphatically denounced as false and merely superstitious.

The so-called contamination by Mahomedan musicians is, in fact, not a perversion of the old Rágas in any sense of the word, but on the contrary they have rather perfected them either by adaptation or by filling up the defects of the original compositions. For instance, an alteration of a Rága, which originally consisted of five notes only (Oḍhava), by introducing into its composition one or two more notes in places calculated to enhance the melody and beauty of the whole so as to make it either Khoḍava or Sampurna, ought rather to be welcomed and admired as a desirable improvement in the art instead of being ridiculed as an unjustified departure from unalterable standard formation. What is wanted in music is the musical value of a particular composition and not its mere form or name, however respectable it may be for its antiquity. The Rágas ought never to be regarded as religiously unchangeable hymns or scriptures good and true for eternity. To preserve the individuality of a Rága is, no doubt, of primary importance, and it is really inartistic to begin a Rága as Oḍhava for a time and then in the course of the same performance to make its features indefinite in the number of its notes. What is meant is that a given Rága, if it admits either of extension or curtailment in its notes, with the effect of rendering it more musical, may be so extended or curtailed as not to lose its distinctive character from other Rágas, and it is of little consequence, as to what name you give to such formations. In practical music, the greatest importance should always be attached to *form* as well as to *substance.* In comparison with Hindustani music (see pp. 31 and 32) the Madras one is more for form than for substance. However, it is a common practice among Indian musicians to preserve the antique form of a Rága, even if, from experience, they find such forms to be inartistic, but with the average Indian artist in music this desirable addition to the art is generally sacrificed to time-honoured rules of form, which it is considered almost sacrilegious to violate.

Before closing this chapter, it must be observed that there is an almost superstitious belief of long standing that a particular Rága must be sung or played at a particular hour of the day or night.[1] This belief has got such a strong hold on the minds of those accustomed to hear the Indian Rágas, that a departure from the practice is regarded by them as

---

[1] The following are the different hours of the day and night and the names of Rágas to be sung or played during those particular times :— from 3 a. m. to 6 a. m.—Lalata, Lalitá, Soheni, Paraja, Panchama, Jogiá, Rámashri or Gunkali, and Bhairava or Jilhá-Kálangḍá ; from 7 a. m. to 11 a. m. —Jogi or Jilhá-Bhairavi, Gurjari, Bilásakháni-Toḍi, Toḍi, Asávari, Jounpuri, Gandhára (commonly known as Deva-Gandhára), Bibhása (this is rarely known and practised), Bhupa or Bibhása (this is known in the Sanskrit works as Bhupáli), Bilávala or Velávali, Aliá-Bilávala, and Kakubha (commonly known as Kukabha-Bilávala) ; from 11 a. m. to 2 p. m.—Bindrábani-Sáranga, Sura-Sáranga, Baḍahansa-Sáranga, Madhumáta-Sáranga, Rámadáshi-Sáranga and Gouḍa-Sáranga (this is a misnomer as said before, pp. 86 and 87); from 2 p.m. to 5 p. m.—Dhanáshri or Jilhá-Káfi, Palása or Jilhá-Barvá, Bhimpalása, and Multáni ; from 5 p. m. to 7 p. m.—Máleshri or Málavashri, Gounḍáshri, Jaita, Puriá or Renki, Marvá or Dipaka, Purvi, Varáṭi or Puriá-Kalyána, Gouḍi, Shri, Jaitáshri, and Purvi-Hindi ; from 7 p. m. to 11 p. m.—Bhupáli (this Bhupáli is Khoḍava—S R G P Dh N S, in the first table, while its namesake in the old works is Oḍhava—S R G P Dh S, and differs in no way from the Bhupa or Bibhása ;

sinful.[2] The treatment of the Rágas and of their formation as given above, though not quite a scientific one, does not support this notion, neither is it warranted by any intrinsic adaptability of particular musical notes to a particular time, nor does it seem to be justifiable on the basis of any distinctive note or notes composing the Rágas being allotted to any particular time. The most that can be said to maintain this conventionalism, is that there are certain Rágas—such as the Bhairava and Sura-Sáranga, Jogi and Megha or Sura-Malhára, Todi and Gound-Malhára, Puriá and Gouda-Sáranga, Soheni and Desa, Lalata and Kalyána, etc., etc.—which are distinct from each other in Murchhanás, in tones and semi-tones, and which, above all, produce different effects on account of their different formations. This

---

see first table), Kalyána, Yamana-Kalyána Hámira, Kámoda or Kámbodi Náta, Chháyá, Kedárá, Shankará Barana, Shankará, Bhyagdá, and Bhyága, from 11 p. m. to 1 a. m.—Náyaki-Kánadá or Karnáti, Madhura-Kánadá, Darbári- Kánadá, Sáhána-Kánadá, Dháni-Kánadá, Sinda-Kánadá, and Jejevanti-Kánadá; from 1 a. m. to 3 a. m.—Koushi, Málakosa or Málava, and Hindola, either from 3 p. m. to 5 p. m. or from 8 p. m. to 12 p. m.—Bangáli, Tilanga, Deshi, Khamácha or Khambáti, Deshási, Sorata, and Desa; during the rainy-season from midday to mid-night—Megha or Sura-Malhára, Gounda or Malhári, Gounda-Malhára and Miyáki or Tánasena's-Malhára; in the spring—Báhára or Bageshri-Kánadá and Basanta (the former is sung or played at any time during the spring, while the latter is sung or played at night). The names of Rágas of which the time is unascertained by the author are:—Tankiká, Susthávati, Madhumádhavi and Janglá. In concluding the above list it may be added that the author has given the times of the several Rágas as observed by the present professional musicians of India.

[2] "रंगभूमौ नृपाज्ञया कालदोषो न विद्यते" नारदसंहिता।
There can be no sin of time (to sing or play any Rága at any hour) on the stage under the king's order.—*Nárada Samhita.*

difference in impression is, however, not due to their being sung or played at different times. If it is assumed that the effect produced by the Bhairava, Jogi, Toḍi, Puriá, Lalata, and such other Rágas, is softer or less excitable or less lively than the one produced by the Sárangas, Kánaḍás, Malháras, Kalyánas and such other Rágas, it must be stated that this liveliness or dullness has nothing whatever to do with any particular time of their execution. It can never be asserted that a particular hour of the day or night in itself causes pleasant or painful feelings or *vice versâ*.

In order to sing or play a Rága at a time other than that allotted to it according to this belief, and to break through this ancient notion, many old artists seem to have mixed, more ingeniously than musically, two Rágas of quite different melodies, such as the Hinḍola-Báhára, Bhairava-Báhára (otherwise called Pancham, but not of our table), and many others. They have also called others by misnomers, such as Gouḍa-Sáranga, Rátki-Puriá, Dinki-Puriá, Kakubha-Bilávala, Sarpardá-Bilávala, etc.

The author sees no necessity for refuting at length the so-called theory of Rágas and their specified times, but he challenges any advocate of this belief to explain on any rational basis why, out of many instances, Toḍi or Bhupa, Bibhasa or Bhupáli should be appropriated for the *morning*, or why Multáni (1 Rupa in the second table) should be touched only in the *afternoon*, or why, again, Kalyána should be allotted to the *evening*.

It is sheer madness to think that Toḍi conveys any idea of the morning, and when its second note (C Sh.) is omitted only in the ascent, which is done in the case of Multáni, it should convey an idea of the afternoon. It may be added that a similar belief obtains about particular Rágas being only adapted to particular seasons. The above remarks are equally applicable to the *season-Rágas*.

Mr. Rámparasáda,[1] in expounding the *Sánkhya-yoga*, says:—"Then, again, sound has a temperature of its own. The mental impression of sound very often becomes the cause of heat. Indeed, it is well-known that music has a warming or cooling[2] effect."

The last sentence of the above quotation ought certainly not to shield the superstitious belief above referred to from the ridicule it deserves. The physical science of sound, or, as one of the greatest physicists of the present age, John Tyndal,[3] calls it "the immoveable truths of Acoustics," teaches us that the difference between the notes of a musical scale solely depends on the *wave*-length of sonorous vibrations of a uniform

---

1 *The Theosophists' Magazine*, Vol. XV., No. 12, p. 755, September 1894.

2 A warming or cooling in physical science conveys an idea of a variation in temperature, heat, or molecular motion.

3 Preface to the fourth edition, "Sound."

temperature which *per se* determine their pitch. To comprehend this subject better, let the reader strike, with a stick, tea-cups of different sizes, of a particular metal, or of China or glass, and try to ascertain for himself, how and why the notes so produced vary. It will be seen that the determination of different sounds, high or low, sharp or flat, depends only on the size and the thickness or thinness of the cups, and has nothing whatever to do with the difference of *temperature*, so far as the pitch of the sounds of the cups is concerned; it is all the same whether he strikes the cups with a uniform or varying strength: the force or strength with which one strikes determines only the *intensity* of sound but not its *pitch.*

The author feels that this view of his, about the absolute want of any intrinsic connection between a particular time and a particular musical note, is so opposed to a deep-rooted conviction and belief in the minds of all who have been either regularly trained in Indian music, or pretend to know anything about it, that it is sure to be taken as presumption on his part to have even doubted the truth of the position. Unhappily, on this as on other subjects, trained and educated persons like Mr. Rámaprasáda, who are expected to bring the same faculty of close and scientific analysis to bear upon this subject, which they do upon any other, either feel absolutely enthralled or are led away by their reverence for antiquity; and, instead of contributing towards the progress of the art by rigidly separating the scientific from the vulgar or the superstitious, try to give some hazy and apparently plausible explanation about which they themselves are sceptical. This is what has given rise to the publication and acceptance of several novel and curious explanations in support of the so-called theory of sympathy between particular Rágas and particular times. As a typical instance, in concluding this subject, may be given the following quotation :—

" . . . . The ancient[1] Indian music is in harmony with Nature (?) so much so that to each tune is assigned an appropriate name after the seasons and other phenomena of Nature. Let us hear music composed on the tune *Prabhát* (dawn) before the break of day and the same piece in the afternoon. It will not sound so sweet in the afternoon as it did in the early morning. In the same way, take a piece of music composed on *Basant* (spring) and sing it in the spring. It will be found as sweet (?) as the spring itself (?). But the same piece sung in autumn or in any other season will not sound so sweetly as it did in the spring. *Malhár*, likewise, is more sweet in Malhár (rainy season) than in any other season. . . . . Why (?) because these tunes are based on the key-notes of Nature, (?) by the first poet (?) who heard the divine music (?) and then could copy it for the instruction of mankind. Indian music is natural (?) if

[1] *The Theosophic Gleaner*, Vol. IV., No. 3, pp. 61 and 62, September 1894.

sung on proper occasions. . . . . The vibrations of the sound of music must be in harmony with Nature, (?) the vibrations of which are not always the same, but everchanging (?). It is not necessary, therefore, that certain tunes sung now should be as sweet if sung at odd intervals. This was well-known to Indian poets, who composed their music on this principle (?)." . . . .

The above advocacy, in spite of its novel treatment, we are constrained to say, is neither intelligible to those who comprehend music as an art, nor is it instructive to those who are ignorant of it. It is evident that the author of the above quotation is an enthusiastic admirer of the *poetical* portion of Indian music only, and this may be inferred from the fact that he makes little or no allusion to the several compositions of musical notes, while he treats of the meaning of the words that may form a piece or Chija in a Rága or Jilhá. His theory, if we may be permitted to call it by such term, may perhaps be acceptable and convincing to those who can understand music only through the instrumentality of descriptive words of a poem, and must be rejected by all who judge of music as a science, on its relative strength of composition of particular musical notes. The instances he cites, of Prabháta, spring and rain, exclusively belong to their description by a poet, for we know that in such songs the words depict a scene of the dawn, spring, clouds, and the like. Let us see, for instance, what rational and logical basis can be found in the following instances of the so-called theory :—

Megha or Sura-Malhára (S R M P Dh S, first table) and Bindrábani-Sáranga (S R M P K-N S, first table) differ from each other in one note only, and should any person make an attempt to account for their adaptability to different times because of this one differentiating note, he must come to the conclusion that he must condemn this doctrine. When one bases his judgment on the composition of musical notes and not on the order or meaning of words in a piece of song, one cannot help discarding the popular notion. No sane person would make bold to assert that by inserting K-N or by omitting Dh which is done in the case of Bindrábani-Sáranga and Megha or Sura-Malhára, he realizes, in one, the perception or sensation of the scorching heat of the midday sun, and, in the other, the pouring noise of the rains. The advocates of this belief can safely be challenged to rationally allot the fractions of the day and night for the two hundred and sixty-four (according to the *Sangit-Ratnákara*) and nine hundred and sixty (according to Soma)[1] modifications or variations of the so-called six Rágas and thirty Ráginis.

It is probable that the origin of this belief is due to a state of things obtaining when music was in its infancy and poetry was its necessary accompaniment.

[1] *Asiatic Researches*, Vol. III., p. 71.

The appreciation of music in its earlier stages must have been based more upon the meaning of the words which a piece contained than upon the musical notes comprising it. Such pieces or poems generally conveyed a particular picture of things or times, so that some happy and popular compositions or poems, in course of time, came to be associated with those things and times; and even when musical art began to be appreciated on the basis of musical notes, showing a comparatively higher stage of musical culture, this same association kept on in the minds of those poets or composers, and they naturally depicted particular scenes or seasons in particular songs. Some songs, for instance, contained descriptions of the Clouds, Thunder, Lightning, Peacocks, etc., and such compositions came to be styled Megha or Malhára. Similarly, descriptions of summer in songs got names like Báhára, Sáranga, Basanta, etc. The Bhairava, and other songs containing descriptions of the early morn, came to be associated with that part of the day. When these songs of a particular kind were fixed according to their notes or set to music as Rágas, the scenes and seasons came to be less attended to. Instead of confining their poems about the scenes and seasons to particular Rágas, they may have arbitrarily fixed their Rágas to a particular time and season, and thus different Rágas came to be appropriated to different times. It need not be added that, if this is perhaps the true origin of the present belief, it must have been owing to purely the poetry of vocal music, and not instrumental music, for it could not have been then regarded as quite a distinct branch or an independent art by itself.

The execution of a particular song on an instrument certainly does not convey to any one the meaning of the words of which it is composed, but can simply be judged of as a pure piece of music.

The reader may be reminded that even in the several *modes* of reciting poetry called Chhandas and Vrattas, there is no special regard to any fixity of time, and there are several standard metres in which opposite feelings are expressed in one and the same Chhanda or mode of reciting poetry. In poetical recitations the names of certain metres, which bear the names of some of the Rágas, as has been already remarked, stand for metres of the words and not for a Rága. Such theories practically assert that in the *notes* of *speech* called alphabets there are some which are reserved for the day and others for the night or for warmth or coolness, but the author submits that nothing could be more absurd.

When it is proved that a particular melody is used as a vehicle to convey two entirely different scenes or seasons, there ought not to be any doubt that it has no connection whatsoever with any fixed time. But the average Indian mind is so conservative that it does not like to part with its notions when those notions have antiquity on their side. Those who appreciate the

Rágas only as music from an artistic point of view, and still adhere to this time-honoured belief, are the Joḍa-singers and instrument-players. In their case particularly and others generally, this belief is so deep-rooted and so rigidly adhered to in practice that it has become an impossibility with them to dissociate a particular Rága from its time, and one can easily understand how, owing to such associations in their minds, the two things are now indissolubly connected. But this is not owing to any intrinsic connection between the two. It is proved physiologically[1] that if any two mental states be called up together, or in succession, with due frequency and vividness, the production of any one of them is bound to call up the other, quite independently of the desire to do so. It may be asked,—to what then is due the peculiar feeling of adaptibility of particular strains to particular emotions, *e. g.*, the martial music accompanying a march of troops, etc.? The answer is that this also is as much an association and convention as the one noted above. The sense of a particular spirit being aroused is, if carefully observed, due not to any particular musical notes, but to the Time or Tála, so that the arrangement based on a particular Tála is calculated to create a sense of activity or otherwise. Take the musical notes composing a march, and change them in time and accent, and it will be found that the same notes will cease to produce the previous impression. This, however, is quite a different subject from the one dealt with above, which relates to

[1] Huxley's *Elementary Physiology*, pp. 284-286.

the relation between musical notes and portions of day or night, and not to the relation between notes and emotions. And this only further confirms the correctness of the view taken in this work, because an emotion, a sense of dullness or activity, for instance, is surely not confined to any particular time. Disjointed words only convey disjointed ideas of things they denote. The same joined together in syntax according to known rules make a complex idea. It is the same with musical notes,[1] and the utmost that can be said is that these notes differently arranged cause different rhythms, and therefore different complex emotions of pleasure, etc., but absolutely without any regard to the time of the day or night.

---

[1] "हास्यशृंगारयोः कार्यौ स्वरौ पंचममध्यमौ ॥
षड्जर्षभौ तथा ज्ञेयौ वीररौद्राद्भुते रसे ॥ ११ ॥
गांधारश्च निषादश्च कर्तव्यौ करुणारसे ॥
धैवतश्च तथा कार्यौ बीभत्से च भयानके ॥ १२ ॥"

—*Brih-Sárangadhar Paddhati*, p. 353, printed at Benares.

The above verse is old and is given in some Sanskrit works on music. In this verse, certain notes, such as the Panchama and Madhyama, Shadja and Rishabha (Rikhaba), Gandhára and Nish áda (Nikháda), and Dhaivata are thought to convey certain passions (Rasas), such as Hásya (mirth) and Shringára (love), Vira (heroism) and Adbhuta (wonder), Karuná (tenderness) and Bhayánaka (terror), and Bibhátsa (disgust). But it is the firm conviction of the author that it is not one note or two notes which by themselves constitute emotion, but it is their grouping together in a composition. It is the unanimous opinion of scientists and artists that it is the business of the musician so to combine sounds (notes) as to awaken emotions of the peculiar kind which are associated with the works of art. He employs various resources to attain this end, but musical intervals occupy the foremost place. It is upon the judicious employment of these that the success of a composition mainly depends.

In treating of the above subject at such length the author's object is, if possible, to get rid of this belief about the fixity of the Rágas in time, because it is really an obstacle in the way of the performer, and prevents the audience from being able to enjoy some melodies at any time they choose. In reading a book or listening to a story the reader comes across different things and scenes, and he enjoys them all the same without any regard whatever to the time of the day or night. Why should the same not be the case with the poetical portion of music? The usual time for entertainments and concerts in advanced countries is usually a couple of hours or so after the worry of a whole day's work and after the evening meals. If such concerts or public entertainments in Indian music ever become the fashion—fancy the absurdity of the audience never being able to get more than two or three Rágas, and the rich and entrancing melodies of some of the best and highest musical compositions shut out from them, because of the belief that they can be sung or performed only in the morning or afternoon!

A reference has been made to the effect of time or Tála above. To realize time (Tála) in concrete is to experience "rhythm" or pulsation (regularity) which is a marked distinction of music, and as such it is treated in the next chapter.

CHAPTER IV.

THE TÁLAS AND THEIR FORMATIONS.

Professor A. Bain says:—"In his very subtle and original analysis, Mr. Sully traces the attribute of unity in variety through all the various guises assumed in musical composition. First and most conspicuous, as a means of unity, is Time. To make a sequence of tone all equal in time, gives the simplest impression of unity in variety. Next is a sequence where the tones are alternated with their sub-divisions—a semibreve with two crotchets, and so on. This is carried up to the Foot or Bar, which confers on music its distinguishing rhythmic character, as triple, quadruple," etc.

Tála (time), which is an important factor in every system of music, regulates the relative durations of musical sounds, and as such seems to have considerably engrossed the Indian mind.

That which the Indians call Mátrá[1] (metre) is a unit of Tála. For the sake of simplification, one may call

The oldest Véda (Rig) is regulated by a metrical system of a very difficult and complicated nature, which the Oriental scholars of Europe have been trying for years to reduce to writing.

The Mátrá (*metre* or measure of duration) is of great importance in the recitation and accentuation of all the Védas. The measure of a Védic Mátrá is one short vowel. The *Prátisákhyas*, as elaborating a most complicated system of the Védic metres, counting the syllables in the most mechanical manner, have

1, 2, 3, 4, 5, 6, 7, 8, 9, etc., when counted or pronounced at a regular and uniform interval (Laya), as Mátrás. Tála is an aggregate of the Mátrás or equal lengths in a piece of music. The number of Mátrás in each Tála is fixed. If a person repeats the word 1 (one) continuously and at a uniform interval and adjusts a stroke either by the hands or by any other means with the very first sound as the word "one" is uttered each time, he gets the Áditála (primary), which is ordinarily known by the name of Dádrá. The Áditála is the foundation on which other Tálas are based. If he repeats 1, 2, and strikes only at the commencement of uttering the word "one," he gets the Zaptála. In repeating 1, 2, 3, and striking at the commencement of the word "one," a person gets the Gajalatála or Dipachandi (practically this is like a treble and is used extensively). In repeating 1, 2, 3, and striking at the commencement of the words "one" and "two," a person realizes the Rupakatála. Before proceeding further, it may be said that, in order to increase the number

---

assigned nearly a hundred names to every variety which they discovered in the hymns of the Ṛig-Véda. But they also observed that the constituent elements of all these metres were really but four (*Sûtras* 988 and 989) :— (1) *Gáyatri páda* (eight syllables), (2) *Vairága páda* (ten syllables), (3) *Trishṭubha páda* (eleven syllables), and (4) *Jágata páda* (twelve syllables). They also called a Mátrá Laghu (light or short) and Guru (heavy or long). Since the *Prátisákhya* deals more with the metres of the Védas than those of music, it would be hardly useful to go further into the subject. We have referred to it with a view to point out that some of the names of Védic metres and their arrangement have a connection with our Tála. Our present Titála or Triavaṭa is a corruption of the Védic Triviṭ (triplets) or Trishṭubha.

Our object being to deal with the Tálas in music in their particular aspect, we need not trace their origin from the Védas and bring them down in their successive forms to their present stage of development.

of Mátrás in a Tála, Indian musicians have devised what are called the Avasána, Tála, and Kála (rests). The first (Avasána) is the beginning or end of a Tála, and it is also the point where the singer or the player on a musical instrument, and the drummer who is keeping time, come to a happy termination and meet each other in their performances and elicit the applause of the audience. The second (Tála) is the point of a stroke, and the third (Kála) is that of an absence of the stroke (rest).

When a Tála is repeated, each repetition is called Avardá, a corruption of Ávritti (repetition). A number of such repetitions does not change a Tála.

In the Zaptála, Gajalatála or Dipchandi, and in the Rupakatála the point of the Avasána is not a Tála (stroke), but a Kála (rest). No satisfactory cause is shown for this deviation.

To simplify the subject we are now treating of, we must allot to the Avasána (stroke)—otherwise called "Sama"—the *first place* in the serial order of the Mátrás in a Tála. We give a *serial figure* to the Tála (stroke, but not the Avasána) which is called "Bhari" (not empty). We will show the Kála (rest)—otherwise called "Kháli" (empty)—by a serial *figure in a bracket.* This process at once teaches us that the first figure stands for the Avasána, the figure without a bracket is the sign of a Tála, and the figure in a bracket is the mark of a Kála.

If one goes by the above method, he reproduces the Titála or Trivaṭatála (4 Mátrás, but 3 strokes) which is as follows :—1, 2, (3), 4.

Here are the Sulafákatála (5 Mátrás, but 3 strokes) —1, (2), 3, 4, (5) ; Chauṭála or Ekká (6 Mátrás, but 4 strokes)—1, (2), 3, (4), 5, 6 ; and Áḍáchautála (7 Mátrás, but 4 strokes)—1, 2, (3), 4, (5), 6, (7).

The above Tálas are the principal ones, and others are their varieties. The varieties of Tála are effected simply by doubling or quadrupling the number of Mátrás of the principal Tálas and by simply changing the order of strokes and rests. For example, the Dhamára or Hori[1] is neither more nor less than the Áḍáchautála doubled, and its strokes and rests changed.

Áḍáchautála—1, 2, (3), 4, (5), 6, (7).
Dhamára— 1, (2), (3), (4), (5), 6, (7), (8), (9), (10), 11, (12), (13), (14)

The Brahmatála and Rudratála are no other Tálas than the Titála and Sulafákatála quadrupled, and their order of strokes and rests changed.

Titála— 1, 2, (3), 4.
Brahmatála—1, (2), 3, (4), 5, (6), 7, 8, (9), 10, 11, 12, (13), 14, 15, 16.

Sulafákatála—
1, (2), 3, 4, (5).

Rudratála—
1, (2), 3, (4), 5, 6, (7), 8, 9, 10, (11), 12, 13, 14, 15, (16), 17, 18, 19, 20.

---

[1] The Dhamára or Hori is difficult and seldom practised. Its Avasána is not on a stroke.

The Savári tála or Kaida, which is generally practised by latter-day musicians, is no other Tála than the Titála, but the real Savári is not used now. It has 7 Mátrás and a half, and this is the reason why it is difficult. This Savári, when doubled and its strokes and rests are changed, goes by the name of Brahmatála (another form of the Brahmatála).

Saváritála —1, 2, (3), 4, (5), 6, (7), ($\frac{1}{2}$)
Brahmatála—1, (2), 3, (4), 5, (6), 7, 8, (9), 10, 11, (12), 13, 14, 15.

The peculiarity of Indian musicians is that, instead of going at a regular interval (Laya), the singer or player, in competing with the drummer, at times changes the point of Avasána of a piece of music to $\frac{1}{2}$ or $\frac{1}{4}$ of that Mátrá. The former is called Aghátа or Atita (no stroke), and the latter is named Anughátа (after the stroke).

To break up the monotony or the dead uniformity of time in a piece of music, the singer or player (who deals more with the simple jumping than with the Minḍa, Ghasiṭa and Murki) sometimes reduces the original time (Barobari) or speed to one-half (Ṭhá), at other times he doubles (Dviguni or Duni) it, or quadruples (Chaugan) it ; and, as a matter of course, the drummer adopts the same procedure. Ṭhá (one-half), Barobari (equal), Duni (double), and Chaugan (quadruple) are the relative terms, and their relation to each other stands thus :—

Ṭhá is equal to a Semibreve, Barobari to a Minim, Duni to a Crotchet, and Chaugan to a Quaver; or, in other words, Ṭhá is equal to 8 annas, Barobari to 16 annas, Duni to 32 annas, and Chaugan to 64 annas to a rupee. The artists also double the Chaugan in Tána, but they never go further than this ; or, in other words, they use a semi-quaver, but not a demi-semi-quaver.

The artists at times accelerate the original time (Barobari) or speed in a piece of music to 1½ (Áḍa or Deḍi) or to 1¼ (Kuáḍa or Savái), but this is very difficult. To realize this difficulty we suggest to our readers to attempt to produce by the hands Titála with Chautála (Áḍa or 1½) and Titála with Sulafákatála (Kuáḍa or 1¼); or in other words, the Titála and Chautála and Titála and Sulafákatála should be regulated in such a way as to converge their respective Avasánas. This attempt is sure to be attended with an abnormal difficulty in the absence of a key. This key we have invented, and it will appear at the end of the description of Tálas.

Indian musicians have evidently taken great pains to formulate, from the artistic point of view, the technical vocabulary of their drumming. The peculiarity of the Indian Pakhavája[1] or Tabalá[2]-Báyá (detached Pakhavája) is that it is generally attuned[3] to the fundamental (Svarita) note S (C or tonic) of the musicians. It is played by the palms and fingers of both the hands at the

[1] This instrument is also called Mridunga. In Páli it is called Maddraka.—See H. Kern's *Saddharma Pundarika*, p. 15.

[2] The Nabla of the historian Strabo.—See Tod's *Rájasthana*, Vol. I., p. 565.

[3] Few drummers know how to adjust their instruments correctly.

edge, at the middle, and on the centre of the two circles, black and white which lie one within the other. The right hand side (not of a left-handed drummer), which is besmeared with iron to make it resonant, is called Dainá or Dakshina ; and the left-hand side, which is also made resonant by pressing it with wheat-flour to adjust it with the right side, is called Báyá or Váma. The instrument is too common to need any further description. The fingers of the right hand are used more freely than those of the left hand. The stroke, which is produced in the middle of the right side of the instrument (*i.e.*, in the middle portion, not the centre of the black circle) by the right palm, is called Tá ; and the stroke, by the same palm on the centre (iron), is known as Tha. The stroke, which is produced at the edge by the index finger of the right hand, goes by the name of Ná. A similar (four fingers, excepting the thumb) arrangement, if manipulated by the left hand on the left side of the instrument is named Ga, Ghi or Ghin, and Ka respectively. When the right palm and the left-hand fingers produce a stroke jointly in the middle of their respective circles, the stroke thus produced is called Dhá—the usual, but not an invariable, sign of the Avasána. It is unnecessary to say that the Dhá is a compound stroke of the Tha and Gha. A compound stroke of the Ti or Tin and Ghin, is named Dhin. This arrangement is slightly changed on Tabalá-Báyá (detached Pakhavája). There is but very little difference between the Pakhavája and Tabalá-Báyá instrumentally. The former is handled more with the palms and the joint fingers of the left hand (sometimes only three fingers, excepting the thumb and the last, are used separately) than with separate fingers of the hands; while the latter is played more by the fingers than by the palms, and even the left-hand fingers (three, excepting the thumb and the last) are used more freely and separately. Pakhavája is generally played with Dhrupada and Dhamára (music set to Dhamáratála), and Tabalá-Báyá regulates (not in Madras) the Khyála, Ṭappá, Ṭhumri, Gajala and Dancing.

By adjusting the palms and the fingers at different points on the right and left sides of Pakhavája or Tabalá-Báyá, one gets in all 13 letters or technical syllables as elements composing the Ṭhekás and Parandas which are played as an accompaniment of music. We shall treat of Ṭhekás and Parandas in their proper place. The letters or technical syllables are :—

Ka, Ga, Gha, Ṭa, Ḍa, Ta, Tha, Da, Dha, Na, Ma, Ra, and La. The last is now obsolete.

A combination of the above letters is formed thus :—

(1st) Ka or Ká, Kḍán, Kiṭ and Kiḍ.

(2nd) Ga or Gi, Gan and Gadi or Gdi.

(3rd) Ghḍán, Ghiṭ, Ghiḍ, and Ghin.

(4th) Ta or Tá, Ti or Tu, Tak, Tag, Tiṭ, Tin or Tun, Tir and Trán.

(5th) Tha or Tho and Thun.

(6th) Di and Dag or Dig.

(7th) Dha or Dhá, Dhḍán, Dhig, Dhiṭ, Dhiḍ, Dhin, Dhir, Dhláng (obsolete), and Dhum.

(8th) Na or Ná, Nak, and Nag.

The one-Mátrá combinations, which are given above, show that out of the 12 (13th being obsolete) letters 8 are used as initial as well as final (Ghi is not final), and the remaining four (Ṭ, Ḍ, M and R) only as final. The way in which the above combinations are made, with the addition of nasal sounds—M and N (in Kḍán, Gan, Ghḍán, Ghin, Tin, Trán, Thun, Dhḍán, Dhin, Dhum, etc.) only in pronouncing and not in playing and the substitution of R for Ḍ (in Trán not Tḍán) in pronouncing and not in playing, seems to be arbitrary, or probably it is a modification or a part of the 14 Sútras,[1] "अइउण् । १ । ऋऌक् । २ । एओङ् । ३ । ऐऔच् । ४ । हयवरट् । ५ । लण् । ६ । ञमङणनम् । ७ । झभञ् । ८ । घढधष् । ९ । जबगडदश् । १० । खफछठथचटतव् । ११ । कपय् । १२ । शषसर् । १३ । हल् । १४ ।" [2] which are attributed to Shiva thus—

"नृत्यावसाने नटराजराजो ननाद ढक्कां नवपञ्चवारम् ।
उद्धर्तुकामः सनकादिसिद्धानेतद् विमर्शे शिवसूत्रजालम् ॥"

" The Lord of Dancing, with the desire of absolving sages like Sanaka and others, towards the close of his dance, struck a drum fourteen times. This (these

[1] Sútras are short aphorisms constituting in their totality a complete body of doctrines upon some subject.

[2] *Sidhánta Kaumudi*, edited by Pandit J. Vidyáságara, 2nd edition, p. 2.

sounds) I consider to be the collection of Shiva-Sútras (aphorisms of Shiva)."

It may not be out of place here to say a word or two about the "Ḍamaru," which is popularly said to have been used as an instrument to produce the 14 Sútras[1] by Shiva.[2] We cannot bring ourselves to believe that the Ḍamaru in any form can sound forth these admirable Sútras, which are said to be the fundamental basis on which the whole superstructure of the Sanskrit grammar is raised by Páṇiṇi.

Since we have given above the one-Mátrá combinations, we also give the two-Mátrá combinations, to show how they are formed in Ṭhekás and Parandas, which are extant :—

(1st) Ka-Tá, Ka-Dhá, Kḍán-Tá, Kḍán-Dhá, Kiṭ-Tá, Kiḍ-Tak, Kiṭ-Thun, Kiḍ-Dhum, Kiḍ-Ná and Kiḍ-Nag.

(2nd) Ga-Tá, Ga-Dhá, Ga-Dhin, and Gdi-Gan or Gadi-Gan.

(3rd) Ghiṭ-Tak, Ghiḍ-Tiṭ, Ghiḍ-Nag, Ghḍán-Tá, Ghḍán-Dhá, and Ghiṭ-Thun.

---

1 Prof. Max Muller in describing Itsing's Chinese work, says among other things that "most likely this refers to the Shiva Sútras, granted by the favour of Maheshvara. But, from the description given, this Sidhánta must have contained much more than the fourteen Shiva-Sútras. 'There are forty-nine letters,' Itsing writes, 'the compounds of which are divided into sections, and of which altogether more than 10,000 words are formed. These words are arranged in 300 Shlokas, of thirty-two syllables each.'"

2 Shiva (one of the Trinity of Hindus) is represented by the late M. M. Kunte, B.A., in his *Vicissitudes of India*, as a fanatical dancer and wanderer.

(4th) Ta-Kiṭ, Tá-Thun, Tag-Tiṭ, and Tir-Kiṭ.

(5th) Thá-Kiṭ or Tho-Kiṭ, Thun-Gá, Thun-Tá, Thun-Thun, Thun-Dhá, and Thun-Ná.

(6th) Dig-Tá, Dig-Dhá, and Dig-Nag.

(7th) Dhá-Kiṭ, Dhá-Tiṭ, Dhig-Nag, Dhir-Kiṭ, Dhi-Láng (obsolete), and Dhum-Kiṭ.

(8th) Na-Kiṭ, Nag-Tiṭ, Nag-Dhiṭ, Nag-Thun, Nag-Dhun or Dhum.

When the above combinations are given the same time, which is given to the preceding ones (one-Mátrá combinations), the speed (Laya) will be relatively double (Duni).

There are other combinations besides, but we have selected those which, according to our taste of drumming, appeared to us the best, and have given them to serve as specimens. The beauty of a combination of the above technical syllables is that it not only sounds well, but it admits of being played swiftly with comparative ease. In short, the above technical syllables andt heir combinations are so exquisitely formed in the different divisions of Tála, and are played so smoothly and artistically that to become an excellent drummer would require a life-long practice. Mathematically Tálas are of no great consequence, but musically they are of the greatest use.

We give below common-place Ṭhekás of the principal Tálas of which we have spoken, and also a few Parandas to show how the technical syllables are combined. It will be observed that the above specimens and the following combinations, if properly read, will assist one in making new Ṭhekás and Parandas.

The difference between a Ṭheká and a Paranda is that the former is a limited and a repeated combination to keep up the Tála, while the latter is an extended and generally changed combination to swell the Tála. There is variation in time, that is to say, the combinations are not of a uniform speed.

Before giving the Ṭhekás and Parandas, it would be well to remark here that a Pakhavája-player can produce more resonant[1] sounds as Dhá and its combinations, Ghi and its combinations, and Tho and its combinations, than a Tabalábáyá player can, the latter generally dealing in Ga and its combinations, Tá and its combinations, Dig and its combinations, and Ná and its combinations. This is in a great measure due to the palms being used more freely in the former than in the latter.

Ṭhekás on the Tabalábáyá.

(1), 2.
Zaptáala—Ghin Tá Tá, Tin Tá Tá (Avasána on the rest, and the first is rest).

1, 2, (3),
Trivaṭatála—Ná Dhin Dhiná, Ná Dhin Dhiná, Ná Tin
4.
Tiná, Ná Dhin Dhiná.

---

[1] The distinction between Ta and Tha, Ga and Gha, and Da and Dha is that the former in each of these pairs s produced by obstructing the free sounds of the instrument, while the latter sounds are produced by so handling the instrument as not to obstruct them.

1, 2, (3), 4.
Trivaṭa or Titála—Dhin Dhin, Dhá Tiṭ, Tu Ná, Kiṭ Tá.

1, (2), 3, 4, (5).
Sulafákatála—Dhin Dhin, Dhá Tiṭ, Tu Ná, Ka Tá, Kiṭ Tá.

1, (2), 3, (4),
Ekká or Chautála—Dhin Dhin, Dhá Tiṭ, Tu Ná, Ka Tá,

5, 6.
Dhag Tiṭ, Dhi Ná.

Áḍá Chautála—

1, 2, (3), 4, (5),
Dhin Dhin, Dhá Tiṭ, Tu Ná, Ka Tá, Dhin Dhin,

6, (7).
Ná Dhin, Dhin Ná.

Savári or Kaid—

1, 2, (3), 4, ("½"),
Dhin Ghin, Dhá Tiṭ Dhin Ghin, Tuná Katá, Dhá,

(5), 6, (7).
Dhin Dhin, Ná-Dhin, Ná Dhin.

If the Dhá (½) is taken away from the Savári it is reduced to Áḍáchautála in another Ṭheká, and if the Dhá (½) or its equivalent is added to the Áḍáchautála it will serve the purpose of Savári. It is not necessary to adhere to the Ṭhekás which we have given above. The same Tálas can be represented by any other combination. The object of giving simple Ṭhekás with a slight alteration in order to meet the different Tálas, is to simplify description, and to give an idea as to how Ṭhekás are ordinarily composed. There are, and can be made, excellent Ṭhekás of artistic combinations, but want of space does not permit us to do so.

A peculiar kind of combination, which is familiarly known by the name of Áḍá, is as follows on the Tabalábáyá :—

Trivaṭa or Titála—

1, 2, (3),
Dhá Ghi Nág, Takiṭ Ghi Nag, Dhá Trak Dhá Kiṭ,
4, 1, 2,
Ghi Nag Tin, Ná Gin Ná Gin, Ka Tak Dhá Kiṭ,
(3), 4.
Dhá Trak Dhákiṭ, Ghi Nag Tagan.

Here are common but artistic Parandas on the Tábalábáyá :—

Trivaṭa or Titála—

1, 2, (3),
Dhiná Kḍadhán, Dag Nag Dig Nag, Tirkiṭ Dag Nag,
4, 1, 2,
Dhig Nag Tirkiṭ, Dhag Tiṭ Tag Tiṭ, Dhá Trak Dhákiṭ
(3), 4, 1,
Ghiḍ, Nag Dhiṭ Kiṭ Tak, Nag Tiṭ Kḍán, Dhá Dhá
2, (3),
Dhi Gan, Dhá Dhi Gan há, Kiḍ Nag Tarkiṭ Tak
4,
Dhir Kiṭ Tak, Dhag Nag Dhag Tiṭ.

Trivaṭa or Titála—

1, 2, (3),
Ta Kiṭ Thunkiṭ Ghiḍ, Nag Dhiṭ Kiṭ Tak, Nag Tiṭ
4 1, 2,
Kḍán, Dhá Dhá Dhi Gan, Dhá Dhi Gan Dhá, Kiḍ Nag

(3), 4
Tar Kiṭ Dhir Kiṭ Tak, Dhag Nag Dhag Tiṭ, Dhag Tiṭ Dhag Tiṭ.

Ṭhekás on the Pakhavája—

(1) 2, 3.
Rupakatála—Dhá Dhá, Tiṭ Katá, Gadigan (Avasána on rest).

1, 2, (3), 4,
Titála—Dhá Dhá, Dhin Tá, Gadi Gan Dhá, Tiṭ Tá.

1, (2), 3,
Sulafákatála—Dhá Dhá, Dhin Tá, Gadi Gan Dhá,
4, (5).
Dhin Tá, Kiṭ Tá.

1, (2), 3, (4),
Chautála—Dhá Dhá, Dhin Tá, Gadi Gan Dhá, Dhin Tá,
5, 6.
Tiṭ Ka Tá, Gadi Gan.

The following is a common Ṭheká for the Dhamára, and a careful perusal of it will show how nicely it is composed:—

(1), (2), (3), (4), (5), 6, (7) (8), (9), (10)
Dhamára—Dh——-á Dhi-ṭ D-há Ga Dhi—n,
11, (12) (13), (14).
Ti—ṭ T——á (Avasána on rest).

If the Ṭhekás of the Titála and Sulafákatála are quadrupled, they will serve the purpose of the Brahmatála and Rudratála respectively. When the Ṭheká of the Savári is doubled, it will represent the Brahmatála in another form.

Now we give the Parandas (common but artistic) on the Pakhavája, which are familiarly known by the name of Áḍá:—

Chautála—

1, (2), 3,
Takk Dhá Kiṭ, Tá Kiṭ Tho Kiṭ, Dhigan Nagan,
(4), 5, 6.
Digg Gadi Gan, Katiṭ Dhá Dhin Tá, Tá Kiṭ Dhán.

Chautála—

1, (2), 3, (4),
Nakiṭ Takiṭ, Katit Dhakiṭ, Dhánn Nán, Dhá
5, 6.
Dhintá Katt, Dhḍán, Nagan Dhán.

Chautála—

1, (2) 3,
Dhá Kiṭ Takk, Takk Thokiṭ, Katt Ghinag
(4), 5, 6.
Ka Tiṭ Dhákiṭ, Nakiṭ Tán, Kḍán Dhán.

It is necessary to mention that the Dvitta (double) K, G, T and N are accents. Wherever any Dvitta comes it should be considered as an accent. The accents are beautifully shown in an artistic drumming.

Parandas on the Pakhavája in the Chautála:—

1, (2), 3, (4), 5,
1st—Takiṭ Tho, Kiṭ Tak, Dhig Tag, Tag Tiṭ, Ka Tiṭ
6, 1, (2), 3,
Ta, Gan Ghi Ghi, Nag Dhigg, Ghḍán, Dhag Ná Ná,
(4), 5,
Kiṭ Takk Thunn, Taká Thun Thun

6.
Kiṭ Takk Gadi Gan (this Paranda is in one Avardá, *i. e.*, in 6 Mátrás, but we have given it in two Avardás, *i. e.*, in 12 Mátrás).

1, (2), 3,
2nd—Ghin Tir Kiṭ Tak Tá, Ka Tá Ghi Ghi Dhinn, Nag
(4), 5, 6.
Dhitt Tá, Ghin Tḍán Dhá, Dhin Tá Ka, Tiṭ
Dhá Kiṭ Tak Gadi Gan.

1, (2), 3,
3rd—Dhiṭ Tiṭ Kiṭ Tak, Dhig Tag Tiṭ Ka Tá, Ghin Tir
(4), 5,
Kiṭ Tak Tag Tiṭ, Tag Tiṭ Dhag Tiṭ, Ka Tiṭ Ta
6,
Gan Dhag Dhitt, Dhḍán Na Gan Dhán

1, (2),
4th—Dhiṭ Tiṭ Trak Dhiṭ, Dhir Kiṭ Tá Ghin Dhi Ka
3, (4),
Tá, Kiṭ Tag Tag Tiṭ, Kiṭ Takk Thun Gá Takk
5, 6.
Thun Gá, Tir Kiṭ Tá Dhiṭ Kiṭ Tá, Dhá
Gi Gi Dha Gi Gi.

The few samples given above, though short and not the best, will, however, serve to give an idea as to how the Ṭhekás and Parandas are formed. There is a general belief, perhaps well-founded, among the Indian musicians that to become a perfect artist[1] in music, one

[1] The late Sádikálikhá (Rabába-player) and Báhádurhusenkhá (Sursingára-player) knew several beautiful Parandas and composed new ones. The late Bábu Jotasingji and Jorávarasing (drummers) kne several Dhrupadas and Dhamáras in the Rágas.

must necessarily be able to appreciate thoroughly the real beauty of the Ṭhekás and Parandas, and be able to utilise them as a guide to compose and execute music. It may also be added that great instrumentalists, such as players on the Biná, Rabába, Saroda and Satára, produce some of the Ṭhekás and Parandas in the Rágas with great skill, and thus compete with an artistic drummer. They imitate some of the strokes of the fingers of a drummer by their Mijráfa or Nakhi and Javá referred to above, *vide* p. 64. Nowadays, however, there are very few artists of this class.

We give below a formula by the aid of which one can easily keep any Tála by the left hand and its Duni or double by the right hand at the same time. It is unusually difficult to practise this without the support of the process we now speak of. Before we give the formula a few preliminary words of explanation are necessary:—A stroke by the left hand should be named "Ka," and one by the right hand "Tá." The joint strokes by the left and right hands at a time called "Dhá," and the absence of a stroke should be denoted "á." This process teaches one to produce the following Tálas:—

Titála—Dhá, Tá, Ka, Tá, Tá, Tá, Ka, Tá.

Sulafákatála—Dhá, á, Tá, Tá, Ka, Tá, Ka, Tá, Tá, á.

Chautála—Dhá, á, Tá, á, Dhá, Tá, Tá, á, Dhá, á, Dhá, Tá.

Aḍáchautála—Dhá, Tá, Ka, Tá, á, Tá, Ka, Tá, Tá, á, Dhá, á, Tá, á.

Instead of giving the strokes and rests, we give below the key which has rendered this process so easy and practical. It is hardly necessary to say that the key will work with all the Tálas.

Titála— 1, 2, (3), 4.
Duni—1, 2, (3), 4, 1, 2, (3), 4.
Dhá, Tá, Ka, Tá, Tá, Tá, Ka, Tá.

Sulafákatála—1, (2), 3, 4, (5).
Duni— 1, (2), 3, 4, (5), 1, (2), 3, 4, (5).
Dhá, á, Tá, Tá, Ka, Tá, Ka, Tá, Tá, á.

Chautála—1, (2), 3, (4), 5, 6.
Duni—1, (2), 3, (4), 5, 6, 1, (2), 3, (4), 5, 6.
Dhá, á, Tá, á, Dhá, Tá, Tá, á, Dhá, á, Dhá, Tá.

Aḍachautala—1, 2 (3) 4 (5), 6, (7).
Duni—1, 2, (3) 4 (5), 6, (7), 1, 2 (3) 4, (5), 6 (7).
Dhá, Tá, Ka, Tá, á, Tà, Ka, Tá, Tá, á, Dhá á Tá á.

A careful perusal of the above process shows that when two strokes meet together, we call them Dhá. When there is a stroke on the Duni or double, we term it Tá; and when there is a stroke on the Tála, we name it Ka. We need not repeat that "á" stands for the absence of a stroke, and whenever it comes it is always on the Duni or double. The only thing to be done in producing the Tálas and their Dunis at the same time is to give equal and uniform time (Laya) to the "Ka," "Tá," "Dhá" and "á" described above.

As a novelty, the Chautála and Titála can be produced by the hands and by a foot at a time in such a way as to converge their (the said Tálas') respective Avasánas. Those who have seen this execution, have admired it much. First, give the Tála and Duni of the Chautála by the hands as shown above, and adjust the three strokes (rest excluded) of Titála by a foot in the following way:—

Hands—Dhá, á, Tá, á, Dhá, Tá, Tá, á, Dhá, á, Dhá, Tá.

A foot—1, 2, (3), 4.

In concluding the description of Tálas, we give below, as has been promised before, a key by the aid of which Titála and Chautála (Áḍa or $1\frac{1}{2}$) and Titála and Sulafáka-tála (Kuáḍa or $1\frac{1}{4}$) can be produced by both the hands at a time in such a way as to converge their respective Avasánas.

Suppose we take a series of 12 consecutive figures beginning from 1 and ending with 12. Now in the Chautála there would be 4 strokes and 2 rests. The strokes will be on 1, 5, 9 and 11, and the rests will be on 3 and 7. The reader must have already learnt from the general description that the first stroke on 1 is the Avasána. In the same manner as regards Titála the series will divide itself into 4 points (Mátrás), composed of 3 strokes and 1 rest—the strokes coming on 1, 4 and 10, and the rest coming on 7, the stroke on 1 being of course the

Avasána. The following is a demonstration of the foregoing :—

Chautála—1, (2), 3, (4), 5, 6.

series—1, 2, 3, 4, 5, 6, 7, 8, 9, 10, 11, 12.

Titála——1, 2, (3), 4.

The 12 figures are to be counted at a regular and uniform interval, and the strokes and rests should be adjusted as shown above.

If the above is rightly understood, it will be plain that the Titála and Sulafákatála may also be similarly realized. As the latter is $1\frac{1}{4}$ times the former, we shall have to take the series of 20 figures, instead of 12 figures. The result will be that as regards the Titála there will be strokes on 1, 6 and 16, and the rest on 11 ; and as regards the Sulafákatála the strokes will be on 1, 9 and 13, and the rests on 5 and 17.

It will be judged from the above description and demonstration that what is necessary to be done, is to take any common multiple of the units (Mátrás) contained in the different Tálas which are to be produced simultaneously but separately by the two hands and to adjust their strokes and rests in the manner aforesaid.

Before dismissing this side of our work, it is absolutely necessary to say that we have purposely omitted the subject of giving a mode of setting the Rágas to the Tálas we have spoken of. This cannot be done artistically in the absence of a *notation* of a general and recognized acceptance. The ancient notations are too complicated to be clearly understood for practical purposes, and those which are invented by our present writers on Indian music are too crude and too many to be of general use. We, therefore, strongly recommend our authors to adopt the European *notation* with certain additions to meet the peculiarities of Indian music as a whole. Such a system of *notation* is sure to lay open the way to the advanced music of Europe, and to serve as a channel of exchange between Western and Eastern music.

The above object would be best secured if music should form a part of school and college curriculum; for, unless this is done, no one will care to have Indian music reduced to writing with the aid of a standard notation. It is attempted to give some idea of practical music in the next chapter with a view to practically illustrate the several details of Indian music which have been given in the preceding pages.

CHAPTER V.

PRACTICAL HINTS ON INDIAN MUSIC.

Notwithstanding the total absence of a standard notation of Indian music, it is intended to give in the following pages a short description of the mode which regulates practical music. This mode will be a popular and a comparatively easy one to show practically the efficacy of the details which have been treated until now. The treatment of this subject, though brief, will require considerable space and a closer attention in the absence of a standard notation. Those who are conversant with music as an art, may find the said details quite sufficient to form a rough estimate of Indian music as an art and to attempt further progress in it; but those who are entirely unacquainted with the A B C of music,[1] will find the reading of the aforesaid details and of the principles underlying them very difficult; and perhaps they may think it to be uninteresting and uninstructive. But it should be borne in mind that the studious reading of this work certainly pre-supposes a familiarity or at least partial acquaintance with music if it is to be utilized for practical purposes.

[1] The A B C of music is the correct understanding of its general aspects, such as the proper appreciation of the notes (स्वर) and sequence (ताल).

It should be clearly understood at the outset that we have been principally dealing with that portion of Indian music which is artistic and not a tom-tom one; and, therefore, we are not expected to deal with the Chijas and Gatis which are very common and inartistic, or which constitute the major or perhaps the whole portion of the stock of our so-called musicians. We shall give a few classical compositions which will be sufficient for our purpose to show a method of utilizing the several foregoing details and enable the reader to form an opinion of the real worth of Indian music as an art.

We use the word *composition* throughout this chapter to denote generally any musical arrangement of words in a poem technically called a Chija (vocal music) or any arrangement of syllables—conveying no meaning—technically called Gatis (instrumental music).

In instrumental and vocal music the words of a musical composition are distributed over the notes of a musical scale or scales—Anudátta, Svarita and Udátta —according to the individual taste of a composer or of an executor. Our present musicians, as a class, are executors and not composers. The general practice adopted by them is not to attempt to sing or play a particular composition in more than one Rága or Jilhá (see pp. 54-55), nor ever to try to set a given composition, either by extending or curtailing its words or notes to more Tálas than one. It must be admitted, however, that there are some high class compositions, which, if transferred from the original Rágas and Tálas to which they have been once set by their composers to other Rágas and Tálas, lose both in poetic beauty and music ; but since we have to show the principles which govern the artistic distribution of the words of a composition to different notes and sequences, we intend giving in this chapter a method by which this transference can be conveniently done.

The compositions of music are regulated more by a Tála to which they are set than by the Rágas in which they are sung or played. Such compositions are called Dhrupada, Dhamára or Hori, Khyála and Ṭappá Ṭhumri and Gajala and Gatis (see pp. 63-65).

Musical compositions are divided into two parts :—the first is called Astái and the second Antrá; the first is so named because it is partly in the Anudátta and partly in the Svarita scale, and the Antrá covers partly the Udátta and considerably the Svarita scale. It is not necessary to treat this subject at length here, for the difference shown above will be made clear by the study of a few compositions later on in this chapter.

It will be seen from the foregoing pages (90-94) that we have begun the extensions (Prastára) of Rágas from the Savrita (register) S or C or tonic, and closed them with the same.

It has been already stated that the compositions, as a class, do not begin from the tonic. Instead of beginning an extension of the Rága, or in other words the distribution of the words of a composition in Savrita S, we may commence it from any one of the notes of a Rága and then distribute the subsequent words of it over the other notes of the same Rága without breaking the principle of ascent and descent; for instance, in Bhupa or Bibhása of the first table:—

5, 3, 1; 8, 5, 3, 1; 10, 5, 3, 8, 5, 3, 1;
G, R, S; *or* P, G, R, S; *or* Dh, G, R, P, G, R, S;

13, 8, 10, 5. 8, 5, 3, 1,
or S, P, Dh, G, P, G, R, S; and so on (see page 93).

It is hardly necessary to say that the above arrangement is one of descent and not that of ascent. We may reverse the above arrangement and turn it into an ascending one without violating the principle of ascent and descent, which, along with other principles, preserves the individual Rága from being confounded with any other Rága.

It is hardly necessary to repeat that our standard note is the *tonic* or the S (c) of the Svarita (register octave) and, therefore, we designate other notes as ascending or descending according to their relation with the tonic S. Generally speaking, the first letter of the first word of a composition is fixed to the first of the two principal notes (Pradhána, *vide* pp. 106-107) of a Rága on which its Murchhanás depend (*vide* pp. 106-107). As regards the Tála (sequence) our treatment of the various details in the last chapter will suffice for our present purpose to mark the words and notes with the figures with their proper signs, such as the Avasána, Tála and Kála (*vide* p. 131).

Before going further into this subject, it is absolutely necessary to say that the words of a composition are not evenly distributed over all the notes of a Rága. Even the fractions of words of a composition may be set to a note or notes either as Jumping, Murki or Miṇḍa or Ghasiṭa; for instance, "Ge" of the word "get" :—

Jumping { 1 3 / S R / G E }

Murki { 1 3 / S***R / G***E }

and Miṇḍa or Ghasiṭa { 1 3 / S—R / G—E }

In Jumping one letter cannot cover more than a note, or, in other words, one stroke cannot cover more than a note, while either in Murki, Miṇḍa or Ghasiṭa we can cover more than one note by a stroke of the index finger of the right hand with a Nakhi or Mijaráfa (triangular ring used for striking the wires of the Biná, Satára, etc.—*vide* pp. 64 and 65) and by a bow as on the fiddle. On the Piano, Harmonium and such other instruments only the Murki, and never the Miṇḍa or Ghasiṭa, can be attempted by making the fractions of a letter which are technically called complimentary notes. In this attempt we are required to give separately as many strokes as are wanted to make the fractions of a letter, for instance, the

	1	3		1	3	5
"*Ge*" of the word "get"	S	R	or	S	R	G
	G	E		G	E	E

In this arrangement we are forced to make the "*ge*" in two or three divisions within the time which "*ge*" takes either in the Minḍa or the Ghasiṭa which does not separate the letter but prolongs it. A careful perusal of the above three illustrations will be enough to show what we are speaking of. These three separate arrangements, which have their respective effects, may be verified by playing on the instruments mentioned above. To make more than one division of a letter to distribute it over many notes in music requires greater skill than the one of fixing one letter to one note; it can also be stated that the distribution of one word or letter over a number of Mátrás is more difficult than to assign the same to one Mátrá, which is a unit of Tála.

As it is intended in the present chapter to give some idea of practical music, we cannot confine ourselves to the Svarita (Register) scale as we did before, but we must now draw upon the two other scales, *viz.*, Anudátta and Udátta. This addition will necessitate an increase in the number of notes from 1 to 36 to cover the three scales —Anudátta (one octave below the Register or the mean), Svarita (Register or the mean), and Udátta (one octave above the Register or the mean).

According to this arrangement the number 1 (s or c) shows the S of the Anudátta, No. 13th, the S of the Svarita, and 25th, the S of the Udátta.

To make the above subject more clear, we give below 36 notes with their abridged names and numbers :—

ANUDÁTTA

1	2	3	4	5	6	7	8	9	10	11	12
S	K-R	R	K-G	G	M	T-M	P	K-Dh	Dh	K-N	N

SVARITA

13	14	15	16	17	18	19	20	21	22	23	24
S	K-R	R	K-G	G	M	T-M	P	K-Dh	Dh	K-N	N

UDÁTTA

25	26	27	28	29	30	31	32	33	34	35	36
S	K-R	R	K-G	G	M	T-M	P	K-Dh	Dh	K-N	N

As Indian musicians, from ancient times, have confined themselves to three octaves, we must necessarily limit the number of notes within that limit. It should be observed here that few voices can touch in artistic singing all the notes of the three octaves.[1] The general

[1] "Helmholtz has recently fixed the lower limit at 16 vibrations, and the higher at 38,000 vibrations, a second. By employing very small tuning-forks, the late M. Depretz showed that a sound corresponding to 38,000 vibrations a second is audible. Beginning with note 16 and multiplying continually by 2, or more compendiously raising 2 to the 11th power, and multiplying this by 16, we should find that at 11 octaves above the fundamental note the number of vibrations would be 32,768. Taking, therefore, the limits assigned by Helmholtz, the entire range of the human ear embraces about eleven octaves. But all the notes comprised within these limits cannot be employed in music. The practical range of musical sounds is comprised between 40 and 4,000 vibrations a second, which amounts, in round numbers, to 7 octaves." —*Sound*, by John Tyndall, pp. 69 and 70, Fourth Edition. Professor P. Blaserna, in

practice is from P of the Anudátta to P of the Udátta, but even this is impracticable for a Tána—*vide* p. 69.

For the sake of brevity we might conveniently do away with the names of the notes, such as S, K-R, R, etc., etc., and adhere only to the numbers which stand for their respective notes as shown above. We think that in the absence of a standard notation the method of denoting notes by numbers, when we have to deal only with three octaves, will be more practicable. Instead of devising various symbols for the Miṇḍa or Ghasiṭa, Murki, Murchhaná and the Shake we adhere, as we have already done, to the following signs:—

(1) The Miṇḍa or Ghasiṭa is denoted by dashes as follows:—1—3—5, or 5—3—1.

(2) The Murchhaná is denoted by $\frac{1}{4}$ of the number on which it is dependent, thus:—1—3—5—$\frac{1}{4}$, or $\frac{1}{4}$—5—3—1.

(3) The Ása will be denoted by one asterisk between two or more notes, for instance:—1*3*5, or 5*3*1.

(4) The Giṭakaḍi is denoted by two asterisks, thus:—1* *3* *5, or 5* *3* *1.

(5) The Murki is denoted by three asterisks, as thus:—1* * *3* * *5, or 5* * *3* * *1 (see p. 67).

(6) The Shake is denoted by italics, thus:—*1 3 5*, or *5 3 1*.

---

his *Theory of Sound in its Relation to Music*, gives recorded instances of some of the great vocalists whose voices were capable of covering about 4 octaves.

From the above arrangement it will be seen that the six illustrations are ascending as well as descending; they are also in the Anudátta. If we want to bring them on the Svarita or Udátta scale, we have only to change the numbers.

Before turning our attention to the Tála, which is an important factor in music, we give below certain practical exercises which will enable the student of music to reproduce the compositions in this chapter with comparative ease. The following are practical exercises not set to Tála:—

Bhúpa or Bibhása.

13—15—17; 17, 20, 22—25—27; 25, 22, 20; 20* 22* 20; 17, 15, 13; 8, 10—13; 15* * * 17; 22, 20, 13; 22, 20, 17, 15, 13.

If we insert in the above Rága only the N, that is, the number 12 of the Anudátta and 24 of the Svarita, the composition is changed from Bhupa to Bhupáli, thus:—

13—15—17; 17, 20, 22—24—25—27; 24, 25, 22, 20*20*22*20; 17, 15, 12, 13; 8, 10—12—13; 15* * * 17 * * 22, 20, 12, 13; 22, 20, 17, 15, 13.

If we add only the T-M, that is, the 7 of the Anudátta and 19 of the Svarita, the Bhupáli is raised to Kalyána.[1]

---

[1] The Bhúpa consisting of 5 notes is one of the Oḍhavas; by adding to it N it becomes Bhupáli, which is one of the Khoḍavas, and by adding T-M to Bhupáli it becomes K refer one of the Sampurnas.

Instead of transcribing the composition of the Bhupáli *in toto*, we make a slight alteration in it, and add the two Murchhanás of the Kalyána:—

12, 13, 15, 17 ; 17$\frac{1}{4}$—19—20—22 ; 24, 24—25, 24$\frac{1}{4}$ —22—20 ; 20, 8—10—12$\frac{1}{4}$—13 ; 17, 15, 24***22, 20 ; 20—19—17$\frac{1}{4}$, 15, 13.[1]

If we substitute R (3 or 15) and Dh (10 or 22) of the Bhúpa given above by K-R (2 or 14) and K-Dh, (9 or 21), the new composition will be one of the Bibhása (see the first table). It need not be said that along with the change of the two notes their Murchhanás must also be changed.

By adding T-M (7 or 19) and N (12 or 24) to the Bibhása and by changing the Murchhanás we get Púrvi. If we replace the K-Dh (9 or 21) of the Púrvi by Dh (10 or 22), the change will make the composition one of Varáṭi or Puriyá Kalyána (see the first table).

From a study of the above details it will be seen that to learn the several Rágas one has in the first instance to

[1] When one succeeds in producing the two Murchhanás of the Kalyána, it becomes very easy to produce other Murchhanás of the same Rága. It has been already stated elsewhere that along with the improvement in the Minḍa or the Ghasiṭa the number of Murchhanás for each Rága is increased from two to more, and that the increased Murchhanás generally depend on the Komala Svaras—*vide* p. 106.

covern

practise the Murki, Murchhanás and the Minḍa or Ghasiṭa in a Rága in its ascending and descending order with limited variation, and then to study the skeleton notes of the Rága to be sung or played. These are the chief principles which underlie the practical art. It is true, however, that the application of these several abstract principles depends completely on the personality of the performer. Such abstract principles are, no doubt, a guide, but they never satisfy the want of a living preceptor. It cannot be denied that more can be learnt from an artist in a day than from a book in a year; neither can a man become a musician solely by the aid of books, although much may be learnt from a good manual, both by a beginner and by his instructor. To conform to the arrangement of a book is to follow some system of teaching, and this, if sound, must help both the master and the pupil.

The distribution of the words over the notes of a Rága is not uniform; the same must be said of the distribution of words of a composition over a Mátrá, which, as has been already stated, is a unit of a Tála. We also know that the number of Mátrás in a Tála is fixed, and that their repetition does not mean the change of that Tála.

A study of the few Ṭhekás and Parandas given as samples will show that the number of words or technicalities is not evenly distributed over the Mátrás of a Tála. If we refer to the Ṭhekás on the Tablá-Báyá and the Pakhavája (pp. 140 to 143) we shall find that the number of words in the Ṭhekás are generally even, and only odd in Zaptála, Gajalatála, and such other Tálas. In all Tálas generally the even number of words for a Mátrá is from two to four, but at times it is raised to eight. The words of a musical composition are divided into two parts, *viz.*, Astái and Antrá. So far as Tála is concerned the distinction between Astái and Antrá is that the words in the former are generally less than those in the latter. Some of these words are generally distributed over the two Avardás (repetition) of a Tála as an Astái, and the remaining words are reserved for the Antrá. The number of words of the Astái and Antrá are not always the same. It is not our intention to measure the words of a composition according to the rules of poetry. We treat the musical poems in the light of music, and deal with their words as they are distributed over the notes of a Rága and over a Mátrá in a Tála. If the poetical words are insufficient for a Tála the deficiency is made up by extending a note or notes or by some such words as "ho," "aré-ho," etc. Sometimes this deficiency is made good by a Tána or a simple sound, or by a pause, of course, consistently with the Rága.

Before studying the following compositions it must be remembered that the Mátrás of a Tála are known as Avasána or Sama, Tála or Bhari, and Kála or Kháli, which means rest (see pp. 131), and their respective figures stand thus :—Titála 1, 2, (3), 4. These signs of the Tála are to be used in the following vocal composition thus:—

A Name of woods peacocks sing or sound

Madhu banaké morélá bolé.

This is an incomplete piece of a Ṭhumri in Gounḍa-Malhára. Before setting this piece to music and Tál, it must be remarked that this piece consists of three Mátrás and a half. Now, if this is to be set to the Titála, which we know has four Mátrás, we shall have either to extend the duration of Bolé or to bring in some such meaningless words as "há há" or "aré-ho," or to resort to a Tána or rest. The first is the easiest and most convenient method, and therefore we follow it here. In order to show how the piece is wanting in half a Mátrá, we shall first give the equal divisions of the piece in time—

1 2 3 4 5 6 7

Mádhu Ban Ké Moré Lá Bo Lé,

and then extend the letter "le" to complete the deficiency, thus—

1 2 3 4 5 6 7 8

Madhu Ban Ké Moré Lá Bo Lé é.

This piece when set to music will stand as follows :—

Notes—	15—18,	18*17*18	22,	20,	18 17	18,	15	13*15	13
Poem	Bo,	lé	é	Madhu,	Ban	Ké,	Moré		la
Tála	1		2		(3)		4		

In the above Astái there is no note of the Anudátta scale, the whole piece being in the Svarita scale. Before going to its Antrá we may analyse the Astái first. The word Bolé is taken first because it is the Avasána. In practice a singer begins a Chija (vocal music) from the Kháli or rest, and the drummer joins him from the Avasána. The letter "Bo" is set to a Minḍa or Ghasiṭa, and therefore has two notes ; the letter "le" is in Ása, and has three notes. ; the letter "re" is also in Ása, and has only two notes ; and the rest of the letters have separate notes. If all the foregoing principles are brought to bear on this piece, it will be quite artistic. The piece is an old and simple one for an artist, and he may extend the Minḍa or Ghasiṭa to more notes than the two given above. He may also extend the range of scales, touch the Murchhanás, resort to Vádi, Samavádi and Anuvádi in the Minḍa or the Ghasiṭa and in the Murki, and may indent on many other principles of music. But, as we do not wish to puzzle a beginner with the *technique*, we allow this piece to stand in its simple form as given above. Let us now take its Antrá. The Astái is only in one Avardá, and the Antrá, which begins from the Kháli, is in two *Avardás*, or repetitions. As we have divided the Astái in Tála, etc. so we do the Antrá.

Bola (voicing), zingarvá (cricket, an insect), ghana (clouds), garjé (roaring), bijali (lightning), chamakat (flashing), hai (is), chana nana nana (a description of the mode or motion of electricity).

1 2 3 4 5 6 7 8 9 10
Bo la zin gar vá ghan gar jé bij li cham kat
10 11 12 13 14
hai chan nan nan nan

From the above letters it will be seen that, like the Astai, they are insufficient in number to suit the four Mátrás of the Titála, and therefore we shall have to extend the "je" to set the words to the Titála, thus :—

(3) 4 1 2 (3)
Bo la zin gar vá ghan gar jé é bij li
4 1 2
cham kat hai chana nana nana (repetition)

The whole Ṭhumri, *i. e.*, the Astái and the Antrá taken together, when set to music, will be as follows :—

Notes 15 15 20 18 18 20 22—25 22—¼ 20
Poem Bo la zin ga ra vá gha—n ga r jé é
Tála (3) 4 1 2

Notes 17-18-17-18 15 20 18 18 20 22—25—27 25—22 20
Poem bi ja li cham kat hai cha——na na——na
Tála (3) 4 1

Notes 17-18 20 22 20
Poem na na Madhu (repetition) Ban
Tála 2 (3)

We have purposely selected this Chija from among several Chijas of the Gounḍa-Malhára, as it depicts a scene in Nature, and is also free from love-affairs.

The foregoing illustration of a Ṭhumri will serve to show how the poetical words of a Chija, in any Rága, are distributed over the Mátrás of a Tála. It should be remembered that, should the words in a Chija be more or less than those in the above example, their distribution over the Mátrás will vary accordingly.

We give below three Gatis of the Gounḍa-Malhára as instrumental music. In these Gatis, instead of poetical words, we use only the technical syllables Dá, Ḍá, Diḍ, and Ḍid or Ḍadá (*vide* pp. 64 and 65).

The commonest and easiest syllables of a Gata in the Titála are sixteen in number, and they are as follows :—

1		2		(3)		4		1		2	
Dá	Dá	Ḍá	Diḍ	Dá	Diḍ	Dá	Ḍá	Dá	Dá	Ḍá	Diḍ
(3)		4									
Dá	Diḍ	Dá	Ḍá.								

The number of syllables in each Mátrá, as shown above, is two. It may be remarked that this Gata nearly resembles the Chija given before. When set to music, the Gata will be as follows (No. 1) :—

Notes	15—18	15—18,	18—15	15 15	15	20 18.
Syllables	D – á	D—á,	Ḍ—á	Diḍ,	Dá	Diḍ,
Tála	1		2		(3)	

Notes	20	22—25,	22-¼	20,	17—18	22 20	18*17*18
Syllables	Dá	Ḍ—á,	Dá	Dá,	Ḍ—á	Diḍ,	D——á
Tála	4		1		2		(3)

Notes	15 13	13	15
Syllables	Diḍ	Dá	Ḍá
Tála		4	

A skilful performer will be able, even with the few syllables of the simple Gata given above, to entertain his audience for at least half an hour with its necessary flourishes and embellishments.

In the remaining portion of this chapter we shall give Gatis of different Rágas instead of Chijas (vocal). The object of this chapter being to give practical hints on Indian music, the Gatis serve the same purpose as the Chijas. In both, Gatis and Chijas, the arrangement, so far as the Rága and Tála are concerned, is precisely the same; the only difference is that, in the place of poetical words (which have of course their peculiar charm), there are the technical syllables.

We give another Gata of the same Rága. The Gata given below is in the Madhya (moderate measure or *adante*), while the one given above is in the Bilambapada (slow measure or *largo*)—*vide* p. 63.

It should be observed that no performance, vocal or instrumental, can be highly artistic unless the performer resorts, so far as the Tála is concerned, to the Bilamba-pada, Madhya and Druta.

1 2 (3) 4
Dáá Ḍá, Dá Diḍ Dá Ḍá, Dáá Ḍá, Dá Ḍá Dá Ḍá,
1 2 (3) 4
Dáá Ḍá Dáá Ḍá, Dá Diḍ Diḍ Diḍ, Dáḍ Dáḍ Dá.

A perusal of the above Astâi will show that the syllables in each Mátrá are two and four. The four syllables take the same time as the two, and therefore they are double (Duni) of the two—*vide* p. 133.

In the above piece it is peculiar to note that the two syllables in a Mátrá in some places are not of equal Laya or duration; the first of the two, *e.g.*, Dá, is longer in time than the second Ḍá, and this is shown in an ása. The last Dáḍ Dáḍ Dá are equal in time with Dá Diḍ Diḍ Diḍ, and are therefore somewhat difficult. Dáḍ Dáḍ Dá, if critically examined, constitute, in matter of time, the four syllables, such as Dá Ḍá Dá Ḍá, but Dáḍ Dáḍ Dá is comparatively artistic and much used in Gatis of the Madhya and Druta. The best way to learn them is to give first the strokes by hands or fingers of an uniform interval (*vide* p. 130) and then to adjust Dáḍ Dáḍ Dá to four strokes, merging the second Dá into the first Dá.

(No. 2) :—

Notes	18*17	18,	15	17	18	20,	17*18	18,	15	17
Syllables	Dáá	Ḍá,	Dá	Diḍ	Dá	Ḍá,	Dáá	Ḍá,	Dá	Ḍá
Tála	1		2				(3)		4	

Notes	18	20,	18*17	18,	17*15	17,	13	15	13
Syllables	Dá	Ḍá,	Dáá	Ḍá,	Dáá	Ḍá,	Dá	Diḍ	Diḍ
Tála			1		2		(3)		

Notes	15,	13	10	13
Syllables	Diḍ,	Dáḍ	Dáḍ	Dá
Tála		4		

The Antrá of this Gata begins from the Avasána thus (No. 2) :—

Notes	10	13	15	17,	18	20	18	20,	18	20
Syllables	Dá	Ḍá	Dá	Ḍá,	Dá	Diḍ	Dá	Ḍá,	Dá	Diḍ
Tála	1				2				(3)	

Notes	18	20,	20	20	20,	18	20	20
Syllables	Diḍ	Diḍ,	Dáḍ	Dáḍ	Dá,	Dá	Diḍ	Diḍ
Tála			4			1		

Notes	22—25—27	22	20,	18	20	18	20,
Syllables	Dáḍ—Dá	Dá	Ḍá,	Dá	Diḍ	Diḍ	Diḍ,
Tála	2			(3)			

Notes	17—18	15	13
Syllables	Dáḍ	Dáḍ	Dá
Tála	4		

So far as the Tála of this Gata is concerned the only thing one has to do is to keep a regular Titála by the hand, and then to adjust the several syllables to their proper Mátrás as shown above. A little practice will enable the student to set the Gata and its Antrá to the Titála. When he has successfully set this Gata with its Antrá to the Tála he can, with comparative ease, set any Gata to the Tála. The syllables which are a little difficult to set to the Tála are Dáḍ Dáḍ Dá and Dáḍ Dá and a few others which he will meet with in some of the following Gatis.

In the following Gatis no attempt is made to divide the syllables first into equal divisions and then to set them to the Tála as has been done in the case of the Ṭhumri, for that process is very long and tedious. We use the simple "a" to show either a pause (rest) or an elongation of a syllable.

The following Gata is modelled by the author after an old Taráná in the Gounḍa-Malhára, which is said to have been composed by two brothers, the celebrated Jáfarkhá and Páyarakhá, Rabába-players. (No. 3) :—

Notes	22—25,	22-$\frac{1}{4}$	20	17—18	15,	15	20	18
Syllables	Dá—á,	Dáḍ	Dá	D—á	Dá,	Dá,	Diḍ	Diḍ
Tála	1	2				(3)		

Notes	20,	17—18	15	13,	10	13	15,
Syllables	Diḍ,	Dáḍ	Dáḍ	Dá,	Dá	Diḍ	Diḍ,
Tala		4			1		

Notes	15--18	15--20	6	8,	8	10—13	10--15,
Syllables	Dáḍ	Dá	Diḍ	Diḍ,	Dá	Dá	Ḍdá,
Tál	2				(3)		

Notes	13	15,	18*17*18	15 13	15,	20*18*20,
Syllables	Dáḍ	Dá,	Dá—á,	Dáḍ	Dá,	Dá—á,
Tála	4		1	2		(3)

Notes	20 18	20,	22—25	22-¼	20,	17—18	15
Syllables	Dáḍ	Dá,	Dá—á	Dá	Ḍá,	Dá	Ḍá
Tála	4		1			2	

Notes	15	20,	15	20	18	20,	20	18	20.
Syllables	Dá	Ḍá,	Dá	Diḍ	Dá	Ḍá,	Dá	Dá	Ḍá.
Tála			(3)				4		

From the Tála of the above Gata it will be seen that it has in all sixteen Mátrás or four Avardás (repetitions) of the Titála and has no Antrá ; the Gata is extended, however, in different ways called Chalat-firat, strain or Táná (*vide* p. 69). It will also be seen from the music of this Gata that G or 17 is touched sparsely but skilfully. If the G or 17 is given more prominence in the Gounḍa-Malhára, it becomes Gounḍa or Malhári (second table). The shade of distinction between Gounḍa and Gounḍa-Malhára is so minute that only those who have closely studied the skeleton notes of the two Rágas can appreciate it. If only G (5 or 17) is totally discarded from the two Rágas the remaining music constitutes the Megha or Sura-Malhára (first table). If N (12 or 24) is added only in an ascent to the Gounḍa with its Murchhaná, the Rága thus formed is Deshi-Malhára. There are other Malháras such as the Tánaseni or Miyáki, Rámadáshi, Haradáshi, Suradáshi, and one or two more, but they are varieties, though very artistic, of the Megha or Sura-Malhára.

The different varieties of Rága should not, even for a moment, be considered to be a mere chance-work or the outcome of the hobbies of vocal or instrumental performers of bygone generations. A close study of the Rágas, both practical and theoretical, will undoubtedly show that these varieties are the highly artistic productions of master musicians, who, preserving the original features of the Rágas intact, inserted, into their skeleton notes, such note or notes as produced a perfect melody. These varieties are, therefore, the artistic modifications of the original Rágas, the perfect music of which was tested by the keen and acute ear of artists of high calibre (*vide* p. 115).

It should be remembered that the Gatis given below are in the Titála. If these are to be set to other Tálas than the Titála, the only thing to be done is either to add other syllables to the Gata or to reduce their number so as to meet the Mátrás of the required Tála. For instance, there are sixteen syllables in the first Gata of the Gounḍa-Malhára in the Titála, but if two syllables Dá Ḍá or their equivalents are taken away, the remaining fourteen syllables will constitute the Âḍáchoutála or Dhamára. But such an inartistic extension or curtailment of the syllables is only puzzling. There are several artistic Gatis in different Tálas; but as we are dealing more with Rágas than with Tálas, we shall take up only the Titála.[1] The first Gata of each Rága is given as an aid[2] to other Gata or Gatis of the same Rága. The first is always to be played as Bilambapada, and the others as Madhya or Druta as the case may be.

Here is a Gata of the Kámoda or Kámbodi second table (No. 4):—

Notes	13*15	15—20,	19—20	15,	13*15	20*19*20,
Syllables	D á,	D á,	Ḍ á	Diḍ,	D á	D i ḍ,
Tála	1	,	2	, (3)		

[1] The author recommends the beginner, who wishes to learn the Gatis, first to reproduce the whole Gata in all its details, and then try to set it to the Tála as shown in this chapter. If he is already acquainted with the Tála, all that is necessary is a little practice; otherwise he will have to seek the aid of a competent musician.

[2] The best way for a beginner is to reproduce the first Gata of the Rágas given in this chapter. If he finds the Minḍa or Ghasiṭa difficult for reproduction, he may omit the joining of notes for a time and touch the notes separately. If he perform on fretted instruments he may produce the Ghasiṭa instead of the Minḍa by slipping over the frets. The only thing to be observed in slipping over the frets is not to touch the intermediate frets forcibly, but only those that are required while the sound of the note to be connected with the other by slipping the finger is not dead. This depends on the smooth way of slipping from note to note and on the resonance of the instrument.

Notes	22—24—25,	24—22	20,	19—20	20***22***20,
Syllables	D á Ḍá,	D á	Dá,	Ḍ á	D i ḍ,
Tála	4	1		2	

Notes	20*19*20	17 18,	15	12—13.
Syllables	D á	D i ḍ,	Dá	Ḍ á.
Tála	(3)		4	

The following Gata of the Kámbodi or Kámoda may be played in the Madhya as well as in the Druta. This Gata is composed by the author (No. 5):—

Notes	15	17—18,	15	20	19 20,	22,	20,
Syllables	Dáá	Dá Ḍá,	Dá	Dá	Ḍdá,	Dáá	Dá,
Tála	1		2			(3)	

Notes	19	20	17	18,	13	15	13	15,
Syllables	Dá	Ḍá	Dá	Ḍá,	Diḍ	Diḍ	Diḍ	Diḍ,
Tála	4				1			

Notes	13	12	13	7	8	8	13,	12 13	15,
Syllables	Dáḍ	Dáḍ	Dá,	Diḍ	Diḍ	Dá	Dá,	Ḍdá	Dá,
Tála	2			(3)				4	

Notes	18	17	15	20*19,	20	19	20***22,
Syllables	Diḍ	Diḍ	Dá	D á,	Ḍdá	Diḍ	D i ḍ,
Tála	1				2		

Notes	20	18*17	18,	15	13*15	12 13.
Syllables	Dá	D á	Ḍdá,	Dá	D á	Ḍdá.
Tála	(3)			4		

The following Gata of the Kámbodi is to be played in the Druta, and is composed by the author in imitation of an old one (No. 6) :—

Notes 22, 20 19 20 17*18, 15 15, 20***22 20,
Syllables Dáá, Dáḍ Dá Dáá, Dá Ḍá, D á Ḍá,
Tála 1 2 (3)

Notes 19 20 17 18, 13 15 13 15,
Syllables Dá Ḍá Dá Ḍá, Diḍ Diḍ Diḍ Diḍ,
Tála 4 1

Notes 13 12 13, 8 8 8 13,
Syllables Dáḍ Dáḍ Dá, Diḍ Diḍ Dá Dá,
Tála 2 (3)

Notes 12 13 15 13, 13 12 13 15,
Syllables Ḍdá Diḍ Dá, Dá Ḍá Dá Dá,
Tála 4 1

Notes 13 15 13 15, 15 20 19 20,
Syllables Ḍdá Diḍ Diḍ, Dá Dá Ḍdá,
Tála 2 (3)

Notes 18 20 19 20.
Syllables Dá Dá Ḍdá.
Tála 4

The Avasána (1) and its succeeding Mátrá (2) in the above Gata are not of an ordinary duration, but a careful study will show that they are very skilful and at the same time easy for one who knows the Tála.

In the Kámoda or the Kámbodi no prominence is given to the T-M. (7 and 19), but it is touched only skilfully. In this Rága the R (15) and P (8 and 20) are given prominence, although its Murchhanás according to our treatment are the sixth and twelfth (*vide* page 105).

Here is a Gata of the Kedára to be played in the Bilambapada (No. 7):—

Notes	13	18	17--18	18,	17--18	20	19--20
Syllables	Dá	Diḍ	D á	Ḍá,	D á	Diḍ	D á
Tála	1				2		

Notes	20,	22--24--25	24--25	25--24--22¼	20,
Syllables	Ḍá,	D á	D á	Ḍ á	Diḍ,
Tála		(3)			

Notes	19--20	20***22***20	18	18,
Syllables	D á	D i ḍ	Dá	Ḍá,
Tála	4			

Notes	18*17*18	20	19	20
Syllables	D á	Diḍ	Dá	Ḍá,
Tála	1			

Notes	20*19*20	22--¼	19	20,
Syllables	D á	Diḍ	Dá	Ḍá,
Tála	2			

Notes	17—8	17—18	18	20*19*20*22,
Syllables	D á	D á	Ḍá	D i ḍ,
Tála	(3)			

Notes	18—17—18		15	12—13	13.
Syllables	D	á	Diḍ	D á	Ḍá.
Tála	4				

By a careful study and the reproduction of all the details of the above Gata it will be seen that, although its syllables are very simple so far as the Tála goes, it is considerably artistic, and gives a fair idea of the Kedárá. When the above Gata is handled with all its details it will prepare a student to produce compound Minḍa, Ghasiṭa, Ása, and Murki. But in the absence of an established and recognised notation it is very difficult, if not impossible, to reduce to writing the exquisite pieces of musical art. What we mean by compound Minḍa or Ghasiṭa is that, instead of touching a few notes only at one stretch or at a stroke, to touch them in the given time more than once. It must be borne in mind that we are dealing more with *notes* than with *time*, our object being to give an idea of the composition of Rágas and not to go deep into the technicalities of Tála. It is really wonderful that, when the *techniques* of notes and time are harmoniously combined, the impression is simply grand and æsthetic. But the space at our disposal prevents our treating this point at greater length.

Instead of giving another Gata of the Kedárá we give below a Gata of the Chháyá (No. 8) :—

Notes	22—25	22—23	22	20,	15—17	15	17—18—20,
Syllables	D á	D á	Ḍá	Diḍ,	D á	Diḍ	D á Ḍá,
Tála	1				2		

Notes	17—18	15	13	15—17—18—20,	17—18	15	13	13,
Syllables	D á	Dá	Ḍá	D i ḍ,	D á	Diḍ	Dá	Ḍá,
Tála	(3)				4			

Notes	10—11	8	15*13	15,	15—17	15	17—18—20,
Syllables	D á	Diḍ	D á	Ḍá,	D á	Diḍ	D á Ḍá,
Tála	1				2		

Notes	17—18	15	13	13,	13—20	20	20	20,
Syllables	D á	Dá	Ḍá	Diḍ,	D á	Diḍ	Dá	Ḍá.
Tála	(3)				4			

In the above Gata there is a long Minḍa from R (15) to P (20) which cannot be conveniently produced on fretted instruments as a Ghasiṭa could, but a careful study of the Minḍa will show that it commences from R (15) and ends with P (20) ; the other notes of Chháyá are included in it. On the Satára, which has no Achala (immoveable) frets, it is comparatively easy to slip first the index finger (of the left hand) from R (15) to G (17) and M (18) and then to connect the M (18) with the P (20) by placing the third finger on the P fret and thus omitting the T-M (19). Those who have seen the ordinary arrangement of frets on the Satára will clearly understand what we mean. As regards the other Minḍa which connects P (20) with S (13), the Minḍa is the best way if practicable; if not, the finger should be moved so smoothly and swiftly that the intermediate notes need not give sufficiently audible sounds; the movement of the finger from R (15) to G (17), M (18) and P (20) should be forcible, but that from S (13) to P (20) smooth.

The following Gata of the Chháyá may be played in the Madhya as well as in the Druta (No. 9) :—

Notes	17—18	17—18,	17—18	15	13	13,	13	15	17
Syllables	Dá á	D á,	D á	Ḍá	Dá	Ḍá,	Dá	Diḍ	Diḍ
Tála	1		2				(3)		

Notes	17—18	15	13	13,	13	10—11	8,
Syllables	D á ḍ	Dá	Diḍ	Diḍ,	Dá	D á	Ḍdá
Tála	4				1		

Notes	13	13	15	17,	18	22—23	22—23	20,
Syllables	Dá	Ḍá	Dá	Ḍá,	Dá	D á	Ḍ á	Dá,
Tála	2				(3)			

Notes	15	17	18	20,	17—18	15	15,
Syllables	Dá	Ḍá	Dá	Ḍá,	D á á	Ḍá	Dáá,
Tála	4				1		

Notes	13	13	13,	22—23	22—23	20,
Syllables	Ḍá	Dá	Ḍá,	D á	D á	Ḍá,
Tála	2			(3)		

Notes	15	17	18	20.
Syllables	Dá	Diḍ	Diḍ	Dá.
Tála	4			

A Gata of the Hámira in the Bilambapada (No. 10) :—

Notes	22—23	22—23	24—25	22 20,	22	24	25	27—29,
Syllables	D á	D á	Ḍ á	Diḍ,	Dá	Diḍ	Da	Ḍ á,
Tála	1				2			

Notes	25	22—23	22	20,	19—20	22	17—18	19—20,
Syllables	Dá	D á	Ḍá	Diḍ,	D á	Diḍ	D á	Ḍ á,
Tála	(3)				4			

Notes	22—23	22—23	22	20,	17	15	17—19—20	20,
Syllables	D á	D á	Ḍá	Diḍ,	Dá	Diḍ	D á	Ḍá,
Tála	1				2			

Notes	17	15—17—15	13	20,	19—20	20	22	17—18	20.
Syllables	Dá	D á	Ḍá	Diḍ,	D á	D i	ḍ	D á	Ḍá.
Tála	(3)				4				

A Gata of the Hámira in the Madhya as well as in the Druta, composed by the late Sáddikálikhá, a Rabába player (No. 11) :—

Notes	22—23	22—23	20,	18	17	18	20,
Syllables	D á á	D á	Ḍá,	Dá	Ḍá	Dá	Ḍá,
Tála	1			2			

Notes 17 18 17 18, 17 15 13, 12 13 13 13,
Syllables Dá Diḍ Diḍ Diḍ, Dáḍ Dáḍ Dá, Dá Diḍ Dá Dá,
Tála (3) 4 1

Notes 17 18 20 19 20, 13 15, 8 13,
Syllables Ḍdá Diḍ Dá, Dáḍ Dá, D á Ḍáá,
Tála 2 (3) 4

Notes 29—30 29 27, 25 24 22 20,
Syllables D á á Dá Ḍá, Dá Ḍá D á Ḍá,
Tála 1 2

Notes 20 22 17 18, 18 20 19 20.
Syllables Dá Diḍ Diḍ Diḍ, Dá Dá Ḍdá.
Tála (3) 4

A Gata of the Gouḍa-Sáranga in the Bilambapada (No. 12):—

Notes 15—17 17—18, 17 17—18, 17 20*19*20,
Syllables D á D á, Ḍá D i ḍ, Dá D i ḍ
Tála 1 2 (3)

Notes 19—20 22—24—25, 25—27 25—24, 22 20,
Syllables D á Ḍ á, D á D á, Ḍá Diḍ,
Tála 4 1 2

Notes 15 13, 12—13 15.
Syllables Dá Diḍ, D á Ḍá.
Tála (3) 4

A Gata of the Gouḍa-Sáranga in the Madhya, composed by the late Sádikálikhá, a Rabába player (No. 13) :—

Notes	17	15,	18*17	17	17,	17	20	19	20,
Syllables	Dá	Ḍá,	Dáá	Dá	Ḍá,	Dá	Diḍ	Diḍ	Diḍ,
Tála	1		2			(3)			

Notes	20	19—20,	22	19—20,	24	22	20	19,
Syllables	Dá	D á	Ḍdá,	D á,	Dáḍ	Dá	Dá	Ḍá,
Tála	4			1	2			

Notes	20	22	19	20,	20	22	24,
Syllables	Dá	Diḍ	Diḍ	Diḍ,	Dáḍ	Dáḍ	Dá,
Tála	(3)				4		

Notes	27	24—25,	24	22	20	19,	20	22	19,
Syllables	Dá	Ḍ á,	Dáḍ	Dá	Dá	Ḍá,	Dá	Diḍ	Did,
Tála	1		2				(3)		

Notes	20,	19—20	17	19,	22	19*20	17*18,
Syllables	Diḍ,	D á ḍ	Dáḍ	Dá,	Dá	Ḍáá	D á ḍ,
Tála		4			1		2

Notes	15	12	12,	13	17	15	18	17,
Syllables	Dá	Dá	Ḍá,	Dá	Diḍ	Diḍ	D i	ḍ,
Tála				(3)				

Notes	17	12—13	13.
Syllables	Dá	D á	Ḍdá.
Tála	4		

Here is a Gata of the Gouḍa-Sáranga in the Druta (No. 14) :—

Notes	12—13	13	13,	17	15	18	17,
Syllables	D á á	Dá	Ḍá,	Dá	Ḍá	Dá	Ḍá,
Tála	1			2			

Notes	17	20	19	20,	20	22	19	20,
Syllables	Dá	Diḍ	Dá	Ḍá,	Dá	Diḍ	Diḍ	Diḍ,
Tála	(3)				4			

Notes	20	15	20,	17	18	12	13,
Syllables	Dáḍ	Dáḍ	Dá,	Dá	Ḍá	Dá	Ḍá,
Tála	1			2			

Notes	13	17	15	18,	17	12—13	13.
Syllables	Dá	Diḍ	Diḍ	Diḍ,	Dá	D á	Ḍdá.
Tála	(3)				4		

From the above two Gatis it will be seen that, though the Minḍas or Ghasiṭas are very few, the Gouḍa-Sáranga is strictly preserved. In the first of these two Gatis the T-M (19) is given more prominence than in the second. When that note (19) is included in this Rága it depends on the individual taste of a composer to give more or less prominence to any note. We have said elsewhere that, with the progress in the Minḍa and Ghasiṭa, the number of Murchhanás is increased. In the above two Gatis the Murchhanás are shown by emphasizing the notes (*vide* p. 105).

From all the Gatis given above it will be perceived that, to preserve and appreciate the *characteristic distinctions* of the Gounḍa-Malhára, Kámbodi, Kedárá, Chháyá, Hámira and Gouḍa-Sáranga, an artistic ear and hand or voice are indispensable. There are several Rágas which differ from one another in the most subtle melody, and it is only the master hand or voice that can do full justice to them. The choice of selecting the notes for a particular piece of music is so much circumscribed in the art of Indian music that only the best composers, whose artistic inspirations are considerably developed by life-long practice and devotion, can venture to compose new pieces in the old Rágas. The Indian musicians of olden times have, however, given a free scope to composers, by allowing them to use any *accidental* notes in the Jilhás or Dhuns, and have thus extended the field of musical activity. We shall revert to this subject when treating of the Gatis in Jilhás or Dhuns.

The following is a Gata of the Shankará in the Bilambapada (No. 15) :—

Notes	22—24—25		25,	25—24—22		20	17	20
Syllables	D	á	Dá,	Ḍ	á	Diḍ,	Dá	Diḍ,
Tála	1			2			(3)	

Notes	17—20		17,	17—15		15,	13	13,	12—13		13
Syllables	D	á	Ḍá,	D	á	Dá,	Ḍá	Diḍ,	D	á	Diḍ,
Tála	4			1			2		(3)		

Notes	12	13,	8	12,	13	17,	17—20		20
Syllables	Dá	Ḍá,	Dá	Diḍ,	Dá	Ḍá,	D	á	Diḍ,
Tála	4		1		2		(3)		

Notes	17	17,	17—15,		15,	13	25,
Syllables	Dá	Ḍá,	D	á	Dá,	Ḍá	Diḍ,
Tála	4		1			2	

Notes	24*25	22	24,	20	22.
Syllables	D á	D i	ḍ,	Dá	Ḍá.
Tála	(3)			4	

Here is a Gata of the Shankará in the Madhya as well as in the Druta, composed by the late Jáfarkhá, a Rabába-player (No. 16) :—

Notes	22—24—25,			25—24	22	20	17,
Syllables	D	á	á,	D áḍ	Dá	Dá	Ḍá,
Tála	1			2			

Notes	17	20	17	20,	17	15	13,
Syllables	Dá	Diḍ	Diḍ	Diḍ,	Dáḍ	Daḍ	Dá,
Tála	(3)				4		

Notes	8	8	8	13,	12 13	17	17,
Syllables	Diḍ	Diḍ	Dá	Dá,	Ḍdá	Dá	Ḍá,
Tála	1				2		

Notes	17	20	17	20,	17	15	13,
Syllables	Dá	Diḍ	Diḍ	Diḍ,	Dáḍ	Dáḍ	Dá,
Tála	(3)				4		

Notes	29	27	25	25,	24	22	25	25,
Syllables	Diḍ	Dá	Dá	Ḍá,	Dá	Ḍá	Diḍ	Diḍ,
Tála	1				2			

Notes	24	22	24,	20	22.
Syllables	Dá	Dá	Ḍdá,	Dáḍ	Dá.
Tála	(3)			4	

Here is a Gata of the Bágesari or Báhára in the Bilambapada. This Rága is a form or variety of the Bágesari of our third table (No. 17):—

Notes	22—23	23,	25*23	25,	22—23	23,
Syllables	D á	Dá,	Ḍ á	Diḍ,	D á	Diḍ,
Tála	1		2		(3)	

Notes	25*23	25	27—28	25,	22—23	18,
Syllables	D á	Ḍá	D á	Dá,	Ḍ á	Diḍ,
Tála	4		1		2	

Notes	20***22	18 20,	16—18	18,	22—23	20,
Syllables	D á	D i ḍ,	D á	Ḍá,	D á	Diḍ,
Tála	(3)		4		1	

Notes	22	18,	20—18	20	16—18	18—20,
Syllables	Dá	Ḍá,	D á	Diḍ	D á	Ḍ á,
Tála	2		(3)		4	

Notes	20—18—16	15,	13	18,	18—20,	20***22
Syllables	D á	Dá,	Ḍá	Diḍ	D á,	D i ḍ
Tála	1		2			(3)

Notes	16—18	18.
Syllables	D á	Ḍá.
Tála	4	

The following is a Gata of the Bágesari or the Báhára to be played in the Madhya as well as in the Druta (No. 18) :—

Notes	22—23	22—23	20,	22	23	25,
Syllables	Dá á	D á	Ḍá,	Dá	Ḍá	Dáá,
Tála	1			2		

Notes	22—23	20,	18	20	16—18	18,	18	25,
Syllables	Dáḍ	Dá,	Dá	Diḍ	D á	Ḍa,	Dá	Ḍḍá,
Tála	(3)		4				1	

Notes	20	23	18	20,	18	20**22	18	20,
Syllables	Dáḍ	Dá	Dá	Ḍá,	Dá	D i ḍ	Diḍ	Diḍ,
Tála	2				(3)			

Notes	16—18—16	15	13,	11	13	13	18—16,
Syllables	D á ḍ	Dáḍ	Dá,	Diḍ	Diḍ	Dá	D á,
Tála	4			1			

Notes	16-18	20	18,	18	20**22	18	20,
Syllables	Ḍdá	Dá	Ḍá,	Dá	D i ḍ	Diḍ	Diḍ,
Tála	2			(3)			

Notes	20	16—18	18
Syllables	Dá	D á	Ḍád.
Tála	4		

The above Gata was composed by the late Báhádur Husenikhá, a Sursingára-player, in imitation of the old Gatis of this Rága by his maternal uncles Jyáfarkhá and Pyárkhá, Rabába-players. We give below a Gata of this Rága composed by Pyárkhá (No. 19) :—

Notes	22—23	22—23	23,	25	23—25	27,	22—23	22	23,
Syllables	D á	D á	Ḍdá,	Dá	Ḍ á	Dá,	Ḍ á	Dá	Diḍ
Tála	1			2			(3)		

Notes	22—23	20	18,	18	25	25	22—23,	20	18
Syllables	D á	Dá	Ḍdá,	Dá	Diḍ	Dá	D á,	Ḍdá	Dá,
Tála	4			1				2	

Notes	18,	18	20**22	18	20,	16—18	15	13
Syllables	Ḍá,	Dá	D i ḍ	Diḍ	Diḍ,	D á ḍ	Dáḍ	Dá
Tála		(3)				4		

Notes	11	13	13	18,	16 18	20	18,
Syllables	Dá	Diḍ	Dá	Dá,	Ḍdá	Dá	Ḍá,
Tála	1				2		

Notes	18	20**22	18	20,	20	16—18	18.
Syllables	Dá	D i ḍ	Diḍ	Diḍ,	Dá	D á	Ḍdá.
Tála	(3)				4		

The above two Gatis are so similar to each other that it is only the individual liking that may decide the superiority of one over the other.

We give below two Gatis of the Darbári-Kánaḍá to show how, if only the Minḍas or Ghasiṭas are omitted from them, they will be reduced to the Sinda-Bhairavi[1] as stated before (*vide* p. 62). It is not only the Minḍas or Ghasiṭas that distinguish a Rága from a Dhun or Jilhá, but also the Murchhanás. We have purposely omitted the Murchhanás from the above Gatis because, if these are reproduced with all the details given above, the insertion of Murchhanás is very easy. The Darbári-Kánaḍá and such other Rágas are associated with more Minḍas or Ghasiṭas than other familiar Rágas, and this is the reason why they are played or sung slowly and only by great artists.

The following is a Gata of the Darbári-Kánaḍá in the Bilambapada (No. 20) :—

Notes	18—16—18	16¼,	13—15	13,	13—11—13—15—11
Syllables	D á	Dá,	Ḍ á	Diḍ,	D á
Tála	1		2		(3)

Notes	11,	11—9—11	8,	6—8	6—8,	6	6,
Syllables	Diḍ,	D á	Ḍá,	D á	D á,	Ḍá	Diḍ
Tála		4		1		2	

[1] If the R (15) is substituted by K-R (14) in the Sinda-Bhairavi, the music comes to Bhairavi, and if the Minḍas or Ghasiṭas and the Murchhanás on the principle of ascent and descent are added to the Bhairavi, it is raised up to the Asávari Rága.

Notes	8	11—9,	11	13,	15—20		20—18,		16	20,
Syllables	Dá	Diḍ,	Dá	Ḍa,	D	á	D	á,	Ḍá	Diḍ,
Tála	(3)		4		1				2	

Notes	18—20		20—25,	23—21		20,	18—16		15,	13	11,
Syllables	D	á	Diḍ,	D	á	Ḍá,	D	á	Dá,	Ḍá	Diḍ,
Tála	(3)			4			1			2	

Notes	11*13*15		11 13,	15	15—20		.
Syllables	D	á	Diḍ,	Dá	Ḍ	á	. .
Tála	(3)			4			.

The above Gata is full of Minḍas or Ghasiṭas, without which a complete idea of the Rága cannot be had.

A Gata of the Darbári-Kánáḍá is only in the Madhya (No. 21):—

Notes	11—9	9—11	9—11,	9¼	8	8	6	6
Syllables	Dá á	Diḍ	Diḍ,	Dáḍ	Dáḍ	Dá,	Dá	Ḍá
Tála	1			2			(3)	

Notes	8	9—11,		9	11	13,	13	15	15—20	
Syllables	Diḍ	D	á,	Ḍá	Diḍ	Diḍ,	Dáḷ	Dáḍ	D	á
Tála				4			1			

Notes	18—16,		16	20	18	23—21,		20	25,	23—25		25
Syllables	Dá	á,	Dá	Diḍ	Diḍ	D	á,	Ḍá	Diḍ	D	á	Ḍá
Tála	2		(3)					4				

Notes	27—28	15—16	18	20,	18—16	15	13,
Syllables	D á	Ḍ á	Diḍ	Diḍ,	D á ḍ	Dáḍ	Dá,
Tála	1				2		

Notes	11	18—16	15	13,	15	13	11	13.
Syllables	Dá	D i ḍ	Diḍ	Dá,	Ḍá	Diḍ	Dá	Ḍá.
Tála	(3)				4			

In the above Gata there is a very long pause or rest on the figure 2 of the second Ávardá. If one is competent enough to utilise this pause either for a long Minḍa or a Ghasiṭa or a Murki, he may attempt it with due regard to the principle of ascent and descent of this Rága. It must be remarked here in passing that the several Gatis given above admit of being rendered more artistic, but our aim is to give a fair idea of the Rágas and not to attempt to render a particular piece highly artistic by giving all its minutest details, for these can be easily acquired by practice and listening to good artists.

We give below a Gata of the Madhya as well as of the Druta in the Sugarái, a beautiful combination of the Sáranga and Aḍáná, a kind of Kánaḍá. This Gata is really beautiful for its *notes* and *Tála*, and was composed by the late Sádakálikhá, a Rabába-player. (No. 22) :—

Notes	25	22—23	20,	20	18	18,	15—18—20	18*20,
Syllables	Dá	D á	Ḍdá,	Dá	Dá	Ḍdá,	Dá á	Ḍá á,
Tála	1			2			(3)	

Notes	18	20	20	25,	23—25,	16—18	16—18,
Syllables	Dá	Diḍ,	Dá	Dá,	Ḍ d á	D á	Ḍ á,
Tála	4				1	2	

Notes	15	15	15	15,	13	13	15	15,
Syllables	Dá	Dá	Dá	Ḍá,	Dá	Ḍá	Dá	Ḍá,
Tála	(3)				4			

Notes	16—18	16—18	15	13,	15	11—13	13	10—11,
Syllables	D á	Ḍ á	Dá	Ḍá,	Dá	Ḍ á	Dá	D á,
Tála	1				2			

Notes	8,	6	8	11	13,
Syllables	Ḍdá	Dá	Ḍá	Dá	Ḍá,
Tála	(3)	4			

Notes	13	15	13	16—18,	18	13,	15	11	13	20,
Syllables	Dá	Diḍ	Da	D a,	Ḍdá,	Dá,	Dá	Dá	Ḍá	Diḍ,
Tála	1				2		(3)			

Notes	20	18	22	20
Syllables	Dá	Ḍá	Dá	Ḍa
Tála	4			

The above Gata, although based on our plan, is difficult in Tála for an ordinary artist. Those who are well versed in Tála will, however, find it easy to perform.

Here is a Gata in the Náyaki-Kánaḍá composed by the author. This Gata is to be played in the Madhya as well as in the Druta. The simple Gata of this Rága is not given because it is shorter than the Darbári-Kánaḍá by one note, *viz.*, K-Dh (9 or 21). We give a first Gata of the Darbári-Kánaḍá as an aid to the other Gata. The former is a Khoḍhava, while the latter is a Sampurna—*vide* first table (No. 23) :—

Notes	15—16,	13—16	18	20	20—23—25,	18	20	25,
Syllables	Dá á,	Dáḍ	Dá	Dá	Ḍ á,	Dá	Ḍá	Diḍ,
Tála	1	2				(3)		

Notes	27—28,	25	23	20,	27	23,
Syllables	Diḍ,	Dáḍ	Dáḍ	Dá,	Dáḍ	Dá,
Tála		4			1	

Notes	25	20,	23	18,	20	23,	25	27—28,
Syllables	Dáḍ	Dá,	Dáḍ	Dá,	Dá	Ḍá,	Diḍ	Diḍ,
Tála	2		(3)		4			

Notes	25	23,	20,	18	20
Syllables	Dáḍ	Dáḍ	Dá,	Dá	Ḍá—á—á
Tála	1			2	

Notes	20—23	20	18	16—18,	16	15	11 13	13 15,
Syllables	D á	Ḍá	Dá	Ḍ á,	Dá	Ḍá	Diḍ	Diḍ,
Tála	(3)				4			

The long pause or rest in the above Gata at figure 2 marked á—á in the third Ávaradá may be utilised for a Minḍa, Ghasiṭa or Murki, of course consistently with the notes of the Rága.

If K-Dh (9 or 21) is added to the above Gata in its proper place, the piece will be raised to a Darbári-Kánaḍá. Instead of K-Dh (9 or 21), if the pure Dha (10 or 22) is added, it will become a Sáháná-Kánaḍá. It is needless to repeat that, if we want to render the above Gata in any of the varieties of Sáranga, excepting the Gouḍa-Sáranga, we shall have to omit the K-G (4 or 16) and play the Gata with the notes of a Sáranga. For want of space we refrain from giving more Gatis of the other Rágas, because to treat this subject exhaustively belongs more to a work exclusively devoted to it than to one like this which treats of the several departments of music and their general outlines. Those who wish to study this subject more fully, must have recourse, as we have said elsewhere, to special works on practical music and their special study. However, to a person well versed in any branch of music the treatment we have given in the second, third, fourth and this chapter, will suffice to enable him to have an idea of singing and playing in the several Rágas, and to form a fair estimate of the practical side of Indian music.

As regards the practical side of vocal music of the Rágas, one has only to substitute the poetical words for the technical syllables, such as Da Ḍa, etc. In doing so the Gatis in the Bilambapada will be of greater use than those in the Madhya or Druta. It will be useful to note that artistic singers can sing or play Gatis of any Rága in the Bilambapada, because this class of Gatis differs but very little from the Khyálas. In lieu of the poetical words of the Khyálas they have only to put in the Da, Ḍá, etc., to meet a particular Tála. This can only be done with real credit by those who can boast of an intimate knowledge of the *skeleton notes* called *Sargam*. Moreover, the real instrumentalists as a class are taught first to sing the Dhrupadas of Rágas, which give them a correct idea of their skeleton notes along with their Mindas or Ghasiṭas and Murchhanás. The Murki, as we have said before, does not form part of the Joḍa and Dhrupada. The Joḍa music, vocal and instrumental, is one and the same thing as far as the Rágas are concerned.

Before giving a few Gatis of the Jilhás, we give below those of a few simple Rágas (first table).

The following is a Gata of the Bhupa or Bibhása to be played in the Bilambapada (No. 24) :—

Notes	17—20	17—22,	20—17	15,	17	20,	22—25	25—27
Letters	D á	D á,	Ḍ á	Did,	Dá	Did,	D á	Ḍ á,
	1		2		(3)		4	

Notes	25—22 20,	17*15 13,	15***17 15*13,	10—13 15.
Letters	D á Dá,	Ḍ á Diḍ,	D á D i ḍ,	D á Ḍá.
Tála	1	2	(3)	4

A careful study of the above Gata will show that if we want to change it to the Bhupáli we have only to add the pure N (12 or 24) in its proper place. Again, if we want to change it into the Kalyána we have to add two notes, N (12 or 24) and T-M (9 or 21). We need not remind the student that the Murchhanás of these Rágas are to be used in their proper places.

If R (15 or 27) and Dh (10 or 22) are replaced by their Komalas (half-notes) 14 or 26 and 9 or 21 in the above Gata it will change the Gata into the proper Bibhása.[1]

In changing the notes of the above Gata we only change its Rága, but the change of notes certainly does not necessarily mean a change in its musical value. The musical worth of a Rága does not depend on its skeleton notes alone, but on the proper adjustment of the Minḍa, Ghasiṭa, Ása, Murki, and Tála. To execute a Rága in its pure and simple form is a matter of practice, but the production of it in its highest musical form is the privilege of a real genius.

[1] The Bibhása of the old works on music does not differ from the Bhupa; but the Bibhása proper, as sung or played now, is of modern Mahomedan invention, and it differs from the old Bibhása in this that it has K-R (14 or 26) and K-Dh (9 or 21) in place of R (15 or 27) and Dh (10 or 22). The late Sádikálikhá and a few other musicians used pure Dh (10 or 22) instead of K-Dh (9 or 21), in this Rága.

Here is a Gata of the Bhupa or Bibhása in the Madhya as well as in the Druta, composed by Pyárkhá, a Rabába-player, and the teacher of Báhádurhusenkhá, a Sursingára player (No. 25) :—

Notes 17*15 17 17, 17 22 20 22, 20 17 15,
Syllables Dáá Dá Ḍá, Da Diḍ Diḍ Diḍ, Dáḍ Dáḍ Dá,
Tála 1 2 (3)

Notes 17—20 22—25, 22 27 25 27, 25 22
Syllables Dá Ḍá Dá Ḍá, Dá Diḍ Diḍ Diḍ, Dáḍ Dáḍ
Tála 4 1 2

Notes 20, 25 22 25, 10 22, 27—25 22—20,
Syllables Dá, Dáḍ Da, Dáá Ḍá, Dá Ḍá Dá Ḍá
Tála (3) 4 1

Notes 22—25 20—22, 17 15 13 15, 8 10 13 15.
Syllables Dá Ḍá Dá Ḍá, Dá Diḍ Dá Ḍá, Dá Ḍá Dá Ḍá.
Tála 2 (3) 4

The following Gata is a little simpler than the one given above (No. 26) :—

Notes 17*15 17 17, 17 22 20 22, 20 17
Syllables Dáá Dá Ḍá, Dá Diḍ Diḍ Diḍ, Dáḍ Dáḍ
Tála 1 2 (3)

Notes 15, 17 20 22 25, 22 27 25 27, 25
Syllables Dá, Dá Ḍá Dá Ḍá, Dá Diḍ Diḍ Diḍ, Dáḍ
Tála 4 1 2

Notes	22	20,	15	17	20	22,	22	27	25	27,
Syllables	Dáḍ	Dá,	Dá	Ḍá	Dá	Ḍá,	Dá	Diḍ	Diḍ	Diḍ
Tála			(3)				4			

Notes	25	22	20,	25 22	25,	10	15 13,	15	22,
Syllables	Dáḍ	Dáḍ	Dá,	Dáḍ	Dá,	Ḍá	Dáḍ,	Dá	Ḍá,
Tála	1			2		(3)		4	

Notes	22	27,	22	25	20	22,	20	17	15	13,
Syllables	Dá	Dḍá,	Dáḍ	Dá	Dá	Ḍá,	Dá	Diḍ	Dá	Ḍá,
Tála	1		2				(3)			

Notes	8	10	13	15 .
Syllables	Dá	Ḍá	Da	Ḍá.
Tála	4			

Here is a Gata of the Kalyána in the Bilambapada (No. 27):—

Notes	19—20—22	24,	20***22	20 19,	17*15
Syllables	D á	Dá,	Ḍ á	Diḍ,	D á
Tála	1		2		(3)

Notes	13,	15	17—22,	19—20	15***17,	13***15
Syllables	Diḍ,	Dá	Ḍ á,	D á	D á,	Ḍ á
Tála		4		1		2

Notes	24*22,	25***27	25,	22***24	22***20
Syllables	Diḍ,	D á	Diḍ,	D á	Ḍ á.
Tála		(3)		4	

We have advisedly given Gatis of the Bhupa (No. 24) and Kalyána (No. 27) to show that the distribution of the syllables or words over different notes in a Rága is not so much circumscribed as it would perhaps appear from the simple extensions we have given elsewhere (pp. 90 to 94). A careful study of these two Gatis will at least teach the student to set these sixteen syllables or their equivalent strokes or words to any simple Rága with the Mindas, Ghasiṭas or Ásas and Murkis. If this be done our aim shall have been attained. It is not our ambition to invent a royal road to the study of the highest art of Indian music, but to instil a true idea of the Rágas into those who are acquainted with music as an art but are unacquainted with the Indian classical music, otherwise called Rágas.

The easiest way to set the above Gata to any simple or compound Rága is first to set the syllables to the skeleton notes as shown in the tables and then to adjust the Mindas, Ghasiṭas, Ásas and Murkis within the notes as given in the above Gata. If the number of notes of a Rága is less, the syllables should be distributed in groups of twos or more ; if it is more, the syllables should be sub-divided either by an Ása or a Minda or Ghasiṭa. On the instruments as well as in the voices where a connection of notes is either impossible or difficult, the notes should be detached and produced separately; but this will not be a perfect form of a Rága. The simple production, however, of the skeleton notes of the Rága with judicious adjustment of its ascending and descending order and the emphasizing of its principal notes, as shown under the head of Murchhanás (pp. 106-107), will give a faint idea of the Rága. This is done even by professional musicians when singing and performing on the harmonium, piano, and such other instruments.

We shall now treat of the Gatis in Dhuns or Jilhás. It is indispensably necessary to remind the reader to note the difference between the Jilhás and Rágas (*vide* p. 83). We consider this to be the proper place to say that we are not prepared to state with certainty which of the two, the Rágas or Jilhás, were first developed. From all that can be gathered it seems most rational that the Rágas presuppose the Jilhás, because the former seem to be an advanced and strictly systematized form of the latter. By this declaration we must not be understood as insinuating that all the Jilhás that are in practice were the bases on which the Rágas were founded, nor that the Jilhás are the degenerated forms of the Rágas, as many Indian artists suppose. What we really mean is that in most cases their influence must have been reciprocal. The old authorities on music have omitted to give the historical nature of the formation of the several Rágas and Jilhás, considering them to have emanated from divine persons, and, therefore, free from the general laws of development. It cannot be gainsaid that in the ordinary course of things every art has its antecedent development; why, then, should the Rágas form an exception to this immutable law? It is our firm conviction that the Rágas were the offshoots of the Jilhás, at least in most, if not all, cases. It is also impracticable to decide whether the simple Rágas as a whole were the basis of all compound Rágas. Those musicians who have devoted their lives to the study and practice of the simple and compound Rágas, can better realise the difficulty in certain cases in executing them vocally, in spite of their being simple. To produce the Hinḍola (one of the Oḍhavas) in a vocal performance is so very difficult that artists of the highest merit only can do justice to the five notes and the two Murchhanás. These remarks are without reserve applicable to the Jilhás also. There were and are a few artists who have devoted their lives with great credit to the performance of the Jilhás. The Rágas, however, are held in such great admiration and the Jilhás in such low estimation that the performers of the latter, if asked about their skill, freely admit that they can only sing or play the Jilhá-Zinjoṭi. We, on the contrary, attach equal importance to both, as we have said in treating of the difference between the Minḍa or Ghasiṭa and the Murki (*vide* p. 65). In performing the Jilhás, the artist has to deal not only with the Minḍás or Ghasiṭas but has also to pay considerable attention to the Murki. The fundamental difference between a Rága and a Jilhá is, as we have said before, that the former is inflexibly strict in its ascent and descent, while the latter is free from it, and also admits of the introduction of *accidentals* (*vide* pp. 55, 96). In the voice or hands of experts the Jilhás are quite as ornamental and artistic as the Rágas. The choice of selecting notes is, however, greater in the latter than in the former. In short there are several Rágas and Jilhás composed by some of the great artists of the last few generations, but they find no place side by side with the Rágas in old Sanskrit works. Some of these new compositions that have come down to us are really musical and highly artistic. These compositions are mixtures of the old Rágas, such as the Megha or Malhára and Kánaḍá (Miáki-Malhára, see p. 104), Tilaka-Kámoda, &c. Two illustrations of such compositions are given at the end of this chapter.

Here we give some Gatis of the Jilhás. Instead of giving simple skeleton notes (*vide* pp. 55 and 99) in the Tála, it is attempted to make these Gatis as musical as those of the Rágas.

It must be remembered that in the following Gatis of the Jilhás the compound Murki which has been treated of before may be used where a simple Murki is shown. The compound Murki on fretted instruments is produced in the following way :—

Instead of fixing the index finger of the left hand as is done in the simple Murki (pp. 65-67), it should be slipped over other notes, while the third and, if practicable, the fourth finger should strike the notes. This compound Murki can be produced both in the ascent and descent.

In the artistic performance of the Gatis generally of the Bilambapada, this slipping of the finger is combined with a Minḍa. The Minḍa and Ghasiṭa or the Ghasiṭa and Minḍa are produced by a stroke of the right-hand finger (index).

Those who can reproduce the above Gatis in all their details, excepting those of the Tála, will not find the subject difficult.

The following is a Gata of the Káfi-Jilhá in the Bilambapada (No. 28) :—

Notes	15	15,	16***18		13,	15	18,	20	20—25,	
Syllables	Dá	Dá,	Ḍ	á	Diḍ,	Dá	Diḍ,	Dá	Ḍ	á,
Tála	1		2			(3)		4		

Notes	23—22		20***22,		18*20		20—21,	18***20	
Syllables	D	á	D	á,	Ḍ	á	D i ḍ,	D	á
Tála	1				2			(3)	

Noets	16—15,	13*15		11*13.	
Syllables	D i ḍ,	D	á	Ḍ	á.
Tála		4			

We have given the above Gata with a short Minḍa or Ghasiṭa and Murki. The K-Dh (21) is an accidental note. In this Jilhá the pure G (17) is also artistically touched. If the pure G (5 or 17) and N (12 or 24) be added as accidental notes to the skeleton notes of the above piece, it will be a Gata of the Sindurá-Jilhá.

Here is a Gata of the Káfi-Jilhá in the Bilambapada (No. 29) :—

Notes	13 25 23 25, 25***27 23 25 22*23 20*22,
Syllables	Dá Diḍ Dá Ḍá, D á Diḍ D á Ḍ á,
Tála	1 2

Notes	25—27—28 27—25 23*25 22 23, 20***22 18 20
Syllables	D á D á Ḍ á Diḍ, D á Diḍ
Tála	(3) 4

Notes	16***18 15, 13 18 20***22 18*20, 20—22—23
Syllables	D á Ḍá, Dá Diḍ D á Ḍ á, D á
Tála	1 2

Notes	20 18 15***16 13, 12 13 15*16 15*16,
Syllables	Diḍ D á Ḍá, Dá Diḍ D á Ḍ á,
Tála	(3)

Notes	16***18 15 13 11.
Syllables	D á Diḍ Ḍá Dá.
Tála	4

This Gata is a combination of the Káfi and Pilu Jilhás. The notes of the Pilu are N (12) S (13) R (15)

K-G (16) M (18) P (20) K-Dh (21) N (24) S (25). From these notes it will be seen that the Pilu differs from the Sinda-Bhairavi, in as much as it has the pure N (12 or 24) while the latter has (11 or 23) K-N. The difference between the Sindha and the common Bhairavis is that in the former the R (3 or 15) is pure, while in the latter it is Komala (2 or 14).

The following is a Gata of the Káfi-Jilhá in the Madhya, composed by the late Báchpaiji of Banáras, the teacher of the late Máharája Shri Jivanlálji of Bombay (No. 30) :—

Notes	20,	17	17	17	17,	18	20***22	18
Syllables	Dáá,	Dáḍ	Dá	Dá	Ḍá,	Dá	D i ḍ	Diḍ
Tála	1	2				(3)		

Notes	18***20,	18	15***16	13	15,	15	23	22
Syllables	D i ḍ,	Dá	D á	Ḍ	d á,	Dá	Diḍ	Diḍ
Tála		4				1		

Notes	23***25,	22*23	20***22	18	20,	27	23***25
Syllables	D á,	D á	D i ḍ	Dá	Ḍá,	Dá	Ḍ á,
Tála		2				(3)	

Notes	22***23	20	20	25,	23	20	18,
Syllables	D á ḍ	Dá	Diḍ	Diḍ,	Dáḍ	Dáḍ	Dá,
Tála	4				1		

Notes	18***20		16	13	11,	13	15	15	16***18	
Syllables	D	á	Diḍ	Diḍ	Dá,	Dá	Diḍ	Dá	Ḍ	á
Tála	2					(3)				

Notes	15***16	13*15.
Syllables	D á ḍ	D á.
Tála	4	.

The above Gata will prove really beautiful when executed with the compound Minḍa, Ghasiṭa and Murki.

Here is a Gata of the Káfi-Jilhá in the Madhya as well as in the Druta (No. 31) :—

Notes	20	20	18,	20	22	23	25,	22—23	20,
Syllables	Dáá	Dá	Ḍá,	Dá	Ḍá	Dá	Ḍá,	D á á	Diḍ,
Tála	1			2				(3)	

Notes	18	16	15	15,	16	20	18	20,	18
Syllables	Dá	Diḍ	Dá	Ḍá,	Dá	Diḍ	Dá	Ḍá,	Dá
Tála	4				1				2

Notes	17	18,	17	18	17	20,	18,	15*16	15
Syllables	Ḍá	Dá,	Dá	Diḍ	Dá	Ḍá,	Dáá,	D á á	Dá
Tála			(3)				4	1	

Notes	18,	16	15	13	11,	13	15	15
Syllables	Ḍá,	Dá	Ḍá	Dá	Ḍá,	Dá	Diḍ	Dá
Tála		2				(3)		

Notes	16***18,	18 20	18.
Syllables	Ḍ á,	Dáḍ	Dá.
Tála		4	

The following is a Gata of the Zinjoṭi-Jilhá in the Bilambapada (No. 32) :—

Notes	18*17	17	17*18		15	17,	13	15	13	15
Syllables	D á	Dá	Ḍ	á	D i	ḍ,	Dá	D i	ḍ	Dá
Tála	1						2			

Notes	20,	18**20	17**18	15**17	13,	15	25*23
Syllables	Ḍá,	D á	D á	Ḍ á	Diḍ,	Dá	D i ḍ
Tála		(3)				4	

Notes	23*22	22*20,	20***22		18	18***20	17,	17*8	17
Syllables	D á	Ḍ á,	D	á	Diḍ	D a	Ḍá,	D á	Diḍ
Tála			1					2	

Notes	15*17	13*15,	13*15	10***13	10*11	8,
Syllables	D á	Ḍ á,	D á	D á	Ḍ á	Diḍ,
Tála			(3)			

Notes	10	13	15	20***22.
Syllables	Dá	Diḍ	Dá	Ḍ á.
Tála	4			

Here is a Gata of the Zinjoṭi-Jilhá in the Madhya, composed by the late Báchapaiji of Banáras (No. 33) :—

Notes	17,	17	18	23	22,	20**22	18**20	18,
Syllables	Dáá,	Dá	Ḍá	Diḍ	Diḍ,	D á ḍ	D á ḍ	Diḍ,
Tála	1	2				(3)		

Notes 17**18 15**17 13, 13*15 13*15*20 18, 17
Syllables D á ḍ D á ḍ Da, D á D á Ḍdá, Dáá
Tála 4 1 2

Notes 11 10, 8, 10 13*12 13, 15 20***22 18 .
Syllables D i ḍ Diḍ, Dá D á Ḍdá, Dá D á Ḍdá.
Tála (3) 4

The following is a Gata of the Gárá-Jilhá in the Madhya (No. 34) :—

Notes *20* 17, *18* 15 17, 18 20**22 18
Syllables Dáá Diḍ, Dáá Dá Ḍá, Dá D i ḍ Diḍ
Tála 1 2 (3)

Notes 20, 18 15***17 13 15, 15 25 22 25,
Syllables Diḍ, Dá D á Ḍd á, Dá Diḍ Dá Ḍá.
Tála 4 1

Notes 15 20, 18 20**22 18 20, 18 15***17
Syllables Dá Dḍá, Dá D i ḍ Diḍ Diḍ, Dá D á
Tála 2 (3) 4

Notes 13 15.
Syllables Ḍd á.
Tála

To the above Gata may be added the following simple piece in Duni (double time). A careful perusal of this piece will show how the Duni is produced. In the above Gata the largest number of syllables is four, while in Duni it will be eight. This Duni begins from the Avasána (No. 35) :—

Notes	10	13	15	17	13	15	17	18,
Syllables	Dá	Ḍá	Dá	Ḍá	Dá	Ḍá	Dá	Ḍá,
Tála	1							
Notes	15	17	18	20	17	18	20	22,
Syllables	Dá	Ḍá	Dá	Ḍá	Dá	Dá	Dá	Ḍá,
Tála	2							
Notes	22	20	18	17	20	18	17	15,
Syllables	Dá	Ḍá	Dá	Ḍá	Dá	Ḍá	Dá	Ḍá,
Tála	(3)							
Notes	18	17	15	13	13	15	13	15
Syllables	Dá	Dá	Dá	Dá	Dá	Diḍ	Dá	Dá
Tála	4							

If for want of practice, the above piece is reduced to the Barobari (same as the Gata or four letters to each Mátrá), it will certainly not be so charming as in the Duni. In the above piece *fastness* is more alluring than the *arrangement* of notes. We have purposely given this piece to convince our readers that *fastness* within certain limits is of paramount importance in increasing the charms of music. This is the reason why one is charmed at times by listening to the Sargams (simple *notes* adjusted to *time*) produced rapidly by the voice or on instruments, such as the Piano, Harmonium, Concertina, Musical Boxes, etc. Sometimes, however, slowness is also a source of pleasure, for in slowness the notes are intensified. This explains why artists of high merits generally give fastness to acute notes and reserve the dull notes for slowness.

If we should want to poduce this piece, of course with certain alterations, in the second Gata (No. 31) of the Káfi, we have only to replace G (17) by K-G (16), and instead of commencing it from Dh (10), begin it from K-N (11). By this procedure we bring in the K-N (11), which is one of the notes of the Káfi. It has been already asserted that the pure N (12 or 24) and G (5 or 17) are added to the Káfi as *accidentals*.

This piece cannot be inserted in any Gata of the Kánaḍás, for this reason, that it is not the notes alone that go to make up a Kánaḍá, but there are other things essentially necessary as previously stated. Whatever permutations we might make of the notes S (1 or 13), R (3 or 15), K-G (4 or 16), M (6 or 18), P (8 or 20), Dh (10 or 22), or K Dh (9 or 21), and K-N (11 or 23), and so on, it will never cease to be a Káfi or Sinda-Bhairavi, unless we produce the Minḍa or the Ghasiṭa with certain Murchhanás, while without the Murchhanás it would not be the Kánaḍá. In the different varieties of the Kánaḍá, extensions called *Chalat-firata or ávajáva* (*Tána* or strain in instrumental music) may be attempted only in the Madhya, because it is impracticable to compound or connect notes in the Druta. In the above piece, in spite of its rapid execution, the impression is of jumping and not of connecting notes.

So far as fastness is concerned simple jumping has an advantage over the Miṇḍa, Ghasiṭa and Murki. In each Rága at least two of its notes on which the two Murchhanás depend must be joined with its other note or notes. This principle is strictly observed even by ordinary performers when executing the Kánaḍá, Miyá ki-Malhára, Bhairava and a few other Rágas. In the Bhupa, Kalyána, and a few other Rágas one need not be so particular as in the Kánaḍá. But an expert in music never performs a Rága without executing almost all its details, however sparingly.

If this piece (No. 35) is to be executed in any Rága, some of its syllables will have to be distributed among the combined notes; but its execution is very difficult in the Druta.

It is not possible to treat at great length, within the limited space of this treatise and in the absence of a complete and standard notation, the execution of various details, such as *Ṭhá, Duni, Chougan and Áḍa*, in the Rágas as is done by great artists.

The signs that have been adopted in this chapter cannot be called notation proper.

The following is a Gata of the Bhairavi-Jilhá in the Bilambapada (No. 36):

Notes	20	20	20	20,	20*21	20	21	25,
Syllables	Dá	Dá	Ḍá	Diḍ,	D á	Diḍ	Dá	Ḍá,
Tála	1				2			

Notes	25***23	21***23	21**20	20 21,	18	20
Syllables	D á	D á	Ḍ á	D i ḍ,	Dá	Diḍ
Tála	(3)				4	

Notes	16	18,	18	23	21***23	20,	20***21
Syllables	Dá	Ḍá,	Dá	Diḍ	D á	Ḍá,	D á
Tála			1				2

Notes	18 20	16	18,	16***18	14***16	13	13*14,
Syllables	D i ḍ	Dá	Ḍá,	D á	D á	Ḍá	D i ḍ,
Tála				(3)			

Notes	11	13	16	18.
Syllables	Dá	Did	Dá	Dá.
Tála	4			

In the above Gata T-M (7 or 19) may be added to M (18) in the descent as an *accidental note.*

This is a Gata of the Bhairavi-Jilhá in the Madhya, composed by the late Gulámáli, a Saroda-player, of Gwallior (No. 37) :—

Notes	16**18	16,	18	20	*23,*	20	21,	20
Syllables	D áá	Dá,	Dá	Ḍá	Dáá,	Dáá	Diḍ,	Dá
Tála	1		2			(3)		4

Notes	18	16	18,	16	21	20	21,	18	20
Syllables	Diḍ	Dá	Ḍá,	Dá	Diḍ	Dá	Ḍá,	Dá	Diḍ
Tála				1				2	

Notes	16	18,	16	20	16	18,	16	14
Syllables	Dá	Ḍá,	Dá	Diḍ	Diḍ	Diḍ,	Dáḍ	Dáḍ
Tála			(3)				4	

Notes	13,	16**18*	16,	14	13	13,	9**11*	9,
Syllables	Dá,	Dáá	Dá,	Dá	Ḍá	Dáá,	Dáá	Dá,
Tála		1		2			(3)	

Notes	11	13	*16,*	*20*	18	18,	16	14	13.
Syllables	Dá	Ḍá	Dáá,	Dáá	Dá	Ḍá,	Dá	Ḍá	Dá
Tála	4			1			2		

Notes	13,	13	20	20	21***23,	20**21	18*20.
Syllables	Ḍá,	Dá	Diḍ	Dá	Ḍ á,	D á ḍ	D á.
Tála		(3)				4	

The piece No. 35 may be inserted in the above Gata without reducing its fastness, provided it is distributed among the notes of the Bhairavi S (13), K-R (14), K-G (16), M (18), P (20), K-Dh (21), and K-N (23), with all their possible permutations. If so distributed the piece will never cease to be Bhairavi, but if the Minḍa or Ghasiṭa and certain Murchhanás be added to the notes with due attention to the principle of ascent and descent it will be Jogi or Asávari (see first and second tables).

We give below, as said before, a piece in the Tilaka-Kámoda. This mixed Rága is either the original work of, or its further artistic development by, the late Sádikálikhá and Báhádurhusenkhá. This piece is not set to Tála here. From the name Tilaka-Kámoda given to this piece it would be seen that it is a mixture of these two Rágas only, but in its present form it is a beautiful mixture of more than two Rágas. The piece should be executed, vocally or on instruments, in the slowest time possible. It is a remarkable fact that in playing the Joḍa the instrumentalists always use the outward stroke, that is Ḍá and not Dá. In the Joḍa (p. 63), the former is more forcible or resonant than the latter, and this is the reason why it is much used in the following piece. In vocal music this Ḍá would show emphasis. In the following piece are inserted the compound Minḍa or Ghasiṭa, Ása and Murki. The following is the piece of the Tilaka-Kámoda :—

Notes 8 12 13 15 15—20 18—17—15—13
Syllables Ḍá Dá Ḍá Dá Ḍ—á Ḍ——————á

Notes 12 8 12 13 15 15—18—17—15—13
Syllables Dá Ḍá Dá Ḍá Dá Ḍ——————á

Notes 12 13 15 18 20 20—23—22—20
Syllables Ḍá Dá Dá Ḍá Ḍá Ḍ————á

Notes 22***20***18***17 13*15 13*15*17*15 13
Syllables Ḍ*** *** ***á Dá Ḍ * * * á Ḍá

Notes 15 15—23—22—20 20—18—17—15 15 18
Syllables Dá Ḍ——————á Ḍ——————á Dá Dá

Notes 20 20—24—25—27—25 25—23—22—20
Syllables Dá Ḍ——————á Ḍ——————á

Notes 20***22***18***17 13*15 13*15*17*15 13*15 13
Syllables Ḍ*** *** ***á Ḍ á Ḍ* * * á D á Ḍá

The following is a sample of the Miáki or Tánasena's Malhára (see p. 104). It is not set to Tála, and must be played as slow as possible :—

Notes 13 10—11—10—11 6 8 10—11—10—11
Syllables Ḍá Ḍ————á Dá Dá Ḍ————á

Notes	12—13	13	15	15—20—18—16	18—20
Syllables	D—á	Dá	Ḍá	Ḍ————á	D—á

Notes	15*13	13*15	13	15	18	20	20—22—25
Syllables	Dá	Dá	Dá	Dá	Dá	Ḍá	Ḍ———á

Notes	25——23	23—24—25	20—22—23—20	20—27—25
Syllables	D——á	Ḍ———á	Ḍ————á	Ḍ———á

Notes	20—23—22—23	24—25—24—25	18	20	15—16
Syllables	Ḍ————á	D————á	Dá	Dá	Dá

Notes	16——23—22—20—18—16	15*13	13
Syllables	Ḍ——————á	Ḍá	Ḍá

The above two pieces, which are given in the simplest and skeleton forms for the sake of brevity, may be extended in the following way:—

In the place of one Dá or Ḍá or its Minḍa or Ghasiṭa, Murki or Ása the student may produce more than one Dá or Ḍá. It is hardly necessary to remind the student that the additions of more Dás or Ḍás involve more notes simple, compounded or trilled, of course consistently with the skeleton notes of the two pieces, which represent, although in a simple and pure form, the two Rágas. It may also be noted that the additions need not necessarily be equal in numbers. It is already stated (*vide* p. 107) that in executing a Rága some of its notes are touched more than others, and that with the progress in the Minḍa or Ghasiṭa the number of Murchhanás in each Rága is increased (*vide* p. 106). The foregoing pieces will really be beautiful if Vádi, Sama-Vádi and Anuvádi (*vide* pp. 95, 96) are inserted in them.

Before concluding this chapter it must be admitted that the subject in hand has not been done that justice which it richly deserves. This is partly due to the limited knowledge of the author and partly to want of space; the absence of a standard notation is also responsible for it to some extent. The signs or symbols used in this chapter to indicate notes, Tálas, Minḍa or Ghasiṭa, Murki, Murchhanás, etc., are so imperfect that the minute details which make the various pieces or Gatis highly artistic have to be unavoidably omitted. It is hoped, however, that, should the student follow the Gatis and pieces as they are treated in this chapter with the imperfect notation, he will have some idea of Indian music, provided he reproduces accurately the notes as they are given with the details in the pieces and the Gatis treated in this chapter.

The next chapter will deal with a short history of the musical scale.

CHAPTER VI.

A SHORT HISTORY OF THE MUSICAL SCALE.

A short history of the musical scale of Europe may be sketched out by drawing on the writing of Prof. Pietro Blaserna,[1] who of all other historians of Greece treats of the subject of music in greater detail and in its technical aspect. It will be enough for our purpose to give here only the names of the *notes* and not their theoretical ratios. To do this we omit figures from our present dissertation, so that the subject may be intelligible to the average reader. Mathematical terms are, as far as possible, avoided.

The Professor says:—"Primitive music is as ancient as history itself. From the high plains of Asia, where many ancient historical traces of it are found, it followed man in his wanderings through China, India, and Egypt. One of the most ancient books, the Bible, speaks of music often and from its earliest stages. David and Solomon were very musical. They composed psalms full of inspiration, and evidently to be sung. To the latter is due magnificent organization of the singing in the temple at Jerusalem. He founded a school for singers, and a considerable band, which at last reached the number of four thousand trumpeters, the principal instruments being the harp, the cithern, the trumpet, and the drum.

[1] P. Blaserna's *Theory of Sound in its relation to Music*, pp. 115-120, Third Edition.

"C, F, G, C. These four notes, according to an ancient tradition, constituted the celebrated *lyre*[1] *of Orpheus.* Musically speaking, it is certainly very poor, but the observation is interesting, that it contains the most important musical intervals of declamation.

"C, D, F, G, ♭B, C. This is the ancient Scotch and Chinese scale.

"C, D, E, F, G, A, B, C. This is the present Diatonic scale of Europe. The *A* and *E* were introduced by Terpandro;[2] the last, the *B*, by Pythagoras, whence the Greek scale still bears the name of Pythagorean scale.

"The Pythagorean third (E) and sixth (A) are decidedly dissonant (p. 120). The Pythagorean scale held almost exclusive sway in Greece. However, in the last few centuries before the Christian era—that is to say, during the period of Greek decline in politics and arts—many attempts at modifying it are found. Thus, for example, they divided the interval between the notes corresponding to our *c* and *d* into two parts, introducing a note in the middle. At last they went so far

---

[1] According to Homer the lyre was first invented by Hermês, a messenger of the gods, and given by him to Apollo. (George Grote's *History of Greece*, Vol. I., p. 58.) This legend is identical with the Indian one which ascribes the invention of the lyre (Biná) to Nárada, a messenger of the gods.

[2] Terpandro flourished in 676 B. C.—George Grote's *History of Greece*, Vol. II., p. 54.

as to again divide these intervals into two, thus introducing the *quarter*[1] *tone*, which we look upon as discordant.

"Others, again, (in subsequent centuries), introduced various intervals, founded for the most part rather on theoretical speculations than on artistic sentiment. All these attempts have left no trace behind them, and are therefore of no importance. But the Pythagorean scale passed from Greece to Italy, where it held sovereign sway upto the sixteenth century (A. D.), at which epoch began its slow and successive transformation into our *two* musical *scales* (p. 121). The different Greek scales underwent much disturbance in Italy. *Ambroso,* Bishop of Milan, and, later, *Pope Gregory the Great*, had the merit of re-establishing the first four.[2]

"In the tenth and eleven centuries (A. D.) an attempt was begun, especially in Flanders, at *Polyphonic music*—that is to say, at music for several voices."

The above is a sketch of the history of musical scale which led to the formation of the present major and minor scales of Europe.

---

[1] This quarter-tone interval is not practised in Europe, the shortest interval in Europe being the semitone. The quarter tone (Murchhaná, Tivratara or Atikomala) forms a part of the Indian system of music (see p. 77).

[2] The Greek scale formed of every fifth note. For further information see Prof. P. Blaserna's *Theory of Sound in its relation to Music*, pp. 116-119.

The reason for calling the Pythagorean[1] third and sixth notes (E and A) as dissonant—with which the reader must be already acquainted—is that the relative ratios of C with E and A are not simple in the Greek scale. To render this clear we give below the comparative ratios of the Pythagorean and the present European scales.

Supposing the fundamental note makes 240 vibrations per second, and calling it *C*, the European major (Diatonic) scale is represented by the following figures :—

	C,	D,	E,	F,	G,	A,	B,	C
European	240,	270,	300,	320,	360,	400,	450,	480
Pythagorean	240,	270,	$303\frac{3}{4}$,	320,	360,	405,	$455\frac{5}{8}$,	480

Supposing the fundametal note (S) makes 220 vibrations per second of a sonorous wave, the Hindu[2] system of the scale, the history of which we wish to trace, represents the following figures :—

S,	R,	G,	M,	P,	Dh,	N,	S
220,	260,	290,	310,	350,	390,	420,	440

[1] The Pythagorean legends tell us that, while the sage (Pythagoras) was passing by a blacksmith's shop, his attention was drawn by the sounds of seven hammers of different sizes, and this circumstance led him to measure the ratios of musical chords (Lewes' *History of Philosophy*, part i., p. 25). According to some historians he had travelled for thirty years and had seen many countries, India being one of them (George Grote's *History of Greece*, Vol. IV., p. 76).

[2] Sir W. Jones says :—"If I understand the native musicians, they have not only the *chromatic*, but even the second, or new, enharmonic, genus; for they unanimonsly reckon twenty-two *Shrutis*, or quarters and thirds of a tone, in their octaves: they do not pretend that these minute intervals are mathematically equal, but consider them as equal in practice, and allot them to the several notes * * (*Asiatic Researches*, Vol. III., p. 69).

Now let us direct our attention to the history of the Indian musical scale, if such history can at all be worked out from the researches into ancient Sanskrit and Páli literature, which oriental scholars of Europe, such as Professors Max Muller, Kern, Oldenberg, H. H. Wilson, and others, have rendered accessible to the English-reading public.

At the outset of our present enquiry, we deem it necessary to state that it is impossible to trace the history of the musical scale with its theory, and to show the chronology of its gradual development in India, as is done by Prof. P. Blaserna in the case of the European scale.

Our principal object in this enquiry is only to find out whether the musical scale was known to the Védic Ṛishis (sages) ; we shall, therefore, limit our investigation within that sphere. To do this we must, in the first instance, enquire whether the musical scale was known to the early Hindus independently of foreign influence, or whether it was imported into India from Greece, which, of all bygone historical nations, possessed the musical scale, and which formed the basis of the present musical scale of Europe. So far as our knowledge of the Greek history is concerned, we are prepared to say that the musical scale of Greece was *not* borrowed by the early Hindus.

It is a fact that the musical scale, Diatonic and Chromatic with the Murchhanás, was in practice in India at the time of the Mahomedan[1] advent in India, because the present as well as the past Mahomedan musicians of India have adopted the Sanskrit scale with its nomenclature intact. It is very much to be regretted that the Mahomedan historians of India do not give us much information of the dates and names of the Emperors and kings who patronized Hindu music, though there are references to music and musicians in certain histories by Mahomedans.

In the absence of such a history of the musical scale, we can reliably depend on the writing of Sáranga-Deva, the compiler of the *Sangîta-Ratnákara*. About the date of Sáranga-Deva, Prof. H. H. Wilson[2] says :— "The *Sangîta-Ratnákara* treats more especially of singing and dancing than that of dramatic literature. It furnishes, however, some curious notices of the theatrical representation and gesture. It is the work of Sáranga-Deva, the son of Shorhala, the son of Bháskara, a Cashmerian Pandit, who sought fortunes in the south. His grandson is patronized by a prince named Sinhala-Deva, but of what time or place he does not inform us. It is clear, however, that he wrote between the twelfth and fifteenth century (A. D.), as he names Bhoja

---

[1] The advent of Mahomedans in India (Panjab) dates from the ninth century A. D. (H. T. Buckle's *History of Civilisation in England*, Vol. I., p. 46).

[2] *Theatres of the Hindus*, Vol. I., p. xxii., Third Edition.

amongst his predecessors in the science; and a comment on his own work was written by Kallinátha, by desire of Prauḍha, or Pratápa-Deva, king of Vijayánagara, from A. D. 1456 to 1477."

Sáranga-Deva treats the musical scale as diatonic and chromatic with quarter tones (Murchhaná) according to the light in which it was treated before him, and also refers to Bhoja as his predecessor.

The *Sangîta-Ratnákara* is not the only work that treats of music; but there are still in existence, though most of them are out of India, a number of works on Indian music (*vide* p. 44). In the *Catalogus Catalogorum* (an Alphabetical Register of Sanskrit Works and Authors, by H. Theodor Aufrecht, pp. 685 to 687) alone we find the following works on music:—

"(1) Sangîta-Kalá Nidhi, by Hári Bhaṭṭa.

(2) Sangîta-Kaliká, quoted by Hemádri on Raghuvansha.

(3) Sangîta-Kalpataruṭiká-Sunodhinî, by Gaṇeshadeva.

(4) Sangîta-Kalpadruma, by Rádha.

(5) Sangîta-Kaumudî, quoted in Sangîta-Náráyaṇa (Oxford).

(6) Sangîta-Gangádharavyákhyá-Shravaṇánandinî, by Káshipati.

(7) Sangîta-Chintámaṇî, by Kamalalochaṇa.

(8) Sangîta-Tála, on Time in Music.

(9) Sangîta-Darpaṇa,[1] Paris (D 281), Rádha in seven chapters, by Dámodhara.

(10) Sangîta-Dámodhara, by Dámodhara—Most likely the Sangîta-Darpaṇa by Shubhamkara, son of Shridhara, Paris.

(11) Sangîta-Nárayaṇa by Náráyaṇa, Jones, Oxford.

(12) Sangîta-Nrittyaratnákara, by Viṭṭhala, Barner.

(13) Sangîta-Nrittyákara, by Bharatácharya.

(14) Sangîta-Párijáta, by Ahobala, Kávyamálá.

(15) Sangîta-Pushpajjali, by Veda, Bikaner.

(16) Sangîta-Makaranda, by Veda, Bikaner.

(17) Sangîta-Mádhava—a poem in praise of Vishṇu, by Prabodhánanda Sarasvati Gausvámi (Oudh.)

(18) Sangîta-Mimánsá Music, by Kumbhakarṇamahimendra.

(19) Sangîta-Muktávali, by Devendra (Nrityádhyáya), Burnell.

(20) Sangîta-Raghunandana, by Vishvanátha (Oudh).

(21) Sangîta-Ratna, by Rádha.

(22) Sangîta-Ratnamálá, by Mammata, quoted in Sangîta-Náráyaṇa (Oxford).

---

[1] Translated into Persian, *Asiatic Researches*, Vol. III., p. 65.

(23) Sangîta-Ratnákara, by Sárangadeva. It consists of seven chapters—(1) Svaragatádhyáya (Oxford), (2) Rágavivekádhyáya (Oxford), (3) Prakirṇakádhyáya (Tüb), (4) Prabandha (Oxford), Tála (Oxford), (6) Vádya (Bengal N. P.), (7) Nritya.

(24) Sangîta-Ratnávalî, by Somarájadeva.

(25) Sangîta-Rágalakshaṇa.

(26) Sangîta-Rághava, verses for singing, by Sinhabhomabhupála (Burnell).

(27) Sangîta-Rája, music by Kumbhakarṇamahindra.

(28) Sangîta-Vinodanrittyádhyáya, Bikaner.

(29) Sangîta-Shástra, quoted by Kaivalyáshrama (Oxford), by Sárangadhara (?), Oppert.

(30) Sangîta-Shiromaṇi, Bikaner.

(31) Sangîta-Sarvasva, quoted by Jagaddhara on Veṇisanhára, by Vasudeva on Karpurmanjari.

(32) Sangîta-Ságara, Rádha.

(33) Sangîta-Sára, Rádha, Bikaner, N. P., quoted in Sangîta-Náráyáṇa (Oxford).

(34) Sangîta-Sárasangraha (Oppert).

(35) Sangîta-Sárámrut attributed to Tulájirája of Tanjore (Burnell).

(36) Sangîta Rochára or Rodhâra (Oppert), by Hárí Bhaṭṭa.

(37) Sangîta-Sidhánta, by Rámánandatirtha.

(38) Sangîta-Sudhá, by Bhimanarendra.

(39) Sangîta-Sudhákara (Oppert) Sangîtaratnákáratíká, by Sinhabhupála.

(40) Sangîta-Sundara, by Sadáshiva Dikshit (Burnell).

(41) Sangîta-Ámrata, by Kamalalochaṇa.

(42) Sangîta-Árṇava, quoted in Sangîta Darpaṇa (Oxford).

(43) Sangîta-Opanishada, composed by Sudhákalasha in 1017.

(44) Sangîta-Opanishására, composed by Sudhákalasha (this name appears above) in 1324."

To the above list the names of a few other works, which Sir W. Jones gives,[1] may be added.

(45) Sangîta-Rágadarpaṇa.

(46) Sangîta-Sabhávinoda.

(47) Sangîta-Rágavibodha, by Soma."

Although the dates of the several works, given above, are not as yet fixed, still we may safely conclude that some of them were the fruits of at least from the tenth century A. C. (see 43rd) to the eighteenth A. C. It is really wonderful that, during the constant fight with the Mahomedans, and in the absence of a settled and peaceful kingdom, the Hindus, Rájas and Pandits, were

[1] *Asiatic Researches*, Vol. III.

devoting their time and leisure in writing on music and thus saving at least a portion of their ancestral music as an art as well as a science. These works do not give only the compositions but treat of music as a science though within certain limits, and must ever possess supreme interest, for they constitute an imperishable record of the state of the written music at a momentous epoch not only of transition but of a revolution in Hindu music. That the several authors of the works might have either registered or contributed to the ancient music is probable enough. Artistic inspiration has been the prerogative of the highest musical genius in all ages and countries.

Most of the works given above may be regarded as representing the end rather than the commencement of the works on music. All the works, if critically studied, may suggest that they did not originate the systems of which they speak but only stereotyped them.

To trace the history of musical scale before the tenth century A. C. we may reasonably presume, from Kálidása's treatment of the art of music[1] as a part essentially associated with drama, that it was practiced in India in the seventh century A. C., the date[2] generally allotted to Kálidása.

---

[1] Act iv. of the Vikrama and Urvashi, *Theatres of the Hindus*, Vol. I., p. 239, Third Edition, H. H. Wilson.

[2] Mr. K. T. Telang fixes the date of Kálidása at the middle of the fifth century A. C. In support of this statement Telang gives the date of the historical translation of the *Panchatantra* by Nushirvan of Persia, about the beginning of the sixth century A. C.—*Sacred Books of the East*, Vol. VIII., p. 29.

The technicalities of Kálidása are so erudite that Professor H. H. Wilson[1] says among other things :— "The names of the airs and measures are not current in the present day, nor known to the Pandits; the explanations of them in the 'Ṭiká,' or 'Commentary on the Drama,' are quoted usually from *Bharata*, whose rules no longer exist in a collective form. The manuscript, however, being full of errors, little assistance has been derived in this respect from the annotator; but his definitions of the airs seem to be extracted chiefly from the *Sangîta-Ratnákara*, from which authority it appears that this subject has yet been very insufficiently investigated, as the modifications of the six *Rágas* amounted to two hundred and sixty-four, with the whole of which we are yet unacquainted. *Some* enumerate, according to Sir W. Jones, nine hundred and sixty variations. (*A. R.*, iii., 71.)"

The late Rao Bahadur Shankararao Pándurang Pandit, M.A., instead of attempting to explain the musical technicalities of which Professor H. H. Wilson speaks with respect, tells us that he has some reasons to believe that the passages in question are of later date. However, he cautiously concludes by saying[2] :—"I have thought, I hope not incorrectly, that the above facts and considerations are sufficient to account for expunging the passages from the main text of my edition. Though I am not at present in a position to pronounce

[1] *Theatres of the Hindus*, Vol. I., p. 239.

[2] Fourth Act of the *Vikramorvasiyám*, Second Edition, Criticial Notice, pp. 6-10, S. P. Pandit.

decidedly on the merits of the passages, I may perhaps be allowed to risk a guess that it may be that the passages were intended to be chanted by some one behind the scenes, and as such anonymous passages without any indications that they are to be repeated behind the scenes are not known to occur in the plays, our passages may or may not have originally belonged to the play, even though they be a production of the author."

To the above conclusion, so guardedly worded, we may also add as a surmise that the author (Kálidása) might have brought in the musical technicalities in the act with an object to render it suitable to the heroine who was a Gándharva, so-called heavenly choirist. It is a well-known fact that singing, dancing and gesticulating have an intimate connection with the idea of dramatic representation, and there is not the least doubt that the classical writers of Sanskrit dramas of bygone times were acquainted with the principal features of the art of music.

When we trace the existence of musical scale further back than the time of Kálidása, we come across the fifth act of the *Mrichchhakaṭi* or the *The Toy-Cart*, in which Kumbhilak only gives the number of the notes of diatonic scale in describing the flute and Viṇá. He says:—"A pretty situation for a man of my talents; for one who can play the flute with seven holes, the *Viṇá* with seven strings * * and who acknowledges no musical superior, except perhaps Tumbara or Nárada."[1] As

[1] H. H. Wilson's *Theatres of the Hindus*, Vol. I., p. 93, Third Edition.

regards the date of the author of the drama of *The Toy-Cart*, King Śúdraka, H. H. Wilson concludes:— "From the considerations thus stated, we cannot but regard the *Mrichchhakaṭi* as a work of considerable antiquity, and from internal evidence may very safely attribute it to the period when Śúdraka, the sovereign, reigned, whether that be reduced to the end of the second century after Christ, or whether we admit the traditional chronology, and place him about a century before our era."[1]

To trace the musical scale further back than the time of Kálidása and Śúdraka we draw on Amarasinha, the celebrated Buddhist compiler of a dictionary called after his name. Amarasinha gives the names of the seven notes in his dictionary thus:—

निषादर्षभगान्धारषड्जमध्यमधैवताः । पञ्चमश्चेत्यमी सप्त तन्त्रीकण्ठोत्थिताः स्वराः ॥
अमरकोशे प्रथमकाण्डे शब्दादिवर्गः ।

The date of Amarasinha has not yet been finally settled; Professors H. H. Wilson and H. Kern assign him to the fifth century A. C., while the late Mr. K. T. Telang, M. A., puts him to fifty-six years B. C.[2]

In the absence of an undisputed date of Amarasinha we resort to the early Buddhistic writings, of which we have got an account from the Páli and Chinese languages, which are preserved with religious devotion in the

---

[1] H. H. Wilson's *Theatres of the Hindus*, Vol. I., p. 9, Third Edition.

[2] *Bhagavadagítá*, Introduction, p. cxii., K. T. Telang.

Buddhist literature of Nepal, Thibet, China and Ceylon.

In the Páli literature the names of the seven notes are not given, so far as our knowledge of the literature is concerned, but the octave is distinctly mentioned along with musical instruments,[1] so also dances of different kinds and various songs. The paragraph in which the scale is mentioned, runs thus:—** "Avalokiteshvara possesses a good voice like Brahma, (voice) going through the whole gamut of tones."[2]

It is hardly necessary to remind the reader that the omission of the names of *notes* may be explained on the ground that the subject in which it appears is not musical. The Chinese version of the *Saddharma-Punḍarîka* was written in 601 A. C.; the contents of the original, however, may be older in date, as its vocabulary considerably corresponds with that of the *Śatapatha-Bráhmaṇa.*[3]

It is not a matter of wonder to find the scale mentioned in the *Saddharma-Punḍarîka*, one of the religious books of Buddha, when we have traditionary proof that the great Buddha Gautama was versed in music. This fact may be verified by the following dialogue between Buddha and his disciple, Sona, a young man:—"Sona, were you able to play the lute (Viṇá) before you left home?" "Yes, sire." "What do you think then,

[1] *The Akáránga Sûtra*, Vol. I., p. 183; *Saddharma-Punḍarîka*, p. 51.
[2] *Saddharma-Punḍarîka*, p. 416, H. Kern.
[3] H Kern's Introduction to *Saddharma-Punḍarîka*, pp. xvi., xvii.

Sona, if the strings of your lute are too tightly strung, will the lute give out the proper tone and be fit to play?" "It will not, sire." "And what do you think, Sona, if the strings of your lute be strung too slack, will the lute then give out the proper tone and be fit to play?" "It will not, sire." "But, how, Sona, if the strings of your lute be not strung too tight or too slack, if they have the proper degree of tension, will the lute then give out the proper sound and be fit to play?" "Yes, sire." "In the same way, Sona, energy too much strained tends to excessive zeal, and energy too much relaxed tends to apathy. Therefore, Sona, cultivate in yourself the mean of energy, and press on to the mean in your mental powers, and place this before you as your aim."[1]

The simile of musical instruments in Buddhist period and writings seems to be general, as will be seen from the following dialogue between the Yavan King Milinda, that is, the Ionian or Greek prince Menander, who flourished in 100 B. C. Such dialogues between the argumentative Greeks with the Indian monks and dialecticians were held in the Indus territory as Dr. Oldenberg[2] shows from the Buddhist literature.

There is a paragraph in the questions of king Milinda which runs thus:—"Suppose, O king, if there were no bridge of metal on a mandolin, no leather, no hollow space, no frame, no neck, no strings, no bow, and

---

[1] *Buddha, His Life, Doctrine and His Order*, pp. 189, 190. Dr. Oldenberg.

[2] Dr. Oldenberg's *Buddha*, p. 254.

no human efforts or exertion, would there be music" ? In short, music was so much liked during the Buddhistic period that the most reliable of the lives[2] of Buddha known in China was written by Bodhisatava Ashvaghosha, who was a musician and a poet, and was the twelfth Buddhist patriarch. Ashvaghosha is generally believed to be a contemporary of Kanishka, who flourished in or about the first century of the Christian era. Buddhaghosha, who flourished according to some writers in the beginning of the fifth century A. C., and who had translated the Páli Buddhist canon from the Sinhalese or actually composed it, was also a musician. Professor Max Müller[3] tells us that Buddhaghosha was so named because he was (*ghosha*) as Buddha himself.

From the above sketch it will be seen that the musical scale has been in practice in India before or since the beginning of the Christian era.

To trace the musical scale further back than the Buddhistic writings we shall have to tread on ground which is a bone of contention between certain Christian missionaries[4] and certain Oriental scholars. Here we refer to the *Bhagavadgîtá*, of which the *Anugîtá* forms a part.

In the *Anugîtá* the musical scale is clearly mentioned

---

[1] *The Questions of King Milinda*, p. 84.

[2] Introduction, p. xxx., to *A Life of Buddha*, by S. Beal.

[3] Introduction, p. xxi., to *Dhammapada-Sutta-Nipata*, by Max-Müller.

[4] See Telang's Introduction to the *Bhagavadgîtá*.

and the names of the seven *notes* are given. The *Anugîtà* does not speak of the chromatic (विकृत) scale (see p. 53). This omission may probably be due to the absence of separate appellations for the five supplementary notes as is the case in the European nomenclature of the notes. The English translation[1] of the text (Chap. XXXVII.) runs thus:—"Now space has one quality and that is stated to be sound only. I will speak at length of the numerous qualities of sound. Shaḍja, Ṛishabha, together with Gándhára, Madhyama, and likewise Panchama, and beyond these should be understood to be Nisháda and Dhaivata likewise, agreeable and disagreeable sound also, compact and of (many) ingredients. This sound, which is produced in space, should be understood of ten descriptions."

Certainly, had the *Anugítá*, which discloses a more advanced form of the Hindu thoughts than the *Bhagavadgîtá*, been favourably disposed towards music, as[2] it is not like Apastambha, Manu and Gautama Dharmashástras, it would have given us more information than the simple enumeration of the seven musical notes as qualities of sound and the ten descriptions of sound.

Professor Max Müller, the editor, and the late Mr. K. T. Telang, M. A., the translator of the *Anugítá*, with masterly treatment of Hindu literature, infer, with

---

[1] *The Sacred Books of the East*, Vol. VIII., p. 385.

[2] See Telang's Introduction to the *Anugítá*, *Sacred Books of the East*, Vol. VIII., pp. 207, 208.

caution, that the *Anugîtá* may have been composed six centuries before Christ.[1]

To trace the musical scale further back than the *Anugîtá* we come upon the *Bhagavadgîtá*, the so-called former portion of the *Anugîtá*. Instead of getting the names of our *notes* in the *Bhagavadgîtá*, we come across the generic name of music. The *Bhagavadgîtá* (tenth chapter), in securing to itself almost all the oldest, the highest, and the best religious and secular things imaginable of the early Hindu institutions, gives preference to the Sáma[2] among the Védas, to the Gáyatri[3] among the Chhands (metres), to Chitraratha among the Gándharvas[4] or the ideal heavenly choristers, and to Nárada *among the Ṛishis or sages.*

The object of the *Bhagavadgîtá* in selecting the Gáyatri from the metres may be for its priority.

The preference which the *Bhagavadagîtá* gives to the Sáma among the Védas may probably be due to its

---

[1] See Mr. Telang's Introduction to the *Anugîtá*, *Sacred Books of the East*, Vol. VIII., p. 225.

[2] 1 वेदानां सामवेदो ऽस्मि । देवर्षीणां च नारदः । गन्धर्वाणां चित्ररथः । गायत्री छन्दसामहम् ।

[3] In the Anukramaṇis there are only seven metres, but in Saunakás list, they are ten : Gáyatrî, Ushṇih, Anushṭubha, Brihati, Panktî, Trishṭubha, Jagatî, Atijagatî, 'Sakvarî, and Atisakavarî.—Max Müller's *History of Ancient Sanskrit Literature*, p. 222.

[4] Instead of specifying music in clear terms the *Bhagavadgîtá* only refers to Chitraratha, who may have been as the head of musicians sometime before the compilation of the *Bhagavadgîtá*.

tones,[1] as it is well known that, with the exception of about seventy-five verses, all the rest of the *Sáma-véda Samhitá* is found in the *Ṛig-véda;* or as Max Müller says:—"The *Sáma-véda* is but a short extract from the *Ṛig-véda,* containing such hymns as had to be chanted during the sacrifice."[2]

That the *Sáma-véda* was intended to be chanted or sung unlike other Védas which were only recited, can be proved not only by the present so-called practice, but by many ancient authorities.

In the first chapter, third Bráhmaṇa of the *Brihadárṇyak-Upanishad,* it is said:— * * This is also Udgitha; Life is *ut;* for by life all this is upraised. Speech is Githa. It is *ut* and *Githa,* therefore, it is Utgitha. * * * Therefore, let one who is to perform the duties of a Ritvig, desire to acquire *the musical notes* together with *speech.* By that speech which has obtained the *musical notes,* let him perform the rites of the Ritvig. Therefore, people are desirous to look during the sacrifice upon *the sweet toned* performer of the Udgitha as upon a rich man."[3] * * *

In this Upanishad, first Adháya third Bráhmaṇa 27, it is said:—"Therefore, let a priest, who is going to perform the sacrificial work of a Sáma singer, desire that

[1] The late Mr. K. T. Telang, M. A., says that the Sáma referred to in the *Bhagavadgítá* means "as being, probably, full of music."—*Sacred Books of the East,* Vol. VIII., p. 88, note 6.

[2] *Chips from a German Workshop,* Vol. II., p. 320, Max Müller.

[3] Tookaram Tatya's *Twelve Upanishads,* pp. 112-114.

his voice may have good tone, and let him perform the sacrifice with a voice that is in good tone.[1]

The Sáma-singer was called Udgátri, the Yajur-reciter was named Adhvaryu, and the Ṛig-véda-reciter was given the name of Hotar. Dr. Martin Houg, in his translation of the *Aitariya-Bráhmaṇa* tells us that the establishment of the two new classes of priests, the Udgátars (singers) and Bráhmaṇas (superintendents) must have taken place in India after the Zoroastrians had separated[2] from the Bráhmaṇas. To support this view, which Max Müller refutes,[3] he says:—"The chanters (singers) and the superintendents are entirely unknown in the Zoroastrian ceremonials. The Hotars are called Zaotar, the Adhavaryus are called Rathwiskare."

Before going further into the pre-Buddhist periods to find out the musical scale, we could have spoken a few words about the controversy, between the Christian missionaries and the oriental scholars, to which we have alluded before, but the said controversy is almost a dead letter now. As the advanced researches in Sanskrit and Pâli literatures by eminent scholars of Europe progress the number of impartial scholars is increasing against the missionary view, and therefore we pass on without saying a word about the controversy.

---

[1] Max Müller's *Upanishads*, Part II., p. 83.

[2] Max Müller says:—It can now be proved, even by geographical evidence, that the Zoroastrians had been settled in India before they emigrated into Persia.—*Chips from a German Workshop*, Vol. I., p. 86.

[3] *Chips from a German Workshop*, Vol. I., pp. 108-110.

The partiality of the *Bhagvadgîtá*, of which we have spoken before, for the Sáma is very singular when we see that in the *Anugîtá*, the so-called portion or part of the *Bhagvadgîtá*, the music is condemned,[1] as is the case in the laws of Apastambha, Manu and others. These law-givers have condemned music wholesale. In attacking music, vocal and instrumental, including dancing, they have forgotten, according to the Brihadánṇyak, Kaushitaki, and Chhandogya Upanishads, the sacredness of the Sáma which is equal to that of the other Védas if not more. This emphatic condemnation of music by such ancient law-givers as Manu and others does not only show that it was all-absorbing or inordinate, but proves that it had reached the stage of a separate art from a mere poetical recitation before the times of these law-givers.

If, owing to some unforeseen researches, the dates of the Buddhist writings and of the *Bhagavadgîtá*, of which the *Anugîtá* now forms a part and in which the musical scale is given, turn out to be later than the Christian era, as the aforesaid controversy involves, we resort to Pingala, the recognized authority on Chhandas or metres. Chhandas (metres) are one of the six Védángas. "षडंगो वेदश्छंद: कल्पो व्याकरणं ज्योतिषं निरुक्तं शिक्षा ॥"

Pingala, also called Pingalanága, compares the seven ancient metres with the seven *notes* in a

[1] Preface to the *Anugîtá*, *Sacred Books of the East*, Vol. VIII., p. 208.

Sûtra (succinct aphorism), स्वराः षड्ज ऋषभगांधारमध्यमपंचमधैवत-निषादाः ॥[1]

To find out the date of Pingala we directly draw on the words of Prof. Max Müller. The Professor says:[2]—"The Pingala Sûtras on metres do not pretend to be of greater antiquity than the *Mahábháshya*, supposing it were admitted that Patanjali, the author of the famous commentary on Páṇiṇi, was the same as Pingala (Colebrooke's *Miscellaneous Essays*, Vol. II., p. 63). There would be nothing extraördinary in the fact that Pingala treats of Prákrit as well as Sanskrit metres. For we have the instance of Kátyáyana Vararuchi, who wrote the Varthikas on Páṇiṇi and *lived before* Patanjali; and is said to be the same who wrote a grammar of the Prákrit dialects. It must be admitted, however, that Pingalanága's metre is one of the last works that could possibly be included in the Sútra period (200 to 600 B. C.); though there is no sufficient ground for excluding it from this period altogether, merely because those rules which refer to metres not yet employed in the Véda are ascribed to the same author. Besides, Pingala is quoted as an authority on metres in the *Parisishṭas*, a class of literature which does not seem to be separated from the Sûtra period.[3]

[1] षड्जऋषभगांधारमध्यमपंचमधैवतनिषादाः स्वराः गायत्र्यादिषु क्रमेण द्रष्टव्याः ।सितसारंगपिशंगकृष्णनीललोहितगौरा वर्णाः । ६०.

Pingalanága's *Chhanda-Bháshya*, p. 13, verse 59th of the Manuscript in Gokulji Zálá's Library, Junagadh, Kathiawar.

[2] See Max Müller's *History of Ancient Sanskrit Literature.*

[3] Max Müller's *History of Ancient Sanskrit Literature*, pp. 147, 148.

Professor Max Müller, in allotting a date to the *Mahábháshya*, says:—"At what time the *Mahábháshya* was first composed it is impossible to say. Patanjali, the author of the commentary, is sometimes identified with Pingala; and on this view, as Pingala is called the younger brother, or at least the descendant of Páṇiṇi, it might be supposed that the original composition of the *Mahábháshya* belonged to the third century (B. C.). But this identity of Pingala is far from probable, and it would be rash to use it as a foundation for other calculations.

"It is on the authority of Shadguruśishya, who says: "सूत्र्यते हि भगवता पिंगलेन पाणिन्यनुजेन ॥," that Pingala is considered to be either the younger brother or the descendant of Páṇiṇi."

Apart from the conflicting traditions about the identity with Patanjali and the relationship to Páṇiṇi, Pingala must have flourished during the latter, if not earlier, part of the Sútra period; and it is enough for our present enquiry to infer that during the Sûtra-period—a period which Prof. Max Müller *with all possible moderation* calculates as an experiment[1] from 200 to 600 B. C.—the musical scale was in existence in India.

If we trace our scale to the Brahmaṇa-period, which Max Müller calculates from 600 to 800 B. C., we shall be irresistibly positive in declaring that the

[1] See, for further information, *History of Ancient Sanskrit Literature*, p. 244.

musical scale, diatonic in its complete form, that is, with seven notes, if not chromatic, was practised by the Hindus before the time of Pythagoras,[1] that is, in the sixth century B. C.

Now we find the musical scale in the Śikshá, or Phonetics,[2] of Yájnavalkya, the recognized author of the Śukla (bright) Yajúr-Véda.

Kátyáyana Vararuchi says :—

"शुक्लानि यजूंषि भगवान्याज्ञवल्क्यो यतः प्राप ते विवस्वंतं ॥"

The *Satapatha-Bráhamaṇa* ends with the assertion that the white (शुक्ल) Yajur-Véda was proclaimed by Yájnavalkya Vájasaneya :—

" आदित्यानीमानि शुक्लानि यजूंषि वाजसनेयेन याज्ञवल्क्येनाख्यायंते ॥"[3]

The verse, in the Śikshá of Yájnavalkya, runs thus :—

"उच्चौ निषादगांधारौ नीचौ ऋषभधैवतौ ॥ शेषास्तु स्वरिता ज्ञेयाः षड्जमध्यमपंचमाः ॥ ७ ॥."[4]

Before enquiring into the date of Yájnavalkya, it will not be superfluous to say a word about the meaning of the verse quoted above. The translation of the verse,

---

[1] Pythagoras was born at Samos in 608 B. C. and died in 543 B. C. *Larcher*. According to Meiners he was born in 584 B. C. See Lewe's *History of Philosophy* Vol. I., p. 18; and C. S. Henry's *Epitome of the History of Philosophy*, pp. 94, 95.

[2] *History of Ancient Sanskrit Literature*, p. 113, and also second *Anuváka Taitiriya-Upanishad. Upanishad*, Part II., p. 46.

[3] Max Müller's *History of Ancient Sanskrit Literature*, p. 353.

[4] The above verse with a very little difference is found in the Śikshá literature, thus—उदात्ते निषादगांधारावनुदात्त ऋषभधैवतौ । स्वरितप्रभवा ह्येते षड्जमध्यमपंचमाः ॥१२॥ —*Páṇiniya Shikshá*.

as made by Dayánanda Sarasvati in his *Hindi Grammar*, runs thus. Among the *notes*, the Nisháda and Gandhára are sung in the Udátta (one octave above the register), the Rishabha and Dhaivata in the Anudátta (one octave below the register), and the Shaḍja, Madhyama, and Panchama in the Svarita (the register octave).

The Hindi translation is as follows:—

" यह वचन याज्ञवल्क्यशिक्षाका है। षड्जादिकों मे निषाद और गांधार तो उदात्तके लक्षणसे ऋषभ धैवत अनुदात्तके लक्षणसे तथा षड्ज मध्यम और पंचम ए तीने स्वरित स्वरसे गाये जाते हैं।" [1]

From the above translation it will be seen that Dayánanda Sarasvati has translated the words उच्चौ नीचौ and स्वरित according to their literal, and not technical, meaning. It is unnecessary to remind the reader that in comparison with the Shaḍja, the first note of the scale, the other six notes are decidedly higher in *pitch*, and certainly there are in the Saptaka (Gamut) no two notes of the same *pitch*. Therefore, the literal meaning of the words उच्चौ, नीचौ, and स्वरित, if accepted on the ground of their *pitch*, would be quite senseless.

In order to unearth the technical meaning of the verse, and to discard the literal meaning we quote below the preceding six verses of the Yájnyavalkya Śikshá.

श्रीगणेशाय नमः ॥ अथातस्त्रैस्वर्यलक्षणं व्याख्यास्यामः ॥ उदात्तश्चानुदात्तश्च स्वरितश्च तथैव च ॥ लक्षणं वर्णयिष्यामि दैवतं स्थानमेव च ॥ १ ॥ शुक्लमुच्चं वि-

[1] See the *Savara* by the late Shri Paramahansa Parivraja-Kácharya Svámi Shri Dayánanda Sarasvati.

जानीयान्नीचं लोहितमुच्यते ॥ श्यामं तु स्वरितं विद्यादग्निमुखस्य दैवतम् ॥ २ ॥
नीचे सोमो विजानीयात्स्वरिते सविता भवेत् ॥ उदात्तं ब्राह्मणं विद्यान्नीचं क्षत्रियमु-
च्यते ॥ ३ ॥ वैश्यं तु स्वरितं विद्याद्भारद्वाजमुदात्तकं ॥ नीचं गौतममित्याहुर्गार्ग्यं च
स्वरितं विदुः ॥ ४ ॥ विद्यादुदात्तं गायत्रीं नीचं त्रैष्टुभमुच्यते ॥ जागतं स्वरितं
विद्यादत एवं नियोगतः ॥ ५ ॥

From the above five verses it will be seen that the Uchcha or Udátta is applied to शुक्ल, अग्नि, ब्राह्मण, भारद्वाज, and गायत्री, the Nîcha or Anudátta is given to लोहित, सोम, क्षत्रिय, गौतम, and त्रैष्टुभ, and the Svarita is reserved for श्याम, सविता, वैश्य, गार्ग्य, and जागत, or probably the Jagatî metre.

From the above classification of the deities, of the castes of the Ṛishis, and of the metres into three divisions under the appellation of Uchcha, Nîcha, and Svarita, it may be inferred that the said three words do not refer to *pitch*. It is too much to presume that a man of Yájnavalkya's learning, who writes not only on the Śikshá, but refers to the sounds of the conch, drum and lute (Viṇá), in explaining the so-called self or **आत्मन**[1] to one of his two wives, Maitreye, has quoted this particular verse which, if admitted as relating to *pitch*, may be quite senseless. It is very difficult to comprehend the real meaning of the verse which appears in the Śikshá literature. We are also at a loss to understand what made the ancient Hindus to classify the two notes (G and N) having two Shrutis

[1] स यथा वीणायै वाद्यमानायै न बाह्याञ्छब्दाञ्छक्नुयाद्ग्रहणाय वीणायै तु ग्रहणेन वीणावादस्य वा शब्दो गृहीतः ॥ See *Brihadáraṇyaka-Upanishad*, 1i Adhyáya, 7, 8, 9. Max Müller's *Upanishads*, Part II., pp. 110, 111.

as Uchcha, the other two (R and Dh) having three Shrutis as Nîcha, and the remaining three (S, M and P) having four Shrutis as Svarita (see p. 51).

Be the meaning of the verse what it may, the connection of Rishabha with Dhaivata, Gandhára with Nisháda, of Shaḍja with Panchama, and of Madhyama with Shaḍja in the verse is very thoughtful when looked at from a technical point of view.

The grouping of Rishabha with Dhaivata, Gandhára with Nisháda, and of Shaḍja with Panchama and Madhyama, as is done in the said verse, shows what we may technically call a more advanced form of the progress by fifths[1] than the Greek one.

It is hardly necessary to remind the reader that the R and Dh, G and N, S and P, and M and S are the fifth of each other (see pp. 71, 72).

If the spirit, and not the meaning, which we ascribe to the verse in question may be correct, we have solid, though fragmentary, datum to infer that during the time of Yájnavalkya, the musical scale was practised in India with a considerable acquaintance of its intrinsic relation and its value or ratio.

As regards the date of Yájnavalkya there is, as is generally the case with the dates of ancient *Ṛishis*

---

[1] How the progress by *fifths* was attained by the Greeks, see Prof. P. Blaserna's *Theory of Sound in its relation to Music*, pp. 117-121.

(sages), no unanimous verdict of Oriental scholars. Therefore, we have no other choice than to resort to an indirect method of ascertaining an approximate date of Yájnavalkya.

Kátyáyana speaks of Yájnavalkya, and therefore the Ṛishi was known in the third century B. C., the date allotted to Kátyáyana. We also find the name of Yájnavalkya in the *Mahábhárata* (xii., 11739),[1] in the Shrutis (revelation) along with Vasishṭa,[2] and in the Smriti[3] (recollection) along with Manu and Parásara.

It is very difficult to fix the date of Yájnavalkya when his name appears in different works of whose dates we have no reliable information to depend upon. In the absence of any other reliable source we do, as Mr. Telang[4] has done in ascertaining the date of Anugîtá, rely on the words of Prof. Bühler.[5] "Professor Bühler appears to be inclined to place Apastambha somewhere about the fifth century B. C., and, though probably he himself does not consider the reasons he adduces as conclusive, they seem at any rate to show that the writer cannot have lived later than the third century B. C. From the fact that Svetaketu, the son of Uddálaka Áruṇi, the reputed teacher (and rival) ot

[1] Julius Eggling's Introduction to *The Satapatha-Bráhmaṇa*, p. xxx.

[2] Max Müller's *History of Ancient Sanskrit Literature*, p. 91.

[3] Max Müller's *History of Ancient Sanskrit Literature*, p. 86.

[4] *Sacred Books of the East*, Vol. VIII., p. 215.

[5] See Julius Eggling's Introduction to *The Satapatha-Bráhmaṇa*, pp. xl. and xli.

Yájnavalkya, is counted by Ápastambha among the *Avarus* or moderns, Dr. Bühler infers that the promulgator of the white (शुक्ल or शुद्ध)[1] Yajus cannot have preceded Ápastambha by a longer interval than, at the most, two or three hundred years."

From the above information it is abundantly clear that Yájnavalkya was a pre-Buddhistic Ṛishi, and, therefore, must have flourished before the Great Buddha Gautama, that is, 623 B. C.,[2] the generally accepted date of the Buddha.[3]

As an additional evidence to support the aforesaid date of Yájnavalkya, we may reasonably infer that the Ṛishi must have flourished during the later, if not earlier, period of the formations of the Upanishad literature or Bráhmaṇa period, 600 to 800 B. C. Professor Max Müller divides the ancient Sanskrit literature into four divisions, *viz.*, Sûtra-period from 200 to 600 B. C., Bráhmaṇa-period from 600 to 800 B. C., Chhanda-period from 800 to 1000 B. C., and the Mantra-period from 1000 to 1500 B. C.

From the foregoing dissertation it will be seen that the musical scale has been in practice in India since

---

1 Dvivedaganga explains :—

शुक्लानि यजूंषि by शुद्धानि यद्वा ब्राह्मणेनामिश्रितमंत्रात्मकानि ॥
Max Müller's *History of Ancient Sanskrit Literature*, pp. 350, 351.

2 Wheeler's *History of India*, Vol. III., p. 3.

3 Max Müller provisionally fixes the date of Buddhá's death, after eighty years of age, at 477 instead of 543 B. C. See *The Origin of Religion*, p. 138; *History of Ancient Sanskrit Lterature, Dhammapada* ; etc.

a very long period, but to trace the exact date is beyond the reach of our work. The history, which we have worked out, takes us back to a time which, though involved in dark antiquity, distinctly shows that the musical scale, which is the fundamental basis of the science of music, and which, as Prof. P. Blaserna says, is the result of the musical activities of many centuries (p. 77), was practised by the later, if not earlier, Védic Ṛishis.

Owing to the present unfinished investigation of all possible resources of our ancient literature, we may presume, though provisionally, that the musical scale, of which Pingala and Yájnavalkya speak, was neither the growth of the Sûtra nor that of the Bráhmaṇa period. Yájnavalkya distinctly says in his Śikshá that the seven notes of which he speaks are the notes given in the *Gándharva-Véda*:—

गांधर्ववेदे ये प्रोक्ताः सप्त षड्जादयः स्वराः ॥ त एव वेदे विज्ञेयास्त्रय उच्चादयः स्वराः ॥ ६ ॥

Yájnavalkya's testimony of the existence of *Gándharva-Véda* being nothing but a piece of historical poem, carries evidentiary value under the same conditions as a published writing on paper. He does not speak of the scale as a fact of contemporary development; but, on the other hand, his poem suggests that he speaks of the *Gándharva-Véda* as belonging to a period long before his own time; his authority certainly counts for much, because we have no reason to suspect misrepresentation by a man of his learning and position, nor is there any possibility of an interpolation; where and by whom this *Gándharva-Véda* was composed, and what were its contents is shrouded in mystery, though almost all the ancient works on Indian music have solely and wholely drawn on the *Gándharva-Véda* when dealing with the technicalities of music. The Gándharva, whether men or a country, is looked upon by ancient Hindus with superhuman reverence, but whether it was a country under Indian influence or in communication with it in earliest times, it is impossible to decide. If it were a country its namesake is found only in one of the ***twenty Satrapies*** of the Persian monarch Darius. In the twenty Satrapies India is included, according to Herodotus and other Greek historians, as the only country, which paid tribute in gold, and whose people formed a portion of the numerically fabulous force which Xerxes, son of Darius, took with him to conquer Greece. If it were a country in ancient India its name is also identical with Gandaridæ of the Greeks. Alexander the Great was told that beyond the Ganges are the Gandaridæ, the most powerful, warlike, and populous of all the Indian tribes, distinguished for the number and training of their elephants.[1]

Professor Monier Williams[2] tells us that "Gándharvas were a people in the Madhyadesha." He

[1] George Grote's *History of Greece*, Vol. X., p. 172.

[2] *A Sanskrit-English Dictionary*, p. 288.

also says :—"Gandhára is considered to be the modern Kandhára, lying to the north of India."

It is true that the verse in which Yájnavalkya speaks of the musical scale is Anushṭûbha (a metre); and therefore many would believe that this metre was not in practice during the Sútra-period. But we have ample evidence to prove that Anushṭûbha and Trishṭûbha metres were practised, though rarely, during the Sútra and Bráhmaṇa periods.

Saunaka and Nárada used the Anushṭûbha metre, and the former is included by **Max Müller** in the Brahmaṇa period. Besides in the ancient Anukramaṇis (indices) and in Saunaka's list, this metre is mentioned. This metre was also known to Páṇini. In short, the Anushṭûbha metre was used even in the Védic period. In the *Rig-Véda* there is a passage which runs thus :—"Anu-stûbham[1] anu Karkur yámaṇam indram ni kikyuh havá-yah manîshá=Poets by their wisdom discovered Indra dancing to an Anushṭûbha."

There is a verse attributed to Nárada, in which the *notes* of the musical scale are compared with the voices of other animals. The verse runs thus :—

[2] षड्जं रौति मयूरो हि गावो नर्दन्ति चर्षभम् । अजा विरौति गांधारं क्रौञ्चा नर्दन्ति मध्यमम् ॥

---

[1] Max Müller's *Védic Hymns*, Part I., Preface, p. xcvi.

[2] Tookaram Tatya's *Twelve Principal Upanishads*, pp. 516, 517.

The above way of comparing the tones or noises of certain animals with musical notes seems to be very ancient and general. The above verse, with but very little difference, is also in the *Śikshá* of Yájnavalkya :—

"षड्जो वेदे शिखंडी स्यादृषभः स्यादजामुखे ॥ गावो रंभान्ति गान्धारं क्रौञ्चाश्चैव तु मध्यमम् ॥ ८ ॥ कोकिलः पंचमो ज्ञेयो निषादं तु वदेद्गजः ॥ अश्वश्च धैवतो ज्ञेयो स्वराः सप्तविधा मताः" ॥

Verse 1 of the twenty-second section of the *Chhandogya-Upanishad* runs thus :—

"2. [A chanter said] I wish for the tawrine-toned Sáma hymn, the canticle of Agni (fire), which contributes to the weal of animals. The hymns of the *Anirukta tone* belong to Prajápati, those of the *Nirukta tone* to Soma, those of the mild sweet tone to Váyu, those of the sweet higher pitched tone to Indra, those of the tone resembling the voice of the crane to Brihaspati and Varuṇa, those of the tone of a broken piece of bell-metal—they are all to be practised, the horse-toned alone are to be avoided."

There is also a verse ascribed to Vasishṭa, in which the noise of frogs is compared with other animals. (The 103rd hymn in the 7th Manḍal. This is called a panegyric of the frogs, and is supposed to be satirical.[1]) "One of them is cow-noise, the other goat-noise, one is brown, the other green ; they are different, though they

[1] Max Müller's *History of Ancient Sanskrit Literature*, p. 495.

bear the same name, and modulate their voices in many ways as they speak."

As we are in no way the advocate of the Hindus in whatever they have said concerning the musical notes, we, of necessity, confine our present subject within its legitimate limits, and only say that this verse is also of the same type as the one of which we have borrowed from the Yájnavalkya Śikshá, in which certain Ṛishis, castes, etc., are classed as Uchcha, Nîcha and Svarita.

Of all the dates of the Védic Ṛishis, the date of Nárada is the most hidden in fables and antiquity; and therefore we leave it for future researches.

Sir W. Jones, in praising the Hindu Rágas or passions as he calls them, says[1]:—"A very distinguished son of Brahma named Nárada, whose actions are the subject of and *Puráṇa*, bears a strong resemblance to Hermes or Mercury: he was a wise legislator, * * and a musician of exquisite skill; his invention of the Viná, or Indian lute, is thus described in the poems entitled Mágha. Nárada sat watching from time to time his large Viná which, by the impulse of breeze, yielded notes, that pierced successively the regions of his ear, and proceeded by musical intervals."

The Viṇá referred to above may probably be the present Biná. This instrument seems to be very ancient, and is found in the ancient Sanskrit and Páli

[1] *Asiatic Researches*, Vol. I., p. 228.

works along with other instruments. The primitive Viṇá, ordinarily called Tambura, and which may have received its name from the Ṛishi "*Tumbar*," may be anterior to Nárada. This Tambura is much used by ascetics and beggars for its simplicity; there was also a caste of musicians who were called *Veṇás*,[1] from Viṇá, the lyre.

Apart from the fabulous pedigree of Nárada, of whom so much is said in music and poetry, it is very anomalous that, if the so-called legislator and musician are one and the same person, a man of his genius should have condemned music wholesale in his *Dharmashástra*. He, however, inserts in his legislation musical instruments as a property which, if stolen by anybody, he would be visited by a punishment. If the reference to musical instruments in the *Dharmashástra* is not of the highest value as a work of musical art, the testimony which it bears to the state of musical activity of the early Hindus is very precious.

Before going further into our present enquiry, it is necessary to say that we have traced the musical scale, Diatonic, from the present times back to a period somewhat earlier than Pythagoras and Buddha, if the date either of Anugîtá or of Yájnavalkya holds good.

To go beyond the time of Yájnavalkya to trace the musical scale with its supplementary five Notes

[1] Max Müller's *Chips from a German Workshop*, p. 348.

Shrutis, Murhhanás, Grámas, etc., we shall have to tread on ground which is thickly surrounded on all sides by the mystical symbolism of ecclesiastical Hinduism, with which the Upanishads are replete. A learned[1] Orientalist says :—"No people have made such efforts as the Hindus to solve, exhaust, comprehend, what is insolvable, inexhaustible, incomprehensible." Kapila[2] says :—"The supreme lord of the mystics is either absolute and unconditioned (Mukta), or he is bound and conditioned (Baddha). If he is absolute and unconditioned he cannot enter into the condition of a creature; he would have no desire which could instigate him to create. If, on the contrary, he is represented as active and entering on the work of creation, he would no longer be the absolute and unchangeable Being which we are asked to believe."

"मुक्तबद्धयोरन्यतराभावान्न तत्सिद्धिः ॥ ९३ ॥

Under these circumstances we leave off the Upanishad literature, remarking only that in the Chhandogya and a few other Upanishads there are certain subtle verses which, if critically examined, and deprived of their spiritual garb, give the corresponding number of our Notes, Shrutis, Murchhanás and Grámas. As samples we give below the following verses :—

---

1 Troyer's *Preliminary Discourse on the Dabistan*, Vol. I., p. cviii.; Buckle's *History of Civilisation in England*, Vol. I., p. 146.

2 Max Müller's *Chips from a German Workshop*, Vol. I., p. 230.

The second verse of the first chapter of the *Chhandogya-Upanishad* runs thus :—

The earth *constitutes* the essence of all substances ; water is the essence of the earth, and annual herbs of water ; man *forms* the essence of annual herbs, and speech is the essence of man ; Ṛig is the essence of speech, Sáma of the Ṛig, and of the Sáma the Udgîtha is the essence."[1]

Here again we detect that link in our subject which we got hold of in the *Bhagavadgîtá*, in which the Sáma is selected from the Védas for its tones. It is again clear that the Sáma referred to in the *Bhagavadgîtá* is a particular portion of it which is set to music—of course vocal. This view is supported by the above verse, which means that the Udgîtha is the cream of Sáma.

Now the third verse of the first section of the first chapter of the same Upanishad runs thus :—"The Udgîtha is the quintessence of all these essences ; it is the Supreme, the most adorable, *the eighth*." (Verse 4, *ibid.*) :—"What? what is the Ṛig? What? what the Sáma? What? what the Udgîtha? These are questioned." (Verse 5, *ibid.*) :—"Ṛig is speech, Sáma is life, and Om, this letter, is the Udgîtha. Verily this and that, speech and breath (práṇa)—Ṛig and Sáma—make a *maithuna* (couple)."[2]

The above short poems have launched us in an enigma well known to every reader of Hindu spiritualis-

[1] Tookaram Tatya's *Upanishads*, p. 474.

[2] Tookaram Tatya's *Upanishads*, p. 475.

tic literature. We have purposely brought the reader to the enigma to prepare him to learn that our much-sought-for object, the musical scale with its treatment of which we have spoken as the Hindu theory of the scale, is to be unearthed from such enigmatic writings, in the absence of a connected and clear evidence of history.

We do not like to go deeper into the Upanishads, and, therefore, directly come to the verses in which we find our object.

Verse[1] second of the fourth section of the first chapter of the *Chhandogya-Upanishad* is as follows :—

"The Dévas dreading death, adopted the *threefold* knowledge of the Védas. They shielded themselves with psalms. The psalms are called chhandas (metres or rhythms), because the Dévas shielded (Achchhádyan) themselves therein (verse 3). As fishermen look at fish in water, so did death behold them in the Rig, Yajura, and Sáma hymns. They, apprised of it, forsaking the Védas, of truth betook to the asylum of *voice—Svara* (verse 4). In reciting the Ṛig hymns Om is articulated (Svarati), so in the Yajus and Sáma, therefore, indeed, is this letter (Udgîtha) possessing immortality and safety, called *Svara*. Adopting its support the gods became immortal and secure."

From the above verses it is clear that the real meaning of the word Udgîtha is Svara or sound pure

[1] Tookaram Tatya's *Upanishads*, pp. 490, 491.

and simple. We pass over many verses when they only tell us that their principal theme is to combine the Ṛig with Sáma, and to show that they go hand in hand; and therefore whoever praises the Sáma necessarily praises the Ṛig. The other verses express the importance of the knowledge of Udgîtha. But as this subject is outside our enquiry, we come to a point of the Upanishad with which we have to deal.

We find at the beginning of the thirteenth section of the first chapter of the Upanishad the *Hai* and *Hou*, the phonetic particles, on which the Sáma-singer makes a stand and compounds two or more notes (verse 2). "The sun (is) U; the hymns of welcome [Nihava] E; the Vishvédévás are *Auhoi;* Prajápati is *Hin;* Life is Svara (sound); Aliment is *yá;* speech is Viráta (verse 3). And, *thirteenthly*, the Anirukta or undecided hymns are the indistinct particle *Hun* (verse 4). Unto him speech grants its blessings, and he becomes the milker of speech and the owner and consumer of aliments who verily knows this Upanishada of the Sáma-Véda as herein described."

Out of the above verses the third is puzzling, because it refers to the number thirteenth without giving its preceding numbers up to the twelfth. This omission of the preceding numbers up to the twelfth is neither explained by Shankaráchárya nor by the English translator. Such are the materials with which, however reluctantly, we have to deal for showing that the present

Hindu theory of the musical scale was in existence during the composition of the Upanishads or Bráhmaṇa period which Prof. Max Müller fixes as covering 600 to 800 B. C.

From the first to the end of the ninth section of the second chapter of the *Chhandogya-Upanishad* there are descriptions of the five-formed and seven-formed Sáma. The mystical meaning of the five-formed Sáma is attempted; but the meaning of the seven-formed Sáma remains unexplained.

We now come to the first[1] verse of the tenth section of the second chapter, which runs thus:—" Next, verily the seven-formed Sáma, which is above death like unto the soul, should be adored. Hiñkára [हिङ्कार] includes three letters, [so] doth Prastáva [प्रस्ताव] include three letters, therefore they are equal (verse second).—[The word Ádi] आदि includes two letters, and [the word Pratihára] प्रतिहार four letters, of which (latter) one letter [being added to the former] they become equal (verse 3).—[The word] Udgítha [उद्गीथ includes] three letters, and [the word] Upadrava [उपद्रव] four; the three [of the former] with the three [of the latter] are equal, leaving one letter redundant, [which being assumed] to be three, they [all become] equal (verse 4).—[The word Nidhan] निधन includes three letters, and therefore it is equal [with the rest]. These well known terms thus verily [include] *twenty-two letters* (verse 5).—" The *twenty-first* is the

[1] Tookaram Tatya's *Upanishads*, pp. 510, 511.

sun [Áditya], for it is the *twenty-first* from this earth. By the *twenty-second* that which is above the sun might be triumphed ; it is heaven [नाक] exempt from pain and grief." The sixth and the last verse of this section runs thus :—" He obtaineth the conquest of the sun, and that which is above the conquest of the sun, who, knowing all this, adores—verily adores—the *seven-formed* which is above death, and like unto the soul."

We need not draw any more upon the mystical literature of the Upanishads, because we have learnt that the much-talked-of Udgîtha with its most abridged sounds (Om) is a composition of musical notes combined with words. This Om was the essence of all the hymns, and its general acceptance may possibly be due to its shortness and simplicity. This Om even now forms the meaningless syllable of the *Joḍa* music (see page 63) under the modified or corrupted form—*Noma* or *Toma* of our present singers.

How much the word "Om" was revered may be seen from the twenty-second verse of the sixth Prapáthaka of the *Maitráyaṇa-Bráhmaṇa-Upanishad* :—" Other[1] teachers of the word, 'Om' (as Brahman) think otherwise. They listen to the sound of the ether within the heart while they stop the ears with the thumbs. They compare it to *seven noises*, like rivers, like a bell, like a brazen vessel, like the wheels of a carriage, like the croaking of frogs, like rain, and as if a man speaks in a

[1] Max Müller's *Upanishads*, Vol. II., p. 321.

cavern. Having passed beyond this variously apprehended sound, and having settled in the supreme, soundless (non-word), unmanifested Brahman, they become undistinguished and undistinguishable, as various flavours of the flowers are lost in the taste of honey."

From the above verses it will be seen that they speak of the numbers[1] which exactly correspond with the musical scale and its ratios or intervals. We know that the Shrutis are twenty-two in number, and that the number of Murchhanás, according to the ancient calculation, and not as we have said (see page 101), is twenty-one.

The strong tendency of the Hindus of the Bráhmaṇa period to mystify everything may be seen from the following verses from the seventh[2] Prapáthaka of the *Maitráyaṇa-Bráhmaṇa-Upanishad*:—

1. "Agni, the Gáyatra (metre), the Trivriṭ (hymn), the Rathantar (song) * *."
2. "Indra, the Trishṭubh (metre), the Pañkdasa (hymn), the Brihat (song) * *."
3. "The Maruts, the Jagati (metre), the Saptadasha (hymn), the Vairupa (song) * *."
4. "The Visve Devas, the Anushṭubh (metre), the Ekavims (hymn), the Vairága (song) * *."

---

[1] सप्त स्वराः त्रयो ग्रामा मूर्छनाश्चैकविंशतिः ॥ द्वाविंशतिश्च श्रुतय एतेभ्यो रागसंभवः ॥

[2] Max Müller's *Upanishads*, Vol. II., pp. 338-340.

5. "Mitrá-Varuṉau, the Pañkti (metre), the Triṉavatrayastrimsa (hymn), the Śákvara-raivata (songs) * *."

From the above five verses it is clear that some of the songs were differentiated from the hymns, and that the names of the metres, hymns and songs were associated with the names of God or gods.

Again, the following verses from the twenty-second[1] section of the second chapter of the *Chhandogya-Upanishad* show how even the vowels and consonants are associated with mythological names:— (2) "[The hymns are to be sung with the wish]: Let me sing for the immortality of the gods. For [the due offering of] oblations to the manes, for the [fulfilment of the] desires of mankind, for securing grass and water to animals, heaven to the institutors of sacrifices, aliment for self, let me sing. Thinking thus without excitement let them be sung. (3) The vowels [Svara] constitute the body of Indra, the sibilants and *ha* [Us mána] that of Prajápati, and the consonants [Sparshá] that of Death * * * (4) Should any revile him (singer) about the sibilants and *ha*, he should say:— "I take protection of Prajápati, he will ground thee down," and should any revile him about the consonants, he should say, "I take protection of Death, he will hurl thee into flames." (5) The vowels are to be recited with sound and force, saying: "I take the strength of Indra."

[1] Tookaram Tatya's *Upanishads*, pp. 516, 517.

The sibilants and *ha* are to be sounded internally, but not uttered out [of the mouth], and yet distinctly, saying: "To Prajápati I resign my life." The consonants are to be repeated slowly and distinctly, saying: "From death, I extricate my life."

From the verses referred to above it is sufficiently clear that vocal music was, in some form or another, recognised as part of the Hindu religion in very early ages.[1] The Védas or songs were revered as divine and eternal[2] (नित्य). Under these circumstances, it is no matter for surprise that the Hindus had made considerable progress, not only in the cultivation of language,[3]

---

[1] "There were some parts of the sacrifice, which, according to ancient custom, had to be accompanied by songs, and hence arose another class of priests whose particular office it was to act as the chorus. This naturally took place at the most solemn sacrifices only. Though as yet we have no key as to the character of the music which the Udgátṛis performed, we can see from the numerous and elaborate rules, however unintelligible, that their music was more than mere chanting."—Max Müller's *History of Ancient Sanskrit Literature*, pp. 472 and 473.

[2] "The *Mimánsá* affirms the eternity (नित्य) of sound. This is contested by the Naiyáyiks, who maintain that, were it eternal, it could not be apprehended by human organs of sense."—Colebrooke's *Miscellaneous Essays*, Vol. I., p. 285, Second Edition.

न नित्यत्वं वेदानां कार्यत्वश्रुतेः ॥ ४५ ॥

"The Véda is not from eternity, and there is scripture proof of its being a production."—*Sánkhya Aphorisms of Kapila*, p. 127, by J. R. Ballantyne, LL.D.

[3] Professor Max Müller in his *Lectures on the Origin of Religion* (p. 150) emphatically asserts:—"I believe I shall not be contradicted by Helmholtz or Ellis or other representatives of Phonetic science, if I say that, to the present day, the phoneticians of India of the fifth century B. C. are unsurpassed in their analysis of the elements of language. In grammar I challenge any scholar to produce from any language a more comprehensive collection and classificaation of all the facts of a language than we find in Páṇiṇi's *Sútras*."

poetry,[1] and a few other subjects,[2] but also in the art of music which was, of course, of a semi-religious character.

In summing up the above evidence, it must be admitted that there does not exist a closely connected history in a chronological order of our present scale with its theory. But we have traced the regular history of the scale backwards from the nineteenth century A. C. to about the sixth century B. C., *i.e.*, possibly to the time of Yájnavalkya. It is true that, in traversing a period of about twenty-five centuries, in the absence of any previous attempt by any scholar in this direction, we are required to jump, as will be seen from the foregoing discourse, from one century to another, in order to preserve the link of evidence. In doing this we have first traced the scale from the advent of the Mahomedans to the twelfth century A. C., the probable date, according to the calculation of Prof. H. H. Wilson, of Sárngadeva, the compiler of the *Sangîta-Ratnákara*. To cover the intermediate period from the twelfth century A. C. to the beginning of the Christian era, we have resorted to the periods of the Sanskrit

---

1 As regards Chhandas (metres) Prof. Max Müller, along with F. Von Schlegel Herene and many others, says :—"We possess in the observations and technical terms of the ancient Indian authors a clear confirmation of the latest theories of modern metricians."

2 "The Arabs, however, far from claiming the discovery of the figures for themselves, unanimously ascribe it to the Indians, nor can there be much doubt that the Bráhmans were the original inventors of those numerical symbols which are now used over the whole civilised world."—Max Müller's *Chips from a German Workshop*, Vol. II., pp. 289 and 290, Second Edition.

works on music, of Kálidása, of Shúdraka, of Amarasinha, and some of the Buddhistic writings. To trace it before the Christian era we have had recourse to the periods of Anugîtá, Bhagavadgîtá, Pingalanága, and Yájnavalkya. To go still further into the earlier literature of the Bráhmaṇa period, we are of necessity forced to grope in the mystical and theological darkness of the Upanishada literature ; and, therefore, we own without any reserve, that our dissertation on the period anterior to that of Yájnavalkya may be taken for what it is worth.

It is not too much to expect, from the present unfinished state of the ever-increasing researches into our ancient literature, that the link of the historical evidence, which we have tried to form in the preceding discussion, may guide us further back by a closer investigation of the subject. We are sure that a further enquiry into the Shikshá literature of the Védas may take us to a period earlier than that of Yájnavalkya. It should not be a matter of wonder if we find the musical scale with an exhaustive treatment of it in the *Sámavéda Shikshá*, when we find the scale with its intrinsic relation in the *Shikshá* of Yájnavalkya. The *Yájnavalkya Shikshá* seems to be intended for the *Yajur Véda*, and therefore it does not treat of the musical scale as exhaustively as would naturally be the case with the *Sáma Shikshá*. The *Sáma* of all the Védas is associated more with the tones than with the words. The name of *Shikshá* as defined by the ancient Ṛishis inspires us with a confident belief that any attempt in this direction may not be altogether unsuccessful.

Taittiriyas,[1] from whose writings Sáyana quotes, have devoted a chapter of their *Áraṇyaka* to the subject of *Shikshá*. In the seventh book of the *Taittiriya-Áraṇyaka* there are the following headings :—"On letters, on accents, on quality, on the organs of pronounciation, on delivery, and on the euphonic laws."

Professor Max Müller[2] tells us that no *Pratisákhya* has yet been discovered, nor is it at all likely that such a work ever existed. The Professor says :—"The *Sáma-Véda* was meant to be chanted, and the rules for chanting, therefore, as contained in the *Sáma-Sútras*, naturally take the place of *Shikshá* or pronounciation. There is a small treatise in the same manuscript of the Bodleian Library which contains the *Taittiriya-Pratisákhya*, and which might be called a *Pratisákhya* (phonetic laws of language) of the *Sáma-Véda*. But it is so badly written, and so unintelligible without a commentary, that little use can be made of it at present. It is called *Sáma-tantra*. It begins (MS. Bodl. W. 505) :—

"श्रीगणेशाय नमः ॥

स्वरो ऽ नंत्यः । नीचानां । उपांत्यं । उपांत्ये । त्रिषु । आदिः उपांत्यं च । द्वितीयं । अंतश्च । उपांत्ये ॥ १ ॥ आद्यो । अंत्यो । मध्यं । विपरीतस्वराणां । जारा । माहङ् । शश्व्यु । उता । पारिख्वु । दिं ॥ २ ॥ बि । पिवा । दाधिविदपूर्वो । जरा परा च । सुध्वाई पाङ्गु । अंतो । शता । ति पौ गु ॥ ॥."

[1] Max Müller's *History of Ancient Sanskrit Literature*, p. 113.

[2] Max Müller's *History of Ancient Sanskrit Literature*, p. 143.

The Professor also tells us that there is another manuscript which contains several small treatises on *Shikshá* matter connected with the *Sáma-Véda*, but more in the form of *Parisishṭas:* one on Avagraha or division of words; another called *Sáma-Sankhyá;* and a third called *Stobhan-sanhára*, beginning with the words अथातो ह्रस्वदीर्घप्लुतमात्राण्यक्षराणि व्याख्यास्यामः ॥

As regards a complete collection of the *Sáma-Véda* literature, H. T. Colebrooke[1] tells us:—"A peculiar degree of holiness seems to be attached to the Sáma for its chanting, and that the chanting was of different kinds, and that a *musical notation* (*vide* p. 5) was invented to denote the *metres* and the *mode* of *chanting*. Not having yet obtained a complete copy of the Véda (Sáma), or any commentary on it, I can only describe it imperfectly, from such fragments as I have been able to collect."

Professor Monier William[2] says:—"*Sáma-Véda-ćchlá* is the name of a short work giving certain musical directions in the form of modulations and intonations of letters or syllables for the chanting of the *Sáma-Véda;* the work contains seven chapters, *viz.*, *Yeya-ćchlá*, *Áraṇáço*, *Úha-ço*, *Úhyá-ço*, *Gána-ço*, *Uttarotarapada-ço* and *Stobha-ço*."

In the absence of a complete literature of the *Sáma-Véda* and the *Gándharva-Véda* of which Yájnavalkya

[1] *Essays on the Religion and Philosophy of the Hindus*, pp. 47-50.

[2] *A Sanskrit-English Dictionary*, p. 1107.

speaks, we, of necessity, close the historical aspect of our scale and turn to the scale itself to see what it may teach us intrinsically.

In the first place we find that there is some similarity between certain names of the Hindu and European (Latin) notes of the Gráma or Gamut. The first syllable of the name of the first note of the scale in Sanskrit is Shaṭ or Shaḍ[1] (Shaḍja means born of or emitted from six or षडजायन्त यस्मात्), which seems to be similar with the Ut (which means eight), the Latin name for C. This Ut was changed into Do by the Italian in the seventeenth century A. C. (*vide* p. 50). There is but very little difference between the Sanskrit Ri of the Rishabha, the second note of the Diatonic scale, and the Latin Re. Besides these close similarities it is very singular that the Sanskrit and European semitones change their names on the same principle,[2] or in other words, the arrangement of calling the five semitones, either flat or sharp (Komala or Tivra), is really the same. This arrangement of the scale is too similar to be accidental, and therefore we shall digress a little to weigh the

---

[1] The number of notes at the time of calling the first note Shaḍja may be six only. The seventh is called Nisháda, that is, low caste or cast off. There was a tribe called Nisháda from the name of their country. The Sanskrit explanation of the six places (स्थान), from which the six notes are emitted, is fabulous:—

पूर्वं नाभिस्ततो हृत्स्यात् पश्चात् कंठः प्रकीर्त्तितः ।
अथ मूर्द्धा तथास्यं स्यादिति स्थानानि मेनिरे ॥

[2] *Asiatic Researches*, Vol. I., Number V., pp. 250-254, in which Francis Fowke, Esquire, describes the frets of the Biná.

historical evidence, if there be any, on which Sir W. W. Hunter, Sir W. Jones, Colonel Tod, Captain C. R. Day, and a few others assert that the Greeks and Europeans were, as they were in certain subjects,[1] the followers of the Hindus. Sir W. W. Hunter[2] says:—"The Indian Art of Music (*Gándharva Véda*) was destined to exercise wider influence. A regular system of notation had been worked out before the age of Páṇiṇi (350 B. C.), and the seven notes were designated by their initial letters. This notation passed from the Brâhmaṇs through the Persians[3] to Arabia, and was thence introduced into European music by Guido d'Arezzo in the beginning of

[1] Colebrooke's *Essays*, p. 265; *Chips from a German Workshop; Asiatic Researches*.

[2] *Impeiral Gazetteer of India*, by W. W. Hunter, Vol. VI., pp. 110-112, Second Edition (1886).

[3] Ten thousand Lurians (musicians of a common type) were sent from India by the King Shaukol of Hinda at the invitation of the Emperor Behrám-i-Gur of Persia (who ascended the throne in 417 A. D. and died in 433 A. D.). The Emperor Behrám once asked his courtiers whether the people of Persia were happy; they said that there was no music in Persia as in other countries. On hearing this the Emperor sent for a large number of musicians.—The *Shdhánámá*, by Firdosi, Persian Edition, 1870, p. 156.

"Under Behrám-i-Gur, whose reign spread joy, minstrels and musicians were first introduced into Persia. Behrám, we are told, observed a merry troop of his subjects dancing without music. He enquired the cause. 'We have sent everywhere,' said one of them, 'and offered a hundred pieces of gold for a musician, but in vain.' The king sent to India for musicians and singers, and twelve thousands were encouraged by his munificence to enter his domains." *Zinat-ut-Tavárikha*, by Malcolm.

Malcolm says:—"There were, no doubt, always a few of this class in Persia; since the days of Behrám they have abounded. The dancing and singing girls in Persia are called Kasuli, a corruption of Cabuli, or of Kabul, which shows the quarter whence they came."

the 11th century (A. C.).[1] Some, indeed, suppose that our modern word *gamut* comes not from the Greek letter gamma, but from the Indian Gáma (in Prakrit; in Sanskrit Gráma), literally, a musical scale.

"Hindu music, after a period of excessive elaboration, sank under the Mahomedans into a state of arrested development. Of the 36 chief musicians in the time of Akbar only 5 were Hindus. Not content with tones and semitones the Indian musicians employ a more minute sub-division, together with a number of sonant modifications, which the Western ear neither recognizes nor enjoys. Thus, they divide the octave into 22 sub-tones instead of the 12 tones and semitones of the European scale. This is one of several fundamental differences, but it alone suffices to render Indian music barbaric to us, giving it the effect of a Scotch ballad in a minor key, sung intentionally a little out of tune.

"Its peculiarities—melodies which the Indian composer pronounces to be the perfection of harmony, and which have for ages touched the hearts and fired the imagination of Indian audiences—are condemned as discord by the European critic. The Hindu ear has been trained to recognize modifications of sound which the European ear refuses to take pleasure in. Our ears,

[1] "Von Bohlen, *Das Alte Indien*, Vol. II., p. 195 (1830); Benfoy's *Indien* (Ersch and Grüber's *Encyclopadie*, Vol. XVII., 1840), quoted by Weber, *History of Indian Literature*, p. 272, footnote 315 (1878)."

on the other hand, have been taught to expect harmonic combinations, for which Indian music substitutes different combinations of its own. The Indian musician declines altogether to be judged by the few simple Hindu airs which the English ear can appreciate. It is, indeed, impossible to adequately represent the Indian system by the European notation; and the full range of its effects can only be rendered by Indian instruments—a vast collection of sound producers slowly elaborated during 2,000 years to suit the special requirements of Hindu music. The complicated structure of its musical notes (Rágas) rests upon three separate systems, one of which consists of five, another of six, and the other of seven notes. It preserves in a living state some of the early forms which puzzle the student of Greek music, side by side with the most complicated developments. ...... No Englishman has yet brought an adequate acquaintance with the *technique* of Indian instrumentation to the study of Hindu music. The art still awaits (*vide* p. 29) investigation by some eminent Western professor; and the contempt with which Europeans in India regard it, merely proves their ignorance of the system on which Hindu music is built up."

Lieutenant-Colonel J. Tod[1] says:—"The Greeks, following the Egyptians, had but six notes with their lettered symbols; and it was reserved for the Italians to add a seventh. Guido Arentine, a monk

---

[1] *Rájasthan*, Vol. I., p. 466.

in the thirteenth century (A. C.), has the credit of this. I, however, believe the Hindus numbered theirs from the heavenly bodies—the Sun, Moon, Mercury, Venus, Mars, Jupiter, and Saturn—hence they had the regular octave, with its semitones, and as, in the pruriency of their fancy, they converted the ascending and descending notes into *grahas*, or planetary bodies, so they may have added to the harmonious numbers and produced the *no-rágnis*, their *nine* modes of music. Could we affirm that the hymns,.composed and set to music by Jydeva nearly three thousand years ago and still chanted in honour of the Apollo of Vrija, had been handed down with the sentiments of these mystic compositions (and Sir W. Jones sanctions the idea), we should say, from their simplicity, that the musicians of that age had only the diatonic scale, but we have every reason to believe from the very elaborate character of their music which is painful and discordant to the ear from its minuteness of sub-divisions, that they also had the chromatic scale, said to have been invented by Timotheus in the time of Alexander, who might have carried it from the banks of the Indus."

Captain C. R. Day, F. S. A., in his Notes[1] on Indian Music, says:—"The Hindu scale has, possibly, from a natural transformation tending to simplicity, become practically a half-tone one, allowing of the performance of expres-

[1] Captain C. R. Day delivered a lecture on February 13th to the members of the Musical Association, entitled "Notes on Indian Music."—*India*, March 1st, 1894, p. 91.

sive melodic music capable of the greatest refinement of treatment, and altogether outside the experience of the Western musician. As regards the apparent similarity of the Indian and European scales, it must be remembered that the latter were evolved, in process of time, from those of ancient Greece. * * * The historian Strabo[1] shows that Greek influence extended to India, and also that Greek musicians of a certain school attributed the greater part of the science of music to India. *Even now most of the old Greek modes are represented in the Indian system.* * * * Indians are extremely conservatives[2] in their tastes, and this is shown in a marked degree by the little change that their musical instruments have undergone during the last 2,000 years. This length of time is great, but is fully warranted by the descriptions contained in the Sanskrit treatises, and even more by other references found in certain Páli works."

We shall now quote an authority on the History of Greece from which we shall learn whether the Greeks were indebted to the Hindus or other nations for their

---

[1] Considering this as a question of more or less probative value from the evidence available, we cannot but infer that, so far as the information within our reach goes, there is stronger reason to believe that, instead of the Hindu musicians having borrowed anything from Greece or any other nation, the Indian music has been the source which has been drawn upon by the Greeks. This conclusion is borne out by the careful researches of an independent historian like Strabo who certainly was not partial to the Hindus.

[2] M. Guizot, in his *History of Civilization*, says :—" Civilization in India has had a different effect; societies have fallen into a somnolent condition." See also Buckle's *History of Civilisation in England*, Vol. I., p. 81.

musical scale or they themselves were the inventors of it.

George Grote[1] says:—"Both Phrygians and Lydians did not only modify the religious manifestations of the Asiatic Greeks, and through them of the Grecian world generally, but also rendered important aid towards the first creation of the Grecian musical scale. Of this the denominations of the scale afford a proof. * * *

"It thus appears that the earliest Greek music was, in larger proportion, borrowed from Phrygia and Lydia. When we consider that in the eighth and the seventh centuries before the Christian era, music and poetry conjoined (often also with dancing or rhythmical gesticulation) was the only intellectual manifestation known among the Greeks—and, moreover, that in the belief of all ancient writers, every musical mode had its own peculiar influence, powerfully modified the temper of hearers and was intimately connected with the national worship—we shall see that this transmission of the musical modes implies much, both of communication and interchange between the Asiatic Greeks and the indigenous population of the Continent. Now the fact of communication between the Ionic and *Æolic* Greeks and their eastern neighbours, the Lydians, is easy to comprehend generally, though we have no details as to the way in which it took place. But we do not distinctly see where it was that the Greeks came so

[1] *History of Greece*, Vol. III., pp. 39 to 41, a new Edn.

much into contact with the Phrygians except in the region of Ida, the Troad, and the southern coast of the Propontis. To this region belonged those early Phrygian musicians (under the heroic name of Olympus, Hyagnis and Marsyas), from whom the Greeks borrowed. And we may remark that the analogy between the Thracians and Phrygians seems partly to hold in respect both to music and to religion; since the old myth in the Iliad, wherein the Thracian bard, Thamyris, rashly contending in song with the Muses, is conquered, blinded and stripped of his art, seems to be the prototype of the very similar story respecting the contention of Apollo with the Phrygian Marsyas—the cithara against the flute; while the Phrygian Midas is farther characterised as the religious disciple of Thracian Orpheus.

"In my previous chapter relating to the legend of Troy, mention has already been made of the earliest fusion of Æolic Greeks with the indigenous population of the Troad. It is from hence, probably, that the Phrygian music with the flute as its instrument—employed in the orgaistic rites and worship of the Great Mother in Mount Ida, in the Mysian Olympus, and other mountain regions of the country, and even in the Greek city of Lampsakus—passed to the Greek composers. Its introduction is coeval with the earliest facts respecting Grecian music, and must have taken place during the first century of the recorded Olympiads. In the Homeric poem we find no allusion to it, but it may probably have contributed to stimulate that development of lyric and eligiac composition which grew up among the post-Homeric Æolians and Ionians, to the gradual displacement of the old epic.

"The early relations between the Lydians and the Asiatic Greeks, anterior to the reign of Gygês, are not so well known to us as those of the Phrygians. Their native music became partly incorporated with the Greek, as the Phrygian music was, to which it was analogous, both in instruments and character, though the Lydian mode was considered by the ancients as more effeminate and enervating. The flute was used alike by the Phrygians and Lydians, passing from both of them to the Greeks. But the magadis or *pectis* (a harp, with sometimes as many as twenty strings, sounded two together in octave) is said to have been borrowed by the Lesbian Terpander from the Lydian banquets. The flute-players who acquired esteem among the early Asiatic Greeks were often Phrygian or Lydian slaves; and even the poet Alkaman, who gained for himself permanent renown among the Greek lyric poets, though not a slave-born at Serdis, as is sometimes said, was probably of Lydian extraction."

Now we turn again to the Indian musical scale to see what it teaches or suggests to us intrinsically.

The fact that the *old Greek modes* are represented in the Indian system—and the supposition that Alexander carried the chromatic scale, attributed to Timotheus, who flourished at the time of Alexander, from the banks of Indus—may be further supported by another fact that, of all historical nations of the ancient world, the Greeks were the only nation, excepting, of course, the Hindus, who had adopted the quarter tone[1] (Murchhaná) at the time of their decline in arts and sciences, and that the identity of the words Gamut and Grâma, and the principle on which the sharps and flats are changed and named, are too similar to be accidental. But in the absence of direct and unimpeachable evidence of history, excepting that of Strabo, it is always desirable to be as incredulous as possible, particularly against oneself, and to keep before our eyes critics who will not yield one inch beyond what they are forced to admit on the strongest pressure of facts.

Under these circumstances, we are totally unable to decide to which of the two nations, the Greeks or the Hindus, may be awarded the palm of priority in the science of musical scale.

Have the Hindu and the Greek scales a common origin, or has one been derived from the other, at the time of the expedition of Alexander, or were fragments of the science of music of the Hindus carried into Greece, while at the same time a portion of the Greek system of music succeeded in penetrating beyond the Indus? Is it the Hindu scale which became Greek, or was it a

[1] See P. Blaserna's *Theory of Sound in its Relation to Music*, p. 120.

parallel and independent development, without any influence of the one upon the other? These questions cannot be answered finally until further researches into the Greek, Roman and the Hindu literatures and archæology from one end of them to the other are made by eminent scholars of history and antiquity. The last supposition, however, appears the most reasonable; whatever may be the truth in regard to the above questions, there are certainly some remarkable points of agreement (which points have been the basis and type of all European music) between the science of music of the Greeks and the musical labour of ancient India.

In the absence of an established historical evidence concerning an exchange of the scale of music or some of its notes between the Greeks and the Hindus, and in the presence of certain remarkable identities between the two systems of music will it be rational to suppose that the two systems were the offshoots or derivatives from a common stock of the Early Aryas before their separation from their home in Central Asia?

It will be seen clearly from Bopp's[1] *Comparative Grammar*, that all the *essential forms* of grammar had been fully framed and established before the first separation of the Aryan family took place. The same is generally said of music; but there is neither evidence to prove that the *musical scale*, even Diatonic

[1] Max Müller's *Chips from a German Workshop*, Vol. II., p. 20, Second Edition.

in its Greek or Hindu form, was known to the Aryan family before they separated, nor have we the slightest reason to believe that it was known to the Egyptians who are supposed to be the teachers of the Greeks in certain subjects.[1] It is a historical fact that the Egyptians had a lyre with three strings.

The early lyre of the Greeks had four, constituting their tetrachord. It is only after some centuries that lyres of seven and eight strings were used by the Greeks. And, at the expiration of a thousand years, they had advanced to their great system of the double octave.[2]

From all the evidence brought forward in the foregoing details it is abundantly clear that the Hindus had a complete diatonic, if not a chromatic, scale, when the celebrated harper Terpander (about 676 B. C.) introduced *a* (ध) and *e* (ग), and the philosopher Pythagoras (born about 580 B. C.) completed the diatonic scale by introducing *b* (नि). (See pp. 50 and 218.)

Before concluding the history of the musical scale, we need not repeat what has already been sufficiently set forth in the preceding pages that the mass of Indian evidence posterior to the sixth century B. C., the latest time possible allotted to Yájnavalkya, appears to us reducable either to history or chronology, and that any chronological systems which may hereafter be applied

---

[1] See F. Von Schll's *Philosophy of History*, Translated by James Burton Robertson, Esquire, p. 166, Seventh Edition.

[2] H. Spencer's *Essays, Scientific, Political and Speculative*, Vol I., p. 26.

to it must begin from the time of the Bráhmaṇa period, 800 B. C., in which the musical scale was not only practised by the ancient Hindus, but its internal relation with the several notes was almost scientifically known. From all the evidence available at present the balance of probabilities seems to be in favour of assigning a more ancient date to the development of the musical scale in India than we have given to it. For the oldest period (Bráhmaṇa) in which we have traced the musical scale must be called a secondary period. It exhibits a stratum of musical activities in ancient India perfectly unintelligible without the admission of a preceding age. It cannot be supposed that those who used the musical scale followed immediately upon an age which had known only the musical scale but no musicians and their music *vocal* and *instrumental*. There are traces, though very dim and obscure, in our ancient literature, to show that even previous to the compilation or composition of the *Gándharva-véda* and of the *Sáma-veda* a free and original spirit of a very long duration was at work in the art of music, and that there was also a succeeding period of longer duration than the preceding one in which that free and original spirit was condemned and lost, as will be seen from the *Dharma-shástras* of the ancient *Rishis* or sages. The supposition of a previous stage or period is based upon the principles that the musical (*vide* p. 77) scale is always the product of the musical activity of many centuries; that it is not established before music, but is developed with it; and that a very perfect form of music must have a perfect scale.[1] When we study the parallel history of the same scale in Europe, we are justified in deciding that, when the Greeks and modern Europeans have conjointly taken at least three thousand years to form it with all their civilization, the early Hindus of the eighth century B. C. must have taken equal, if not more, time with their so called lethargic civilization.

As references have already been made to dancing, as a branch[2] of music, in the preceding pages, that subject is treated of in the following chapter.

---

1 Professor P. Blaserna's *Theory of Sound in its Relation to Music*, pp. 113, 114, Third Edition.

2 "Saugíta (music) means *gáṇa* (voices), *vádya* (instruments) and *nṛttya* (actions), or song, percussion, and dancing."—*The Works of Sir William Jones*, Vol. I., p. 416.

CHAPTER VII.

DANCING.

Dancing, which has, all over the civilized world, been recognized as an art, is dependent on the muscular action generated by some elevated feeling. Feelings are the concomitants of nervous changes. There is a recognized relation between the quantity of feeling (pleasurable or painful) and the amount of motion generated. Dancing, which is a mode of expressing joyous emotions, is performed not only by the human race but is considerably exhibited by animals.[1]

It is to be regretted that dancing, which is so natural an expression[2] of joyous feelings, and which is and has

[1] Charles Darwin says:—"In Northern America, large numbers of grouse meet every morning during the breeding season on a selected level spot, and here they run round and round in a circle of about fifteen or twenty feet in diameter, so that the ground is worn quite bare, like a fairy-ring. In these partridge dances, as they are called by the hunters, the birds assume the strangest attitudes, and run round, some to the left and some to the right. * * During the spring our little white-throat (*sylvia cincrea*) often rises a few feet or yards in the air above some bush, and flutters with a fitful and fantastic motion, singing all the while, and drops to its perch." *Descent of Man*, p. 380. Second Edition. There may be very few of us who have not watched and enjoyed the Chandọla (sky-lark), Bulbul (big lark), and a few other birds undergoing manœuvres of the above description.

[2] Professor A. Bain, "*The Emotions and the Will*," p. 113, says:—"Next to experience of Feelings is experience of the Signs. These are—the recognized expression of human and other sentient beings, by Voice, Movement, Gesture, and Demonstration of every kind. * * * * We, therefore, infer that, when music or other genial stimulation wakens up past occasions of pleasure, these echoes do greatly increase the emotional glow; and the highly educated emotional man is necessarily much more elated under the circumstance than the poor, the out-cast, the emotionally famished man."—*Ibid.*, p. 104.

been, practised by all civilised nations[1] of the world, has been totally ignored and discarded by the Indians. They consider dancing to be an undignified act, and hence its practice is confined only to the fair sex. But it was not so with the ancient Hindus. Both males and females used to take delight in dancing in religious and social ceremonials, not only up to the time of "Krishṇa," but long after it. Dancing was held in so much reverence by the early Hindus that its name (Nrîttya) is found in the *Ṛig-Véda* (p. 249) and other ancient Sanskrit and Páli works (p. 231) of great sanctity. It is exhaustively treated in the Sanskrit works on music. According to the latter complete music consists of vocal and instrumental art and of dancing. गीतं वाद्यं नर्तनञ्च संगित मुच्यते ॥

The word dancing must be understood in a broader sense than that in which it is now employed in Europe. It comprises every variety of rhythmical movements or gesticulations, or postures of the body, from the slowest to the quickest; or it is the decorous and expressive movements of the features, especially those of hands and feet. This kind of dancing was also practised by the Greeks.[2]

---

1 "To the Ionians nothing was pleasant without song and dance. The Greeks expressed their joy by dance and song, both of these necessarily became constituent parts of their religious festivals."—Heerne's *Historical Researches in Ancient Greece*, pp. 24, 34. "Among the Spartans the dancing was a public entertainment, and even Kings used to take a part in it."—G. Grote's *History of Greece*, Vol. III., p. 308. The Bible says that David and Solomon were good dancers and musicians. The Egyptians were not dead to the charms of music and dancing.

2 G. Grote's *History of Greece*, Vol. III., p. 308.

The present mode of dancing in India, both private and public, though performed, at times, by a few male artists, is generally confined to females. Private (non-professional) dancing, occasionally practised among higher families and even in the most secluded part of the "Janáná" (harem) as Rásaḍás,[1] is inartistic. Hámchi (in Guzerat), Féra (in Southern Maratha Country), Fugaḍi,[2] etc., are rustic; but the professional (of course not the tom-tom Nácha which is seen at the marriage and other ceremonials at times) or artistic dancing on the contrary is refined.

The artistic mode of dancing has less technical syllables than those of the drumming. These syllables are worked out with the soles of the feet of which the ankles are ringed with a belt of small bells (Zálara or Ghungru), which are sounded in concert with music. The right foot performs the major part of such syllables,

---

[1] In Rásaḍá each lady catches the hands of her neighbours and bows and moves round and round in a circle, slow in the beginning and fast in the end; when separated or not supporting each other by the hands, they perform a zig-zag motion, and clap and flourish their hands. Those who possess a sweet voice, take the lead, and others follow in their train. A female drummer or regulator of the voice and of the measure of the feet, sits in the centre. Ashvaghosha who flourished during the first century A. C. depicts the dance (which may be the Rásaḍá of the ancient Hindus), which was ordered by Saddodan, the father of the great Buddha, to reclaim his son from his ascetic inclination, thus:—"Each one (virgin lady) setting herself off to the best advantage or joining together in harmonious concert, clapping their hands or moving their feet in unison, or joining close, body to body, limb to limb, &c."—*Sacred Books of the East*, Vol. XIX., p. 38, *A Life of Buddha*, by Ashvaghosha Bodhisttava, translated from Sanskrit into Chinese by Dharmaraksha, A. D. 420, and from Chinese into English by Samuel Beal.

[2] Two females support each other by crossed hands, and revolve with a tremendous speed.

and "Parandas" are resorted to as a means to an artistic performance. The technical syllables are these :—Tá, Tak, Tad, Thai, Tho, Thun, etc. These are combined like drum syllables and executed by the feet as Ṭhá, Duni, Áḍa, etc., referred to in Chapter IV.

An artistic dancer has not only to attend to Tálas (time), but has also to exhibit different emotions by means of attitudes, postures and gestures, in accompaniment of vocal and instrumental music. The flourishing of the hands is a necessary condition for performing a dance. To understand the real importance of the flourishing of hands in dancing, as a necessary condition, it will not be quite out of place to note that acrobatic feats are facilitated by flourishing the hands or the poles. We may, therefore, digress a little from our immediate subject to study the movements of the arms in walking.

"If we place," Herbert Spencer says, "our arms close to our sides, and keep them there while walking at a quick pace, we shall find that the shoulders unavoidably fall into a backward and forward motion of a wriggling (ungraceful) character. After persevering in this mode of walking for a time, we shall find that the action is not only ungraceful but fatiguing. Now let us suddenly allow our arms to swing as usual. The wriggling of the shoulders will cease, and the body will be found to move easily. We will also notice that the backward motion of each arm is simultaneous with the forward motion of the corresponding leg; and, if we will attend to our muscular sensations, we shall find that this backward swing of the arm is a counter-balance to the forward swing of the leg, and that it is easier to produce this counter-balance by moving the arms than by contorting the body, as we must otherwise do."

An artistic dancer is one having so acute a muscular sense as at once to feel in what direction the hands should be moved to most readily counter-balance any motion of the body or leg, and also having an artistic sense to gracefully adjust them in such a way as to add to the general effect of different postures, attitudes and movements. Those who fail to adjust their hands in an artistic way, make an impression upon the audience that their hands are a trouble to them; they are held stiffly in a meaningless attitude, they are checked from swinging in the directions in which they would naturally swing, or they are so moved that, instead of helping to maintain the gracefulness (the principal aim in a dance), they diminish it. Artistic dancers, on the contrary, make the audience feel that, so far from their hands being an impediment in the way, they are most useful. Each motion of the hands, while it seems naturally to result from a previous motion of the body, is turned to some advantage. One perceives that they facilitate instead of hindering the general action of the body or the gracefulness of dancing. As in walking nobody praises a walk that is irregular and jerking, so in dancing nobody admires that sort of dancing which is speedy, perfectly *unrhythmical*, and accompanied by violent swinging of the neck and hands.

In common with the artistic mode of dancing the Aratha or Hávabháva[1] (pantomime) is so much connected that we cannot pass it over without saying a few words on the gesticulations. The expressions of emotion by the features and movements of the body which are used in dancing appeal to the eye. In dancing, the expressions of emotion of pain or pleasure, suitable to the poetic words of a song, are exhibited more vividly by movements of the body than by the voice which appeals to the ear. When these two organs are æsthetically touched together in music the feeling thus aroused is entrancing beyond description.

The songs which accompany artistic dancing are simple, and they generally relate to love. The majority of such songs are composed with an object to suit the delicate feelings of the fair sex. It is a common thing in artistic dancing that painful feelings are shown more skilfully than pleasurable ones, because the muscular action in the former is better imitated than that in the latter. A convulsive start of the whole body (not regardless of Tála or time of the general piece of music) is shown by a sudden twinge. The

[1] "The *Bhávas* are therefore divided into *sthâyin* or lasting, and *Vyabhicharin*, transitory or incidental. There are also other divisions * * ".— H. H. Wilson's *Theatres of the Hindus*, Vol. I., pp. xl.-ix.

feeling of an ordinary pain is shown by a knitting of the brows, by a biting of the lips, and by the contraction of the features generally; and that of persistent pain is shown by different attitudes and postures; the body is made to swing to and fro and the hands are clenched. Grief is shown by a wringing of the hands, by sighing and the shedding of tears, and often a pretended action of tearing the hair, clothes and ornaments or adornments is resorted to. A pretended mode of besmearing the body with ashes and of committing suicide by poisons or by some instruments of Asiatic warfare is also adopted. Anger is shown by frowns, by distended nostrils, by compressed lips, and by stamping the ground; it is also expressed by the action of clenching the fingers, by blows of the shoulders and of elbows, and by throwing about clothes and ornaments. Discontent is shown by raised eyebrows and by wrinkled forehead. Disgust is shown by a curl of the lips, and offence is shown by a pout. Joyful feelings are expressed by flourishing the whole body, by brightening the eyes and by a gentle or graceful smile.[1] Each word of a song is interpreted into its proper action regulated by the general time (Tála) of the song. In fact, this sort of performance is an artistic

[1] Sir C. Bell says:—"In all the exhilarating emotions, the eyebrows, eyelids, the nostrils, and the angles of the mouth are raised. In the depressing passions it is the reverse. Under the influence of the latter the brow is heavy, the eyelids, cheeks, mouth, and the whole body droop, the eyes are dull, the countenance pallid, and the respiration slow. In joy the face expands, in grief it lengthens."—Charles Darwin's *Expression of the Emotions* (1873), p. 213.

acting accompanied with vocal and instrumental music.[1] In short, some of the natural expressions of emotion are so artistically performed in dancing (there are very few dancers of this class), with due regard to decency and to music, that they give to a patient observer much material which a painter or a sculptor may turn to great advantage. Instead of treating the subject of dancing at greater length, suffice it to say that the movements of the limbs or the whole body, which in ordinary use are comparatively irregular, are regulated and advanced in dancing as a means to express emotions or centrally-initiated feelings.

If dancing in itself, like an art, is undignified, so are also rhetoric, poetry and music. Regarded from this point of view one cannot comprehend why the present agitation in Southern India is directed wholesale against dancing.

It is not only in an artistic mode of dancing that the efficacy of certain gesticulations is observed, but even educated men use them, though unconsciously, in their daily life. To show the utility of certain gesticulations we shall draw upon the most thoughtful writing of Herbert Spencer, who is at one with the illustrious Charles Darwin. Herbert Spencer says:—

1 "Such dancers' steps are not so mazy as ours, but are much more interesting as the song, music, and motions of the dance continue to express love hope, jealousy, and other passions, which can all be understood by those who are ignorant of the language of the song."—*India Pictorial, Descriptive and Historical*, p. 238.

"How truly language must be regarded as a hindrance to thought, though the necessary instrument of it, we shall clearly perceive on remembering the comparative force with which simple ideas are communicated by signs. To say 'leave the room,' is less expressive than to point to the door. Placing a finger on the lips is more forcible than whispering 'do not speak.' A beck of the hand is better than 'come here.' No phrase can convey the idea of surprise so vividly as opening the eyes and raising the eyebrows. A shrug of the shoulders would lose much by translation into words."[1]

To add to the above subject it may be said that a nodding of the neck with an indistinct "*ye* or *hn* or *hun*" is more expressive than any words of affirmation and approval. A slight shaking of the neck with an indistinct "*n* or *an* or *un* or *hn*" is more impressive than any words of negation and disapproval. A slight wrinkle of the nose and of the forehead and a little raising of the cheeks and closing of the eyes with an indistinct "*ish* or *hish* (or something expelling out)" is stronger than any amount of words of disgust and disapprobation. In short, there are numerous yet impressive expressions of simple feelings which no form of orthography and of articulate language can attempt to imitate.

Professor Thomas Brown[2] says:—"After the remarks on this advantage received from language, which

[1] *Essays, Scientific, Political and Speculative,* Vol. II., p. 11.

[2] *Lectures on the Philosophy of the Human Mind,* p. 127, Twenty-first Edition.

is unquestionably and beyond all comparison the most inestimable benefit which the sense of hearing affords, it would be improper to omit wholly the mention of the pleasure which we receive from it as a source of musical delight—of that expression of feeling, which itself, almost like verbal discourse, may be said to be a language, since it is the utterance of thought and emotion from heart to heart, but which has a voice as independent of the mere arbitrary forms of speech as the tears of gratitude or the smiles of love that may, indeed, give eloquence to words but require no words to render them eloquent."

Professor W. D. Whitney[1] says :—"In the domain of feeling and persuasion, in all that is intended to impress the personality of the communicator upon the recipient it (Expression) possesses the highest consequence. We say with literal truth that a look, a tone, a gesture, is often more eloquent than elaborate speech. Language is harmed for some uses by its conventionality. Words of sympathy or affection can be repeated parrot-like by one whose heartless tone takes all value from them ; there is no persuasion in a discourse which is given as if from a mere animated speaking-machine. And herein comes clearly to light the true sphere of natural expression ; it indicates feeling and feeling only. From the cry and groan and laugh and smile up to the lightest variations of tone and feature which the skilled elocutionist uses, it is emotional, subjective."

---

[1] *The Life and Growth of Language*, p. 283, Fifth Edition.

The subject of dancing and gesticulations with all their artistic details cannot be treated at length for want of space. But it may be safely pronounced that what expresses feelings by bodily actions and movements to which the human flesh is heir is the manifestation of the waves of nervous influence, which waves are the correlative of feelings, presentative, representative and re-representative.

Instead of treating the law of *reflex action* again, suffice it to note that—from that expression of the features indicative of slight displeasure of a *Savant* at a false deduction upto the roaring of anger of a savage—and from that mechanism of the grief muscle (commonly called) in weeping of a gentle woman upto the heart-rending cries of a sufferer—and from that contraction of the zigomatic muscles in a smile of a civilized man upto the paroxysm of laughter of a rude man—and from that mechanism of the vocal cords in a whisper upto the most complex song of a singer—one finds that mental excitement exhibits itself in bodily activity.

Herbert Spencer[1] says :—"Before proceeding to the synthetic interpretation, it may be well to remark that even in our ordinary experiences, the impossibility of dissociating the psychical states classed as intellectual from those seemingly most unlike psychical states classed as emotional, may be discerned. While we continue to compare such extreme forms of

[1] Herbert Spencer's *Principles of Psychology*, Vol. I., p. 473, Third Edition.

the two as an inference and a fit of anger, we may fancy that they are entirely distinct. But if we examine intermediate modes of consciousness, we shall quickly find some which are both cognitive and emotive." (See pp. 26 and 27.)

In closing this chapter we trust that the broad outlines of Indian music, which are treated of in this and the preceding chapters, cannot be said to have been accidental and to have been progressed when the said music was in its infancy; neither can they be said to have been borrowed (*vide* Chapter V.) by the ancient Hindus from their contemporary nations. Unhappily, that part of Indian music, which is more interesting and instructive from a scientific point of view, has been entirely neglected by latter-day Indians. They give no theory, but confine their sphere of investigation to the narrower limits of calculating Svaras (notes), Tálas (time), Nrittya (dancing), and Hávabháva (gesticulations), and thus degrade music from its higher aspirations to lower pleasures. However, we believe that the evidence, which has been set forth in the preceding pages, though of a small magnitude, is sufficient to warrant the leading proposition (page 7) that Indian music is of higher origin and of nobler development than it is generally supposed to be, and that it is dying out for want of support.

We shall now, in conclusion, turn our attention to the present state of Indian music in the last chapter.

CHAPTER VIII.

THE PRESENT STATE OF INDIAN MUSIC.

It is far from our intention to speak sarcastically of the present Indian singers. It may, nevertheless, be permitted us to remark that they are, as a class, lacking in that artistic training or cultivation which is so essential to the attainment of any degree of proficiency or excellence in the art of singing. This defective training is due, partly to the proverbial unwillingness of Indian musicians to impart their skill unreservedly, and partly to the want of ambition to excel on the part of learners because of the lack of encouragement from the public. No sooner is a voice of some sweetness discovered than it is forced into a hurried drill for a time, the possessor of it is taught to sing a few Chijas, and is straightway thrust before the public with as much trumpeting as his circumstances can permit. The singer, after a short-lived splutter, gradually subsides into a dead level of mediocrity; or supposing him to be possessed of taste and perseverance, continues practising, and by the time he has learnt to sing he outlives much of the sweetness of his voice. In a good many instances, the possession of a sweet voice is regarded by the owner as amply sufficient for his purpose, and he discards all attempt to acquire an artistic management of it. It is really a puzzle that so many of the vocalists should think it not worth their while to cultivate sweetness of the voice as being essentially an adjuvant to good singing. There are now, and will no doubt always remain, a few notable exceptions to the above rule; but with the generality of singers there is not the remotest realization of concordance, and no endeavour is made by them to hide the defects of their voices by a careful and properly directed practice. It is enough that mere accident has given them a sweet voice, and henceforth let indiscriminate praise and patronage do their worst. Smooth and easy singing and graceful and finished phrasing go for nothing, and in their place an amount of shouting, shrieking, violent gesticulations, and comic grimaces are performed. Natural means are always preferable, but the necessary cultivation is of great utility. For Art is after all, as J. S. Mill defines, a part and parcel of Nature.

Other false methods of splitting the ear of the groundlings, have also come into vogue, namely, the introduction of high notes screamed out to the fullest extent of the singer's lungs, and the practice of Tána has reached such a tremendous speed, that it can hardly be followed by an artistic ear. Such a tremendous velocity is evidently a poor makeshift for the want of consonance in Svaras (notes) and in Rágas. It is ridiculous to presume that with such an undue haste in producing the notes, one can to any degree preserve the integrity of the Svaras (notes), the principle of ascent and descent of the Murchhanás, or the distinction of the Rágas. The practised ear is so much accustomed to the principles of Sura (concordance), of Komala-Tivra (half or sharp notes), of Árohaṇa, of Avarohaṇa, of Minḍa, of Ghasiṭa, of Tána, of Murchhaná, of Murki, of Kampa (shaking or *vibrato* tones), and of Tála, that even a slight defect in any of them is at once detected, and the performance is regarded not only as inartistic, but most unmusical. It is manifestly evident that the primary pleasure of hearing includes, not merely the agreeable effects of simple tones, but concord and melodious sequences. These are varied by *time*, *intensity*, *volume*, *emphasis*, etc., and, as such, constitute the groundwork of the musical art.

In addition to the aforesaid defects of high notes and speedy Tánas, there is one which is especially intolerable, namely, the introduction of the most complicated mazes of Tálas. Of what earthly advantage could it be to the singers to give more of their attention to the intricate technicalities of Tála than to the Svaras they alone know?

The Tálas, if normally utilised, add to the charm of musical sounds, but, if introduced by way of intricate technicalities, they are more puzzling than charming. However, such screaming notes, speedy Tánas and chronometric Tálas are unfortunately mistaken for real excellence of the vocal art.

The high notes, swift Tánas and puzzling Tálas of claptrap are wholly undeserving of the attention and support they receive; yet some of the highly praised singers do bring in these sensational means to pander to the liking of the undiscerning and shallow portion of their audience. Stooping to such an unworthy device to obtain applause and patronage from their incompetent hearers, who, unhappily, too often form the modern patrons of Indian music, should be repudiated and eschewed by the singers who are capable of better things, and whose artistic conscience must cry shame at such slidings and presumptuous and fallacious devices. Moreover, those on the topmost rung of the ladder should set a noble example to their brethren below. These abnormally high notes and undue liberties and licences in music are always more or less disagreeable to the practised ear.

In connection with the overstraining of voice of which we have just spoken, the subject of Kharaja (grave or bass sound), perhaps, deserves a little attention. That the Kharaja has gradually been lowered to a pitch, which to singers is almost beyond endurance, is an undeniable fact; and it is within the bounds of possibility that further lowering may yet be made. Lowering of voice to the lowest pitch, when its natural harmonics are hardly appreciable by the ear, is not a vocal charm; but is a kind of voice considerably shorn (though a skilful and difficult thing to do) of the harmonics which alone adorn the voice as an indispensable medium to express our thoughts and feelings in their most complex shades. It is true that the tones, in which feelings express themselves, are not always high, but are also deep in comparison with the register or Svarita.

The tendency to produce a tone of *a very low* pitch is an established and well-understood sign of anger eventually being used consciously as a threat. The low pitch is indicative of disagreeable feelings, such as growling, grumbling, indignation, etc. It is true that disagreeable feelings are also shown in screams and shouts.

When our by-gone artists composed Chijas they knew that they (the Chijas) were within the compass of most voices, and could be rendered without violent efforts; but transpose them either to a higher or a lower pitch, and see how striking is the difference. The result in most cases is neither pleasant to the hearer, nor graceful to the performer, but very often greatly tends to bring splendid natural means to premature decay. Whom are we to blame for such intolerable transpositions of high and low pitches? The former fault must, we think, be laid at the door of instrumentalists. It is a well-known fact that the higher the pitch, the greater the brilliancy of tone produced on most instruments. The latter fault lies with the singers, who, in their eagerness to compete with the instrumentalists, lower the pitch to such a depth that most instruments are incapable of following the voice. It is, however, to be hoped that further steps in the above directions may be stayed and discouraged. One of the best indications in this direction is the adoption of European wind-instrument, *e. g.*, the Harmonium (the only defect in it being that when it gets out of order or tune it cannot soon be attuned except by a professional repairer), to replace the string-instruments which do not give a long current of sound unless produced by a bow, and which, again, is not in unity with, or quality of, the voice. It is absolutely necessary that the accompanying instruments, excepting the drum, should not be only in *unison*, but should be in quality or *timbre.*

To secure the above end, the best possible way is to adopt the "voice" as an accompaniment to some wind-instruments as an adjunct. The accompanying voice should only support and intensify the performing one when it makes a stand. Such an effect is not only capital, but most touching and impressive. It cannot be gainsaid that the wind-instruments, such as the Harmonium, organ, etc., are wanting in Ghasiṭa, but the performing voice can do its Ghasiṭa without any adjunct after a long practice. The present mode of accompaniments is an anomaly, because the singer and his co-adjutant players on instruments seldom produce that complete concert which the word Sátha (accompaniment) implies.

The high and low pitches, the swift Tánas and difficult Tálas have enormously contributed to ruin many a voice and to spoil music. It is most intolerable that musicians, as a class, try to test the appreciative competence of their audience instead of consciously trying to please them. In attempting to astound their audience (who in retaliation frighten the performer with Farmás, *i. e.*, by calling for abstruse and difficult Rágas and Tálas) with intricate technicalities of music, they miserably overlook the pleasurable effect of their art. This stratagem leads to many difficult branches of music, which are more calculated to astonish or amaze than to please. Every attempt to purge music of the above defects should always be encouraged by true lovers of the art.

It may be remarked *en passant* that another cause of the deterioration in the singing of the present day, is the excess of Sátha (chorus or accompaniment), which is simply an unmitigated hindrance. It is perfectly useless for an excellent singer to attempt to make himself heard above the sound of a number of voices, strings, pipes, bells and drums played simultaneously. No human lungs could do such a feat with ease and grace. And yet the experiment of many instruments as accompaniments is being constantly tried. Most singers attach too great an importance to their own band, as if it were an indispensable necessity ; and this seems to absorb their main attention, and good many of them appear to study nothing else.

The majority of singers are accompanied by 2 boys or adjutants, 2 big Tamborás, 2 big fiddles with as many strings and holes as the instrument can bear, and a noisy Pakhavája or Tablábáyá. In some performances the above list is greatly swelled, with the idea of securing so many adjuncts of all possible means of these incoherent and unsympathetic instruments. It should be borne in mind that the audience are always eager to hear the vocalists as well as the instrumentalists. Singers, in making their head-way against so many odds, and so much power brought literally to their aid, look as merely opening their mouths, as if they are singing ; but, honestly speaking, nothing comes out of their mouths, except the pantomimic action, contortion of the features, and above all the most funny and comic expressions of the different phases of anthropomorphous animals, the band effectually drowning whatever vocal effect there might be intended.

Nothing is more pleasurable, elevating and ennobling than to listen to melodies and harmonies produced by trained and sweet voices ; and nothing is gained by submerging them or drowning them, when it can be easily so avoided.

Singers ought to contrive to keep their band in playing with as little din and noise as possible, and to enhance the pleasure of their audience, and thus be appreciated. It is necessary for an artistic performance to have an accompaniment of a few instruments as a support and addition to the voice, but it is also very desirable that the instrumentalists should rest satisfied with their opportunity for displaying their skill without attempting to ruin the voice of their co-operator.

In the human voice, which constitutes the richest and most agreeable and monotone musical instrument, the variety is immense. Then it is self-evident that the organ of voice is a musical instrument by the aid of which we communicate our emotional and intellectual feelings and thoughts in their most intimate and delicate shade —an instrument so flexible and complete that the most perfect musical instrument cannot imitate it in the diversity of shades and qualities, which enable the human voice to reach the heart.[1]

The most that can be said of instrumental music is that it is supplementary. However, in an advanced stage of the musical culture, the instrumental music is specialized, and has its own charms.

Tito Vignoli[2] says:—"Instrumental music, considered in itself, with the symphony as its highest expression, has been declared by a learned writer to be the grandest artistic creation and the ultimate form of art in which the vast cycle of all things human will find its development. * * Yet we must not seek in instrumental

[1] H. Spencer says:—"It is generally agreed that the tones of the human voice are more pleasing (because they are very rich in harmonics) than any others. Grant that music takes its rise from the modulations of the human voice under emotion, and it becomes a natural consequence that the tones of that voice should appeal to our feelings more than any others; and should be considered more beautiful than any others."

[2] Tito Vignoli's *Myth and Science*, pp. 318, 319, Third Edition.

music for that which it cannot afford, such as the ideas contained in words." (See pp. 124, 125.)

Apart from the above consideration, it may be asserted that, on the whole, many of the defects of our modern singing are obviously due to the increased dimensions of the Sátha (accompaniment) and its difficult and fortuitous ways of playing. In this connection we cannot pass over without strongly protesting against the false notion of drummers that their co-operation is indispensable to test the vocalist's or instrumentalist's steadiness (Laya) in Tála (time) by harassing him with the most abstruse technicalities of drumming, as if he had to attend only to Tálas and not to Svaras (notes). A vocalist is a real prodigy when assisted by instrumentalists, but is a helpless victim in the hands of instrumentalists when assailed by them with noise and in time by the drummer. These beatings of drums, clapping of hands, clashing of cymbals, playing of instruments, and these bowing and blowing with might and main by the instrumentalists, lead to shouting, shrieking, screaming and to the roughness of style on the part of singers, to say nothing of the loss of the purity of tone and the spoiling of voices. It would have confounded our bygone celebrities to have their voices drowned in a tremendous noise, which is not uncommonly employed as an accessory to the charm of the voice.

It was observed more than once that, when the late Haddukhá of Gwalior used to sing in his best style and mood, his band (accompaniment), which consisted of two Tamborás (unfretted four-stringed lyre), two Sárangis (fiddles), two boys or assistants (his sons), and a drummer, left off playing, and, when called to attention, confessed that they were so much overpowered with admiration as to be unable to accompany him. No such effects are produced in our days, perhaps, because we are getting more technical than æsthetical! It may also be observed *en passant* that the great singers as a rule always held their band in subordination. They used it only to keep up the tonic S, and never allowed it to follow them when performing the details of a Rága, such as a Ghasiṭa, Gamaka, Murchhanás, Tána, Ṭhá, Duni, etc., referred to in Chapters II., III., IV., and V. They also took care to see that all the instruments were scrupulously concordant. Only those who have heard such master performances can form an idea of the artistic way in which each detail is minutely and artistically attended to.

Haddukhá had held an undisputed sway over his contemporary Khyála-singers, and was credited with having preserved some of the cadences and Khyálas of Tánasena and his successors, though he (Haddukhá) belonged to another family of the great singers of the present century. The cadences of Tánasena and of many others of the by-gone generations were transmitted from generation to generation as a patrimony or heritage to their trustworthy and deserving relatives.

This mode of confining the transmission and diffusion of music in the possession of limited families, and of dealing with it as an article of monopoly, was and is so strictly observed that it was and is very difficult, though not impossible, for other families of musicians and amateurs to learn the real art of music and to compete on terms of equality. This check has told very heavily on the circulation of Indian music, and has not only retarded further progress of the labour and thought of the bygone generations, but has injured the art most vitally.

The artistic musicians usually belonged to a few families, and it was their earnest desire to retain their music and its technicalities to themselves, and to transmit them only orally, generation after generation, in their families. In short, such families were very jealous of their art, and took great pains to keep the art of music in their families as their exclusive property. These and other circumstances, we have more than once noted in this work, have been the real obstacles to consigning the Indian art of music to writing and to its circulation. These circumstances are not unfamiliar to those amateurs who have studied and acquired music as an art even in our days. In spite of so many difficulties the art of music was comparatively considerably attained even at the end of the last century as will be seen from the following personal experience of Sir W. Jones.[1] He says:—"The unexampled felicity of our nation . . . . would enable us to attain a perfect

[1] *Asiatic Researches*, Vol. III., p. 62.

knowledge of Oriental music, which is known and practised in the British dominions not by mercenary performers only, but even by Musalmans and Hindus of eminent rank and learning."

Instead of showing at length the patronage which music received at the hands of some of the Hindu and Mahomedan princes of India of the last two or three centuries, and of giving the names of the various celebrated musicians of those days, we quote the personal observations of so keen and sympathetic a critic as Colonel J. Tod.[1] He says :—" The Maharaja Sheodansing was proficient in musical science, and could discourse most fluently on the whole theory of the *Sangîta*, which comprehends vocal and instrumental harmony . . . . He had attached to his suit the first vocalists of Méwar, and occasionally favoured me by telling them to sing at my house. The chief *cantatrice* had a superb voice, a *contra-alto* of great extent, and bore the familiar appellation of '*catalni*.' Her execution of all the *Bussant* or spring-songs, and the *Megh* or cloud-songs of the monsoon, which are full of melody, was perfect. But as she had a rival in a singer from Oojein, we made a point of having them together, that emulation might excite to excellence. The chieftain of Saloombra, the chief of Suktawats, and others, frequently joined these parties, as well as the Maharaja : for all are partial to the dance and the song. Sadoola,

[1] Tod's *Râjasthan*, Vol. I., pp. 556, 557.

whose execution on the guitar would have secured applause even at the Philharmonic, commanded mute attention when he played a *tan* or symphony, or when, taking any of the simple *tappas* of Oojein as a theme, he wandered through a succession of voluntaries.

"Every chief has his band, vocal and instrumental; but Sindia, some years since, carried away the most celebrated vocalists of Oodipur. The Rajpoots are all partial to music."

Even in our generation Their Highnesses the late Rámsingji, Mahárájá of Jaipur, the late Jivájiráo, Mahárájá of Gwalior, the late Ishvariprasáda Náráyansinh, Mahárájá of Banáras, and the late Kalbéalikhá, Naváb of Rampur, were themselves artists to a great extent, and had a passionate liking for music and musicians. But the time is now changed. There may be very few princes of our day who can execute music, European or Indian, with any credit, or even appreciate it as an art. Most of them fancy that it is only practised by professional or mercenary musicians, notwithstanding the general practice of their predecessors and of the present European Royalties doing it as an art with great credit.

In speaking of the last prodigies of the Hindustani music [page 32] we cannot pass on without mentioning the names of a few of these artists. They are :—

Vajirkhá—Dhamára-singer; Hasukhá, Haddukhá, and Tánraskhá—Khyála-singers; Aliján, Tasduk-Husen, and Devaji—Ṭappá and Tiravaṭa Taráná-singers; Bábu Jotsingji, Kudausing, Jorávarsing, and Násarkhá (alive) —drummers; Gulámali—Saroda-player; Várasalikhá—Bina-player; Sádakalikhá—Rabába-player; Báháder-senkhá—Rabába and Sursingára-player; Imratsen and Rahimsen—Satára-players; and last but not least the late Gausvámi Mahárájá Shri Jivanlálji, an amateur Satára and Biná-player. The Mahárájá was an artist in Joḍa [page 63], in the Bilambapada, and in the Madhya.

The abovenamed artists and a few others were the real artists of our time, and whoever has heard them and knew their real worth, could not but be touched and moved to the very core. These artists are not only dead and gone, but with them many Rágas, cadences, songs, tunes, and Parandas of the Hindu design and Mahomedan cultivation are irretrievably lost, never to reappear in their true form and force.

Language, intellectual or emotional, like organized beings, when once extinct, never reappears. The same language, as has been said by Western philosophers, never has two birth-places. Distinct languages may be crossed or blended together, but the dominant (not always superior in every respect) languages spread widely, and lead to the gradual extinction of other languages. The same may be said with equal truth of the art of Indian music.

The Rágas, which were composed by Haradása (Tánasena's last Ustáda or teacher), Rámadása, Suradása,

Tánasena, Biláskhána, and others, and called after their names, indicate a remarkable degree of the power o musical composition. The Rágas composed by these artists were not new, but consisted of more than one old Rága melodiously combined. It may be observed *en passant* that there has been a general belief among the Indian musicians that, however new and accomplished a composition of the notes may be, it could be classed under the names of some one or more of the old Rágas, singly or combined.

Oh, but where are our Tánasenas, Báhádarsenkhás, and Jivanlálji Mahárájás now? Alas, neither the pathos nor the Joḍas exist! It is true that occasionally some imitations of the great vocalists and instrumentalists are heard, but nothing unusual occurs except a fair execution of a few Rágas and Tálas.

Many vocalists get a name solely for the so-called *musical literature* and *Tála-Prastára* (extension), others are liked for Rágas and Tánas, some are praised for the Gamaka and the Ghasiṭa, a few are valued for the Murki and Giṭakaḍi, and others again are patronized *for vigour and vocal fire-works.* But is there ever heard a mastery of beautiful style combined with a sweet and forcible voice, skill in the management of it, purity of intonations, clearness of phraseology, and, above all, a capability to entrance the feelings of the hearers, the only object of the evolution of music?

It is regrettable to observe that the recitative singing in the Indian Náṭaka (drama) of the present day is getting abnormally degenerated and hybridized. It is true that we may find in them certain mixed airs of the so-called Indian and European music, but they cannot be classed as musical. This class of singing is neither European nor Indian in substance, but a curious medley of the present dramatist's invention. This branch of music seems to be quite misunderstood, because of there being no heart, no earnestness and no intelligence thrown into the practice or performance of legitimate music. It will scarcely be exaggerating the deplorable faults in Ṇáṭaka singing, if we say that it is an exception and not the rule to find actors among them who can, in singing, adjust their voices to the keys of the Harmonium which accompanies their performances, so as to spare the audience from that discordant and incoherent clatter which counts for music. Such actors are anything but musical, and anything but artistic in the delineation of the genuine expression of emotions. And yet such actors are allowed to act at least one half of their parts in mere singing, to the disgust of the true appreciators of music and emotions, and are not only patronized, but succeed in creating quite a fervor by their so-called musical songs among their patrons.

It is moreover to be deplored that the dramatists of the present Indian theatre are ridiculous enough to put forth on the stage a parade of lads in fantastic and dazzling female costumes, meant to represent female parts but exhibiting fortuitous female feelings and charms by violent swingings of the neck and body! These interlopers in music think that, by reciting their poems aloud or *falsetto*, and by a lower or a higher tone at times or alternately, they execute the truly artistic modulations of the voice. Among the present set of actors there may hardly be one in a hundred who has received any regular musical training in the proper sense of the word, or has ever attempted to adjust a Tamborá, the A B C of Indian music, and to sing in accompaniment to it. Yet most of these actors are often made to sing in their acting. Even the hero and heroine are not spared from making such a poor show of the vocal art. However, it must be admitted that some of the present dramatists have made great improvements in certain branches of the Náṭaka. The present Náṭaka is incomparably superior to its immediate predecessor that was in use for the last good many years, and which was an eye-sore and most barbarous for its dresses, dances, and screams.

Many actors sing as if they had been taught to do certain things without understanding the motive for so doing. Any intelligent critic has only to attend a Náṭaka (Drama) to see the above facts fully demonstrated. Will the newly-started and much-made of Gáyan—Samájas (musical academies or clubs) and schools of music of our towns and cities tend to mitigate the evil by convincing such actors that what they perform as singing is no more than a curious jumble of music and poetry? This question must, it is feared, at present at all events, remain unanswered. If the Samájas and schools are unable to improve the Náṭaka-music, which is the more valued and appreciated by the present masses and classes, how are they to be credited with regenerating the art of music which is unalloyed by poetry and stage scenery, and which is not now-a-days a marketable commodity?

It cannot be gainsaid that the present dramatists cannot do without some sort of music, and it is only a question with them as to the form of that music. It must also be admitted that at least twenty-five per cent. of their singing is attempted in the ordinary type of old Indian music. Then, it is inexplicable why they should not soar higher in their musical art as they do in the matter of scenes and dresses. It is a lame excuse of the present dramatists that their audience have neither capacity nor taste for the real art of music. Any one who has closely studied the present state of Indian music from all its sides can venture to say without fear of contradiction, that, if one or two dramatic companies take to improving their music, they can do more for the art of Indian music than all the Samájas combined, constituted as they are at present, because the former have sufficient means and opportunities, while the latter have only an intention or desire. It is an idle dream to expect that the dramatic companies will ever be induced to send their actors to any existing schools of music to learn the art of proper music. It is a matter of fact that the present schools of music are either started by so-called musicians as a means to maintenance, or supervised by musicians who fail to get their footing among the real artists. There are very few artists of music in India, and they are proof against any ordinary inducement to associate themselves with such schools and impart their art. This fact is well-known to those amateurs who have succeeded in learning music as an art, or have heard the *Ustádas* (artists) at their best. These few artists are mostly in the service of different Native States of India as pensioners, and they are kept in the States because their keeping is one of the old institutions in large States, whether the ruling princes have a liking or no for their art.

It is a healthy sign that one or two leading dramatic companies of the present day have retained the services of good Mahomedan musicians to supervise their music and to give it a more artistic form, and that, instead of recruiting their actors from stray boys, they have selected many of their recruits from the Bhavaiyás. These Bhavaiyás are the descendants of the once common professional musicians of old India, although they believe that they are the true descendants of the Gándharvas, of whom mention is often made in ancient Sanskrit literature. By recruiting from the class of the hereditarily professional musicians, the present dramatists may be able to confer a great boon on them. This class of people possesses a good deal of stuff, but for want of opportunities to improve their talent, remains undeveloped and uncultivated.

Apart from the above consideration it must be admitted that the higher class of Hindus of olden times had a better sort of drama, so far as poetry and music were concerned, than the present ones. That the ancient composers of dramas in India were well acquainted with the art, and, perhaps, science, of music, is an admitted fact. Professor H. H. Wilson[1] tells us that the Fourth Act of the Vikram and Urvashi, by the immortal Kálidása, is without a parallel in any of the dramas yet met with. It is almost entirely in Prákrit, and is arranged not only in metrical forms, but according to particular musical rhythm as intended to be sung and performed with proper gesticulations. This fact shows that the ancient Hindus had the dramas of operatic and melo-dramatic characters with the technical music for both.

"The Theatre," as Schlegel says, "is an institution, where many arts are combined to produce a magical effect. In it the most lofty and profound poetry has for its interpreter the most finished action, which is at once eloquence and animated picture. The architecture contributes its splendid decorations, and painting

[1] *Theatres of the Hindus*, Vol. I., p. 239, Third Edition.

its perspective illusions. The aid of music is called in to attune the mind, or to heighten by its strains the emotions which already agitate it. The theatre, in short, where the whole of the social and artistic enlightenments which a nation possesses, the fruit of many centuries of continued exertion, are brought into play within the representation of a few short hours, has an extraordinary charm for every age, sex, and rank, and has ever been the favourite amusement of every cultivated people."

Again, how seldom singers are met with who can sing the ancient and old composers' florid music with clearness and flexibility? And how few, even in the simplest passages of the *Kirtana*[2] (something like the *Oratorio*), are capable of singing with sufficient religious pathos and fervency, to reach the hearts of their hearers, and thus to create in them those agreeable and pleasur-

---

[1] A. W. Schlegel's *Dramatic Art and Literature*, translated by J. B. Black, Esq., p. 41, 1861 Edition.

[2] The *Kirtana* or *Hari-kirtana* is a musical performance, vocal and instrumental, of a sacred character, the theme of which is always a moral. I consists of from four to six men; the principal one—always a Brahmin—is called the Haridása, the others, the drummer, the player on the harmonium (new accompaniment), and the assistants with cymbals, sit and stand behind him. He is the foremost standing figure of his company. His function is first to sing a poem with his band, then to render it into prose, and to make its inculcation as impressive and effective as possible by resorting to the embellishment of *rhetoric*. If he is skilled in vocal music, he entertains, at intervals, his audience with the Sargams, Taránás, Ṭhumaris, and the Dhrupadas. In short, the *Kirtana* is a beautiful combination of *rhetoric*, *rhyme* and *rhythm*. This institution seems to be a graft upon the ancient practice of reciting the *Paurânas* (*vide* pp. 8-34), and also seems to have been much in vogue during and after the rise of the Maráṭhás in India; but like other branches of Indian music it also is on its death-bed.

able sensations (peripherally-initiated feelings) and emotions (centrally-initiated feelings), which are the most coveted and supposed to be the means to reach—total absorption or eternal happiness—the principal ambition and end of all religious beliefs?[1] This want

---

[1] Tito Vignoli (in his *Myth and Science*, pp. 315, 316, Third Edition) says:—"The deep and sonorous music of bells of organs, and other ecclesiastical instruments, the chants which resound through vaulted roofs amid the assembled worshippers, ecclesiastical lights, and the fumes of incense, inspire many Christians with a deep and æsthetic sense of the divine presence; and at such moments their vivid faith joins heaven and earth in the same harmonious emotion. The music, chants, and harmony, combined with other solemn rites, are unconsciously embodied by us, entering into our hearts as they circle round the Church, and they become the mysterious language of celestial powers. We are once more immersed in the world of fancy and of myth, purified, however, by the evolution it has undergone. This exalted state of mind is also experienced by those who listen to profane music, since the harmony and modulation of sound, and the expression given to it by the combination of various instruments, immediately affect the soul of the listener as a whole, without the aid of reflection, and a substantial entity which deliberately fulfils its spontaneous cycle of development is thus created; in a word, the harmonies they hear are unconsciously personified. Anyone who makes a deep and careful analysis of his states of consciousness in these circumstances will admit the truth of this." He also says (p. 314):—"Music, which is always becoming more elaborate, continued to be the highest inspiration, a divine power, an external and harmonious manifestation of celestial beings, of eternal life, and the order of the world. This conception was shadowed forth in the Pythagorean theory of the mythical harmony of the spheres; that school regarded the world as a musical system, an harmonious dance of planets." In the ancient world, as Gaston Vuillier Heinemann tells us, dancing was a priestly exercise, an almost scientific ceremony with movements to correspond with the movements of the heavenly bodies. There are beliefs in India which run thus:—"शाब्दे ब्रह्मणि निष्णातः परं ब्रह्माधिगच्छति—He who is proficient in Shábda-Brahma (Náda, sound or Véda) attains Para-Brahma, and the phenomenon of sound is universal and eternal" (*vide* p. 261). The present state of physical science conclusively proves that sound is *not universal* like gravitation but is confined only to the Earth within the limits of its Atmosphere; that it is conspicuously absent from the antarctic, arctic, and frigid zones; that it is totally absent from a complete vacuum, the moon (our next-door neighbour), and interstellar spaces—due to the absence of

of skill to produce certain notes in a given time, is sadly observable in our days, and yet instances have been known of the astounding effect and influence, which some of the great religious singers of past ages had had over their hearers. It is a historical fact that Ashvaghosha (first century A. C.) was successful in converting a number of orthodox Hindus to Buddhism by means of his tenets in singing. Such instances are many, but we have selected this as a typical one.

In connection with the above subject it may be noted that the devotional singing in our Prárthaná-Samájas is not musical at all. And yet some poems in their prayer-books are intended to be sung in certain Rágas. If an impartial listener compares the devotional singing of the Prárthaná-Samájas and of the Christian churches, he will find that the latter is far grander than the former, because the average educated European knows more of the elements of music than the average educated Indian.

The less we say the better of our modern poets who unnecessarily mar their otherwise good poems by encumbering them with the big-named Rágas and Tálas.

---

elastic bodies and tangible media—the necessary condition of the expenditure of heat or manifestation of sound; and that sound is a transformation or equivalent of heat or molecular motion and in itself is a wave of sonorous vibrations caused by the percussion or friction or by both, of solids, liquids, and gasses against each other or between themselves (see p- 45). Ganot says:—" The presence of a ponderable medium is necessary for the production of sound."—*Physics*, p. 103.

Do they know that there are many difficulties[1] in their way to render their poems in the big-named Rágas and Tálas ?

The mode, in which all poems were circulated and brought to bear upon the public, in former times, deserves our particular attention. They were not read by individuals alone and apart, but sung or recited by

[1] The poets who compose songs in Rágas and Tálas must know, in addition to the principal features of music such as the notes (स्वर) and sequence (ताल), the relative adaptability of the vowels and consonants for an artistic effect ; for high notes singers always prefer the vowels *e* and *i*, and find the *a* and *u* unfit for them. Vowels are, as their name implies, the only real vocal sounds ; it is only in a vowel that a note can be said or sung. The Tána, excepting the Bola-Tána, wholly depends upon the vowels.

The Bola-Tána, as its name implies, is a Taná in which the words of a song are not suspended but varied in स्वर (notes) and ताल (sequence) ; while in a Tána they are abandoned, and in their stead pure vowels are used. The variations of a Tála, such as Ṭhá, Duni, Áḍa, Kuáḍa, etc., seem to be the principal aim in a Bola-Tána.

Doctor G. P. Field (*Diseases of the Ear*) says :—" Vowel sounds are rich in overtones, and can therefore be heard at a much longer distance. Hence whispering, in which as the vowel sounds are abated, the consonants are relatively strengthened." Doctor Wolf states that " the broad *a* is heard further than any other vowel, and also that *h* without an added vowel is the weakest of all the consonants." Professor Max Müller says :—" The vowels are produced by the form of the vibrating air. They vary like the timbre of different instruments, and we, in reality, change the instrument on which we speak when we modify the buccal tubes in order to pronounce *a*, *e*, *i*, *o*, and *u*." It is simply presumptuous on the part of a poet to compose the poems of Chijas in Rágas and Tálas without first learning the rudiments of music such as the notes (स्वर), sequence (ताल), and the skeleton notes (सरगम) of Rágas and Jilhás. There is an ancient adage (by Socratés) which runs thus :—" Men cannot know that on which they have neither bestowed consciencious effort, deliberate pains, systematic study in learning." These are the preparatory conditions for a poet to qualify himself to render his poems in the Rágas and Tálas. The poems in song are regulated more by the rules of music than by those of poetry.

trained bards, at festivals, or to assembled companies which were stimulated by community of sympathy and by listening to measured and musical recitals. The training of the bards consisted of hearing and repeating of poetical compositions as well as the practice of exact and elegant pronunciation—which latter accomplishment in languages like the Sanskrit and its later offsprings the Mágadhi and Prákrit, with long words, measured syllables, and great diversity of accentuation between one word and another must have been far more difficult to acquire than it is in any modern language. It will also be seen from our ancient literature that that class of men, who formed the medium of communication between the verse and the ear, were of the highest importance in the ancient world—the bards (Hotars and Adhvaryus, *vide* p. 237) for the epic, the singer (Udgátris, *vide* p. 237) for the lyric, the actors and singers jointly with the dancers (Náṭya, *vide* pp. 45-137) for the drama. The lyric and dramatic (the latter is the last in order of time) poets taught with their own lips the delivery of their compositions. The general effect of poetry greatly depends upon the voice and accompaniment, and pointedly distinguishes from the mere solitary reading of the words. Now, both, dramatic effect and song, are familiar in our times, so that every man knows the difference between reading the words and hearing them under appropriate circumstances.

Strictly speaking, the laws of music, which are being accumulated and systematized by Western philosophers and scientists, and which we have been using throughout our work, were certainly not known in their present forms[1] to our poets of genius and the musicians of olden times, who have left an imperishable mark on their respective arts. They were guided in their arts by feelings,[2] fancy and artistic inspirations.[3]

---

[1] Herbert Spencer, in his *Philosophy of Style*, says:—"Commenting on the seeming incongruity between his father's argumentative powers and his ignorance of formal logic, Tristram Shandy says:—'It was a matter of just wonder with my worthy tutor, and two or three fellows of that learned society, that a man who knew not so much as the names of his tools, should be able to work after that fashion with them.' Sterne's implied conclusion that a knowledge of the principles of reasoning neither makes, nor is essential to a good reasoner, is doubtless true. Thus, too is it with grammar. Doctor Latham, condemning the usual school drill in Lindley Murray, rightly remarks:—'Gross vulgarity is a fault to be prevented; but the proper prevention is to be got from habit—not rules.' Similarly, good composition is far less dependent on acquaintaince with its laws than on practice and natural aptitude. A clear head, a quick imagination and a sensitive ear will go far towards making all rhetorical precepts needless."—*Essays, Scientific, Political, and Speculative*, Vol. II., p. 333, Library Edition.

The above remarks are, with equal force, applicable to music and musicians.

[2] "An unusually emotional nature being thus the general characteristic of musical composers. Intenser feeling produces intenser manifestation, any cause of excitement will call forth from such a nature, tones and changes of voice more marked than those called forth from an ordinary nature."—Herbert Spencer's *Essays, Scientific, Political and Speculative*, Vol. I., p. 227.

[3] "I should not wish these words of mine to raise in the minds of my readers the idea that a science can be or desires to be substituted for art. In art there is one thing that escapes all calculation which science indeed can explain up to a certain point when it has taken a palpable form, but which it can neither predict nor modify: this is the poetic inspiration."—Pietro Blaserna's *Theory of Sound in its relation to Music*, pp. 175, 176.

"High scientific knowledge manifestly transcends the sphere of Art, just as a highly artistic form transcends the sphere of Science."—*The Emotions and the Will*, p. 233, Third Edition. By A. Bain.

As the most profound knowledge of Grammar, Syntax and Prosody is not sufficient to make even a mediocre *poet*, so no complex study of the laws[1] of harmony and instrumentation would be sufficient to create a *musician*.

The three principal kinds of poetry in general are the epic, the lyric and the dramatic.[2] All other subordinate species are either derived from these, or formed of

---

[1] "If we mean by musical sounds those which an artist thinks right to introduce into his work to add to the desired effect, not only must those sounds be closely connected by bonds, which are determined by the pitch, but they must also unite certain particular qualities, the examination of which pertains more to the domain of art than that of science."—N. Lockyer's *Forces of Nature*, p. 185, Third Edition.

Professor Everett (Deschanel's *Natural Philosophy*, p. 898) says:—"It is the musician's business so to combine sounds as to awaken emotions of the peculiar kind which are associated with works of art."

"The artist without considering, and even without knowing, any of the sublime theorems in the philosophy of sound, may attain his end by a happy selection of melodies and accents."—The works of Sir W. Jones in six volumes, p. 414.

History and the living artists of Europe amply confirm the above remarks.

[2] Bharata, in his *Sútras* (Aphorisms) on the diction or the language of a drama, says:—"The poet is to employ choice and harmonious terms, and an elevated and polished style, embellished with the ornaments of *Rhetoric* and *Rhythm*."—H. H. Wilson's *Theatre of the Hindus*, Vol. I., p. i.-xii., Third Edition.

So powerful a body of poetical compositions as those of King Shùdraka, Kálidása, and Bhavabhuti, which have come down to us, has probably never been brought to act upon the emotions of any other people; and when we consider the extraordinary beauty of these immortal compositions (*vide* p. 46) as a separate department of poetry, and give it a dignity and the maximum of elaboration consistently with full poetical effect never since reached, we shall be justified in saying that the tastes and the sentiments of the Hindus of early centuries after Christ must have been much improved and exalted, so far as the dramatic poetry is concerned. This rise and development of dramatic poetry in old India—so abundant, so varied, and so rich in genius—could not have been possible without its corresponding demand and appreciation by the people.

combination from them. The spirit of epic poetry is the calm, quiet representation of an action in progress; the lyric poem is the musical expression of mental emotion by language; the dramatic poetry is a combination of the epic and lyric, to represent events and things as real and present. This description of the three kinds of poetry is a popular one. That these three varieties of poetry were much developed in olden times in India, is also an admitted and well established fact.

Now let us say a few words about the capability of Indian music, of which we have given the principal details in Chapters II., III., IV., and V. It will create a capital effect if some of the Indian airs and tunes of artistic value, which are peculiarly adapted to be played by a number of instruments at a time, are widened, extended, and consigned to the European *notation*, and are heard through their *bands*. The so-called Native airs, which are played by the bands, and which are selected for the musical boxes, are too unmusical to interest the cultivated ear. Some Native princes, no doubt, have their bands taught to play Native airs, and the impression, so far as that goes, is pleasant, but the airs selected are inartistic. If any enterprising artist of high culture and taste were to devote himself, with an object to popularize Indian classical music, to compose new airs and tunes of certain simple and compound Rágas and of certain Dhunns with due regard to Tála, and get them performed by a European band, the result cannot be otherwise than charming. As a matter of fact, all the technicalities of Indian classic music cannot be done adequate justice to by the European instruments as they stand at present. We must, however, admire and frankly admit that the European instruments, as a class, are superior to the Indian instruments in every respect, excepting the individual string-instruments which are specialized to execute the Minḍa or the Ghasiṭa, the Murchhaná and the Murki, which are the real artistic peculiarities and the charming influences of Indian music. At the same time it must be admitted that the European fiddle can do full justice to all the details of vocal music.

No one can gainsay that the civilized nations of the West have advanced their music to such a degree of perfection, according to their standard of taste, that they utilize different melodies and harmonies to be sung or played by different voices or instruments simultaneously and successively, and produce an effect which, to an Indian ear, is too complex to know and judge. But it may be safely stated that the Europeans as nations are really civilized, progressive and considerably free to shake off the old ways which on examination prove to be of no use, and to take to new and better ones. It is, therefore, to be presumed that the effect produced by the singing and playing of so many voices and instruments at a time, might not be unmusical, but might be a necessary consequence of constructive, distributive and collective skill which progress involves. Broadly speaking, the present music of Europe seems to be on the ascending branch of the parabola.

It is absurd to say that every form or system of music is absolutely charming to all humanity, but may be relatively so to those who have imbibed any particular form or system from their infancy, and have been taught individually, socially, and above all hereditarily. Hereditary transmission applies to psychical as well as physical peculiarities. Hence the difference even in the Christian nations of accents and music (p. 79).

Generally speaking, the Italian music is called simple, intelligible, and melodious; and the German music is named studied, obscure and transcendental. In short, every nation has its special marks in national music.

Doctor Seemann,[1] in some interesting remarks on the subject of music, doubts " whether even amongst the nations of Western Europe, intimately connected as they are by close and frequent intercourse, the music of the one is interpreted in the same sense by the others."

In sitting in judgment upon foreign systems of music, the critic, as a rule, anticipates certain kinds of composition and their associated effects, and when he finds, to his

[1] Charles Darwin's *Descent of Man*, p. 570, Second Edition.

disappointment, that the other kinds of composition, which have also their associated effects, are formed in such a manner that his antecedent associations and expectations are not realized, he hastily comes to the conclusion that there is nothing in them to warrant his admiration; and if he casually comes across any similarity, even of the smallest magnitude, between his and foreign compositions, he asserts that a very limited portion of them, at times, gives him pleasure. But if he analyses his conclusion he will certainly find that the compositions, which he likes or dislikes, have no other warrant than his association of music. He totally forgets that it is the compositions, and not the notes in themselves, that differ from each other (*vide* p. 48); and if he be told that even other critics of his own system of music considerably differ in estimating the agreeable or disagreeable effect of the compositions of their own system he admits as an escape, that it is a question of individual liking and training.[1] If the critic is assisted by certain researches which science has ever been increasing in number and definiteness, he maintains certain com-

---

[1] Professor P. Blaserna in his *Theory of Sound in its relation to Music*, pp. 109 and 110, says:—" Strictly speaking, much greater satisfaction is felt when a dissonant chord is resolved into a consonant chord than when nothing but consonant chord has been heard. It is the force of contrast which produces these sensations in us, just as we doubly appreciate a calm after a storm. There can be no absolute rule for the admission of dissonance, and for determining the limit up to which it may be used. All this depends on the degree of musical culture and on habit. Discords which now are perfectly permissible would have appeared monstrosities in the time of Palestrina. It is rigorously true that music, if confined only to consonant chords, and it if does not adopt dissonant chords, would be extremely poor (monotonous)."

positions on the grounds of science as æsthetic[1] and others are abandoned to the average taste of musicians of his country or system.

The way in which an acquired faculty of the parent animal is sometimes distinctly transmitted to the progeny as a heritage, instinct, or innate endowment, is conclusively proved by the European philosophers and scientists. Power, that has been laboriously acquired

---

[1] The illustrious Herbert Spencer, in his finishing remark on *The Principles of Psychology* (Vol. II., pp. 646-648, Third Edition), philosophically says:—"The æsthetic feelings and sentiments are not, as our words and phrases lead us to suppose, feelings and sentiments that essentially differ in origin and nature from the rest. They are nothing else than particular modes of excitement of the faculties, sensational, perceptional, and emotional—faculties which, otherwise excited, produce those other modes of consciousness constituting our ordinary impressions, ideas, and feelings. The same agencies are in action; and the only difference is in the attitude of consciousness towards its resulting states. Throughout the whole range of sensations, perceptions, and emotions which we do not call as æsthetic, the states of consciousness serve simply as aids and stimuli to guidance and action. They are transitory, or if they persist in consciousness some time, they do not monopolize the attention: that which monopolizes the attention is something ulterior to the effecting of which they are instrumental. But in the states of mind we class as æsthetic, the opposite attitude is maintained towards the sensations, perceptions, and emotions. They are no longer links in the chain of states which prompt and guide conduct. Instead of being allowed to disappear with merely passing recognition, they are kept in consciousness and dwelt upon: their natures being such that their continued presence in consciousness is agreeable."

"Perhaps among gratifications of the æsthetic class, that which music yields is that which may be indulged in most largely without evil consequences. Though after a concert, as after a fiction or a play, life in general seems tame; yet there is a less marked reaction, because the feelings excited are more remotely akin to those associated with daily intercourse. Still the pleasures of music are frequently enjoyed to an excess which, if not otherwise injurious, is injurious by the implied occupation of time—by the filling of too large a space in life."—Herbert Spencer's *Principles of Ethics*, Vol. I. (1892), p. 527.

and stored up as statical in one generation, manifestly in such a case, becomes the in-born faculty of the next; and the development takes place of increasing speciality and complexity of adaptation to external nature which is traceable through the animal kingdom; or, in the words of European savants, the law of progress from the general to the special in development, which the appearance of nerve force among natural forces and complexity of the nervous system of man both illustrate, is a law of Nature. Walter Bagehot[1] says:—"The present individual is the inevitable consequence of his antecedents in the past."

From the treatment of the above subject in the way we have done, it is on no account to be understood that we wish to dogmatize that heredity (law of inheritance) is an obstacle in the way of appreciating the various systems of foreign music. What we desire to impress upon the reader is that in judging the merits or demerits of a foreign system of music, one must acquaint himself with all its details and then to test it by the details of his own system. Each and every good canon of a system of music must be recognized, and its defects, if any, must not be allowed to obscure its good features. If this be done with the Indian classical music, we are confident that there will be more Jones, Tods, Max Müllers, Wilsons, Hunters (*vide* p. 269), Days, etc., to appreciate it and to advo-

[1] Walter Bagehot's *Physics and Politics*, p. 8, Seventh Edition.

cate its study and revival than they are now. Such was the case with the Sanskrit language a few decades of years back, but its study and advocacy by eminent European scholars have raised it from its neglected condition to the high level (*vide* pp. 46, 47) which it richly deserves.

In returning to the subject in hand, we must observe that on enquiry it has been found that even Europeans, with all knowledge and notation, are, at times, at a loss to reduce to writing (*vide* pp. 95, 216) the most touching and charming cadences of their great singers. Every art has its own secrets, which are acquired by natural aptitude (personal equation), personal tuition and apprenticeship. These difficulties, as we have more than once stated, stand in the way of many musicians, whose performance does not go, as a rule, beyond tom-tom music, and is confounded with music proper. Tom-tom music is as separate from the Indian classic music as vulgar language is from Sanskrit.

The principal difficulty of our present music is that there is neither a standard work on it nor has it a standard notation. Hence it is a matter of pure accident to come across the real art of Indian music. The absence of a standard work and standard notation may cause the art as practised by one generation to be changed by another ; indeed, it is liable to undergo a change in the same generation. It is true that there are still a few artistic songs, tunes, Parandas, and some teaching from master to pupil, but in the absence of a standard work and notation the art of Indian music may be said to be floating in the air, and each musician, professional or amateur, takes as much as he can or his circumstances allow. Under these circumstances it is not a matter of surprise that accounts[1] given by different musicians of one and the same Rága and Tála vary from each other as do black and white.

Before closing this work we may give below a few popular hints, which, if properly adhered to, will considerably improve the present defects of Indian music.

1st—There should be a sweetness of voice and instruments, and a complete concordance (स्वर) of all the notes to be touched in a piece of music.

2nd—There should be a sympathetic correspondence of the voice and its accompaniments, and the drummer should try to keep up his time (लय) with as delicate a handling as possible and to keep his instrument in tune.

3rd—The number of the notes of a Rága should be scrupulously preserved even in the Miṇḍa or the Ghasiṭa

---

[1] Indian musicians (professional and amateur), as a rule, dispute with each other about the number and the sharp or flat notes of a Rága, and about the number of Mátrás and the strokes or rests of a Tála.

in the Murki, in the Vádi,[1] in the Graha,[2] and Nyása (*vide* p. 99), in the Kampa[3] (shake), in the Tána, or in each and every way of going from a note to a note with due regard to the principle of ascent and descent.

---

[1] "By the word *Vádi* (see pp. 95-97)," says the commentator, "is meant the note, which announces and ascertains the Rága, and which may be considered as the parent and origin of *graha* and *nyása* (see p. 99): this clearly shows, I think, that the *ansa* must be the tonic; and we shall find that the two other notes are generally its third and fifth, or that the mediant and the dominant * * * From the greatness, from the transcendant qualities, of the Hero eager for conquest, other kings march in subordination to him, as other notes are subordinate to the *Ansa*" (see pp. 106, 107).—The works of Sir W. Jones, in six volumes, Vol. I., p. 134.

"The relations existing between the notes (see p. 50) are these:—C, E, G form a major triad, G, B, *d* form a major triad, and F, A, c form a triad (see pp. 71, 72). c, G, F have, for this reason, special names, being called respectively the *tonic*, dominant and subdominant, and three triads the tonic, dominant, and subdominant triads or chords respectively."—*Physics*, by Ganot, translated and edited by E. Atkinson, p. 216, Twelfth Edition, 1886.

[2] "Mirjakhan says, but Sir W. Jones refutes, the Graha is the first note of every mode (Rága) with which every song, that is composed in it, must invariably begin *and end*" (see p. 99).

"Three distinguished sounds in each mode (Rága) are called *graha*, *nyása*, and *ansa*, and the writer of (Sangita) Náráyana (as Sir W. Jones tells us) defines them in the following way:—'The note, called *Graha*, is placed at the beginning, and that named *nyása* at the end of a song (*vide* p. 99): that note, which displays the peculiar melody (Rága), and to which all the others are subordinate, that, which is always of the greatest use is like a sovereign though a mere *ansa* (see pp. 106, 107) or portion.'" The works of Sir W. Jones in six volumes, Vol. I., p. 433.

[3] स्वरस्य कंपो गमकः स तु पंचदशाविधिः ।

Whatever might have been the practical meaning of the word "Gamaka" in the pre-Mohomedan period, it now practically means a Tána (*vide* p. 69) in which all the notes are joined only by the process of Ghasiṭa or Minḍa or both (*vide* p. 203) and never by the means of simple jumping and trilling of the notes. In this process (Gamaka) it is very difficult to touch the notes in a Rága in their ascending or descending order from one octave to the other.

4th—The Murchhanás'[1] should be touched by a Minḍa

[1] क्रमात्स्वराणां सप्तानामारोहश्चावरोहणं=the regular rising and falling of the seven sounds is मूर्च्छन.

मूर्छयन्ति स्वरान् यत्र तत्र जायेत्सुमूर्छना।
तस्मात्स्वरत्रैरात्रमा मूर्छनास्त्वेकविंशतिः ॥

In the above verses the action or process of the word Murchhaná is given. The word Murchhaná, " मुर्छा कौटिल्ये in its musical sense, means a sudden pull, twitch, thrust or a twist. If this be the real meaning of the word, which is quite in accord with the present practice, the view taken of it throughout in this work is fully supported. The real difficulty lies in explaining its number which is stated as twenty-one, and not twelve as is maintained in this work. If one admits the number twenty-one as the number of Murchhanás, he virtually transforms it into a note of the Diatonic scale, and, therefore, cannot, with any process of mathematical calculations, make three *equal* parts or divisions of the five tones and the two semitones of the Diatonic scale (*vide* p. 52), although they are generally called seven sounds or स्वरा. From the interval between each note of the scale (*vide* p. 50) it will be seen that these intervals are not equal. The greatest, although unequal, are called major seconds or tones, and the smallest minor seconds or semitones (*vide* p. 52). Although the major seconds are not equal, it is agreed to place them under the same denomination. These seven notes are also called Avikrit (unchanged or natural) as distinguishable from the twelve Vikrit (changed or tempered, p. 78) notes of the chromatic scale (*vide* p. 53). The words Avikrit and Vikrit, indeed, do not mean or imply the Murchhaná. Murchhaná means a particular part of a note produced in a particular way. Again, if the Murchhaná means nothing but a note with another name of the Diatonic scale, then there must be only seven notes per scale or Gráma or twenty-one notes in three scales or Grámas (*vide* p. 97) सप्त स्वरास्त्रयो ग्रामा मूर्छनाश्चैकविंशतिः ॥. Practically this is not the case. There is another verse which also shows the action or process of the Murchhaná as extending or contracting a sound and gives its number as fourteen only :—स्वराणां कुंचनं चैव अविकुंचनमेव च। मूर्छना च समाख्याता सा चतुर्दश संख्यका ॥ Murchhaná means a quarter tone and is produced only by the Ghasiṭa (longitudinal combination of notes) or Minḍa (transversal combination of notes) (*vide* p. 99), and its number must be twelve only (*vide* p. 101).

The Mahomedan, and even some of the Hindu, artists, who lay no special claims to the literary aspect of music, simply enumerate three kinds of notes, *viz.*:—Shuddha or Purá (tone), Komala or Tivra or Áddhá (semitone), and Atikomal or Tivra-tara or Ausat-Darjá (quarter tone).

In treating of the Indian technicalities of music one must always try to avoid the wrong side of the original features of the ancient words and the

or a Ghasiṭa along with the notes on which they depend, and never separately, and there should be no stand made on them.

5th—There should be moderation in pitch, in the Minḍa or Ghasiṭa, in the Murki, in the Tána, and in the Tála, and the activities, often wasted away on bodily actions and movements (*vide* p. 301), should be concentrated in the voice and instruments.

In concluding this work, it may be said once more, that at a very early period of History, Indian music had developed into a regular science, rich and perfect in composition, combining in a high degree the requisite virtues of melody and symphony.[1] It is not the

wrong side of the ancient works to see what proper bearing they have on the practical side of the art, and to separate the unscientific from the scientific, despite the general reverence for old writings which are received almost as divinely inspired (*vide* p. 2), and passing unexamined from generation to generation, accepted with unsuspecting faith, and consecrated by intense sentiment. Some of the trained and educated natives instead of freely admitting the mythical and defective portion of their arts and sciences and of getting it corrected by Western researches into those arts and sciences, subject it to such alteration as might make it look more like a plausible matter of fact or cast it into historical statement with more or less of transformation as the case may require. Such writers, who always assume that there is a basis of truth which may be discovered by removing poetical exaggeration, lay down that to give pure fiction or to commit any mistake without any foundation of fact is, in their opinion, utterly unworthy of so great a nation as the ancient Hindus who were the most civilized among their contemporary nations.

If we were to deal with each and every detail of Indian music in its entirety, this work would swell far beyond the limits assigned to it. The aim of this work is to deal with the less popular but more important details of the art of Indian music.

[1] "Symphony is the highest differentiation (*vide* pp. 300, 301) of musical art. In it music had wholly discarded its relationship with words, and attained its highest independence (see Joḍa). Hence the symphony is the most musical of all that music can produce. To disown it is to disown that music is a special, differentiated art."—*Degeneration*, p. 203, 1895, by Max Nordau.

province of this small treatise to trace historically the causes which not only stopped all further progress and development of music but made the country practically unconscious of the existence of such treasure. It may be that the chronic perturbed state of the country, the subject of wave after wave of foreign invasion and the internecine warfare helped, among other things, to bring about the present neglect and degeneration of music as a science and art, in which is to be discovered the synthesis of one of the grandest evolutions of human feelings,[1] an evolution that in itself forms one of the most brilliant pages in the history of human culture. There

---

1 "A final remark worth making is, that the æsthetic activities in general may be expected to play an increasing part in human life as evolution advances. Greater economization of energy, resulting from superiority of organization, will have in the future effects like those it has had in the past. The order of activities to which the æsthetics belong, has been already initiated by this economization, and will hereafter be extended by it: the economization being achieved both directly through the improvement of all appliances, mechanical, social, and other. A growing surplus of energy will bring a growing proportion of the æsthetic activities and gratifications, and while the forms of art will be such as yield pleasurable exercise to the simpler faculties, they will in a greater degree than now appeal to the higher emotions."—*Principles of Psychology*, Vol. II., pp. 646-648, Third Edition, by Herbert Spencer.

"A man may be a good economical unit of society, while remaining otherwise an almost worthless unit. If he has no knowledge of the arts no æsthetic feelings, no interest in fiction, the drama, poetry, or music—if he cannot join in any of those amusements which daily and at longer intervals fill leisure spaces in life—if he is thus one to whom others cannot readily give pleasure, at the same time that he can give no pleasure to others; he becomes in great measure a dead unit, and unless he has some special value might better be out of the way (see p. 280, note 2nd). Thus he may add his share to the general happiness, each should cultivate in due measure those superfluous activities which primarily yield self-happiness."—Herbert Spencer's *Principles of Ethics*, Vol. I., 1892, p. 530.

can hardly be said to exist any national taste for music as such in India. Every civilized nation (past and present) believes that in its bearing upon human happiness, the emotional language which musical culture develops and refines, is second to none, and that music has an effect beyond the immediate pleasure it produces, because every class of rational enjoyment does not end with itself but ministers to bodily and mental well-being. This lofty and ennobling source of happiness—or as Professor A. Bain puts it:—"We wonder how life could ever have been passed without it" (*vide* p. 29)—is entirely absent in India. The practice and execution of the art in its purity and exquisite perfection is rarely to be met with: and such as it is, it is confined to a class of people who have no high status and position in society: indeed, the practice of the art is thought socially to degrade an individual from his otherwise high status. There is no standard work on Indian music in any of the spoken languages of the present age, no academy or school is regularly constituted, no competent masters to teach music unreservedly, no examinations held by any professor of music, and in fact no knowledge of the art whatever. Those who profess to be the modern authors and critics on Indian music in most cases have themselves hardly anything beyond a flippant and common-place knowledge of the rudiments of music. Those who profess to have the good of the country at heart, hardly appear to recognize the claims of this art and accomplishment to be cultivated as a means for securing the happiness of the masses.

Had there been a few authoritative and well constituted academies of Indian music the immediate result would have been the creation of standard works and notation and of such a respect for music and musicians as this country has not seen since the last good many centuries; that there would have been an attention paid to music far surpassing the attention now paid by the general run; that there would have been fewer extravagances to run after the present Náṭaka (*vide* p. 308) and Tamáshá music; that music would have been at once raised to higher level; that the good old canons of music would have been revived and established and the tom-tom stuff, which now too often passes for Indian classic music would have become impossible. Indians are now at that stage of education at which they should learn and be taught why music must be honoured; why the music of a country is its choicest possession, how, at any period it reflects the standard of emotional culture of that period. To raise the ideals of a country, to make the people understand the real worth of music, to introduce it as such in Indian homes, to raise the happiness of mankind, and to alleviate the toil and cares of life from which even princes are not exempt—this is the true function of academies[1]

[1] In a few places an attempt has been made in this direction by the establishment of what are called "Gáyana-Samájas," but either from want of earnestness or funds or proper patronage these have not yet been able (*vide* pp. 309, 310) at all to advance the original aim with which they were started and credited.

of music. There is, as is said before, a noted prejudice that musicians are a helpless and contemptible people. Musicians themselves have been somewhat ashamed of their calling; they are ignorant of the fact that by resolutely acting together and trying every means in their power to popularize and disseminate their music, and to set at naught the present bogus writings and criticisms on it, they could raise their profession into the most honourable, and the most independent of any, as it is in the most civilized nations of Western Europe. Such a state of music and musicians, which, at present, is neither more nor less than an idle and sickly dream of an enthusiast (*vide* p. 28), can only be attained when its teachers are the men of the most distinguished abilities and training; this is possible only when Government and the Native States patronize and encourage it by introducing it in the curriculum of schools and colleges (*vide* pp. 29, 30, 150), or by devising special and separate arrangements and means for it. Unless this is done Indian classic music will never be encouraged and revived as we have stated before (*vide* pp. 29, 30).

Indian music, practical, theoretical, and historical, with most of its details—as marked out in the preface—has been brought down in the preceding pages (though not in an exhaustive and a connected form) from the Sáma-Véda (*vide* p. 5), as a musical declamation, to the highest development of it as Rágas and Jilhás. This development is neither mixed nor influenced by any foreign system of music. It is a pure and genuine growth of indigenous musical labour of ancient India, and is one of the noblest amongst the few varieties of musical system of the civilized world. It possesses within itself a pervading melody, and in its intrinsic merits can bear comparison with any other system. It also contains a varied mine of musical materials, though scarcely at all known and explored (*vide* pp. 47, 48). The Sáma-Véda (*vide* p. 236) and the Rágas[1] and Jilhás with all their artistic

---

[1] In the present musical systems of Europe there seem to be no fixed melodies like the Indian Rágas. In European music there seem to be no two songs or tunes (instrumental music) of different arrangements, but of the *same* melody in its strict sense. In it each and every composition has its own melody or harmony, and is known by its own individual name; there is nothing like generic names for melodies and harmonies, as there are in the Indian system of music. In the Greek system of music there seem to have been fixed melodies like the Indian Rágas, and they were called musical *nomes*. "Every nome was the general scheme or basis of which the airs actually performed constituted so many variations, within certain defined limits. The nomes were not many in number; they went by special names."—George Grote's *History of Greece*, Vol. III., p. 301, New Edition.

The author's object in giving this note is not to find fault with the present musical systems of Europe, which are the real wonders of the present century, but to show an anology between the Greek and Hindu systems.

A distinguished and valued friend of the author, a Pársi educationist of eminence in Káthiáwád, has kindly supplied him with the following note and the Latin hymn (*vide* p. 50) with its translation :—"In the European system of Music the approximate equivalent for a Rága is a *Mode*. One can safely say that there are at present two Modes generally adopted—the Doh-mode and the Lah-mode as the Tonic Sol-fa-ists call them. The tunes are Melodies in accordance with certain rules containing what are called 'accidentals' which are sharps and flats of some notes admitted in order to produce certain 'Mental Effects' into the body of a Tune. It may be here observed that the mental effects of the notes as well as of the accidentals in a tune are known, studied and analysed by experts only in vocal and instrumental music. Harmony in the strict sense of the term in Europe is *a pleasing combination of notes*—not

details are the two extremes of the musical activities in India—the activities extending over a very long period of history and tradition. From all that can be gathered it seems probable that the real declining period of Indian music, written, as well as practised (*vide* pp. 226, 227), is co-eval with the ascendancy of the Mahomedans in India; although some of them[1] have patronized and encouraged it as an oral art to the best of their means (*vide* p. 30), and also have left their

---

simply octaves higher or lower—but of *different* notes that all together, *simultaneously*, contribute to the strengthening or sweetening of the original Melody. It must in all fairness be acknowledged that in this science of Harmony the Occidentals have far surpassed the Orientals. On the other hand in Melody which is defined as 'a sweet succession of musical sounds or notes,' the Hindus have in their turn excelled the Europeans by their elaborate rules, of Rágas and Ráginis with their minute Shrutis, Alápas, Mindhas, etc., etc., to heighten or modify the 'Mental Effect' or excite the emotions, pleasurable or otherwise, all which combine to constitute the charm and distinguishing characteristics of their Melodies." From the *Encyclopædia*, article "Guido of Arezzo" (*vide* p. 267). "The six lines from a hymn addressed to St. John the Baptist are :—

Ut queant laxis resonare fibris,
Mira gestorum famuli tuorum,
Solve polluti labii reatum,
Sancte Joannes.

Freely translated, these lines mean :—"In order that the servants (सेवक) be enabled to sing to the free strings (of the musical instruments) thy miraculous deeds, oh thou Sacred John, remove the sins of their polluted lips."

[1] "There is abundant evidence to prove that Akbar was not only fond of music, but was very musical himself * * * The same authority (Abulfazl) states 'his Majesty had such a knowledge of the science of music as trained musicians did not possess' (see p. 8). Every day the court was treated to an abundance of music (see p. 268), the sounds of which have in all times been especially agreeable to Eastern monarchs. Babar, the grand-father of Akbar was fond of music, and was no mean poet."—*Rulers of India, Akbar*, pp. 47, 179, 180, by Colonel G. B. Malleson.

imperishable marks[1] (*vide* Preface) on its features (*vide* p. 31). Its arrested growth, and also the decay of productive genius in it, date from the decline and fall of the Mahomedan Empire. The times between the downfall of the Mahomedans and the supremacy of the English in India seem to have played havoc on the remaining vitality of Indian music which was already crippled if not quenched by the Mahomedans in the beginning of their conquest and authority (*vide* pp. 30, 31).

The present state of Indian music, from all its aspects, indicates but too clearly that, as an art or as a science, it no longer exists in a complete form. Some portion of it, as an oral art, which is also dying out for want of

[1] The Khyála and Ṭappá (*vide* pp. 67, 68) seem to be of later origin and development, because they, or their artistic equivalents, are not mentioned in any of the Sanskrit works on music. In the Khyála and Ṭappá, the Murki or Jamjamá is extensively used; while it is not touched at all in the Alápa or Joḍa, Dhrupada, Taráná and the Sargam (*vide* p. 68). It cannot be satisfactorily ascertained whether the Murki or Jamjamá (*vide* pp. 65-67) belongs to the Mahomedan invention or it was only in practice and not incorporated into the written works on music, much before the Mahomedan advent in India, but it is a fact that it is neither mentioned nor defined in the Sanskrit works. By this declaration it is not intended to prove that each and every detail of the practical art of music was reduced to writing and incorporated into the manuscripts at a time when writing was comparatively not so popular as it is now. It is an established fact of the history of each and every progressive art that the stock of written knowledge concerning it, is always less than that of the practical experience. From all the sources of information concerning the Murki it seems probable that the highest development of it which has its own charms when executed by a *soprano* (*vide* p. 65), belongs to the Mahomedan period and encouragement, if it is not their own invention. The same may be safely asserted about that branch of the instrumental music which goes by the name of Gatis (*vide* p. 152) as distinguished from the Alápa or Joḍa (*vide* pp. 63, 64). Each detail of Indian art of music in itself forms a subject for a separate chapter, but the scope of this work compels us to be as brief and short as possible.

popularity (*vide* p. 28) and support (*vide* pp. 7-291) is, no doubt, preserved and practised by a very few musicians (*vide* p. 2) that are dispersed in, and supported by, a few Native States.

Had it not been for the patronage given by some good and enlightened native princes by attaching to their Darbars the few good artists there were and are, Indian music would by this time have been perhaps completely extinct. These, however, are preserved and exhibited more as Indian curiosities than as the exponents of an art in which there are ennobling materials of Aryan feeling or emotion in a far earlier stage of growth and development than any which survive beyond the borders of India, and which, in its later stage of growth and development, had been drawn upon by the Greeks, the Persians, the Arabians and through the last the present Europeans, if we are to believe the Historian Strabo[1] (*vide* p. 271), the Historian and the Poet Firdosi (*vide* p. 267), and Sir William Wilson Hunter (*vide* p. 267).

This art (music) appeals to the hearts of people at large, and is also recognized as having humanising and elevating influence[2] on the minds of the human

---

1 Mountstuart Elphinstone (*History of India*, 1874, p. 254) says :—"Strabo was the most critical and judicious of all the writers on India."

2 "This art (music) borrowing no part of its material from the experience of our senses, not attempting to describe, and only exceptionally to imitate the outer world, necessarily withdraws from scientific consideration the chief points of attacks which other arts present, and hence seems to be as incomprehensible and wonderful as it is certainly powerful in its effects."—*Popular Lectures on Scientific Subjects*, by Hermann, von Helmholtz, translated by E. Atkinson, pp. 53, 54, Vol. II., First Series, 1893.

race as a whole—a whole consisting of in its lowest scale the most horrible savages of the forest and esquimaux, and in its highest scale the most thoughtful philosophers of the civilized world.

An elegant writer, in the Orchestral Association Gazette, says:—"The South Sea Islander still bangs his tom-tom and shrieks discordantly to express his grief or joy. To him the divinest Sonata of Beethoven is doubtless like a delirium—or does him strike only as noise. But both are music, and one is an evolution of the other." *** Music has never been without its influence on men and things, and has been one of the greatest known powers for civilisation."

Music (as is said by Western philosophers like Professor Max-Müller and others), in an extended sense of the word, is not a new invention of whimsical men. It is older than any human institutions, including language and religion. As soon as we know anything of the thoughts and feelings of man, we find him in *possession of music* or *rather possessed by music*. The oldest literary documents are almost everywhere poetical. Even if we go beyond the age of literature, if we explore the deepest levels of human thought and feeling we can discover, in the crude ore which was made to supply the earliest materials to express external feelings[1]

[1] Herbert Spencer teaches us that what we call feelings, sensational, perceptional, and emotional, are the concomitant nervous changes or the waves of nervous influence in virtue of the general law of nervo-motor action; every feet.

of internal impressions, the presence of musical ingredients. We also find in the higher orders of animals the inborn tendency, which we have inherited from them, and which is becoming more and more complex as we progress from simple enjoyments of life to complex enjoyments, of enjoying life[1] by adapting to ever-

ing has for its primary concomitant a diffused nervous discharge, which excites the muscles at large, including those of the vocal organs, in a degree proportionate to the strength of feeling, and therefore muscular activity increasing in amount—be the nature of feeling what it may. Deep down in the nervo-muscular structures, as they have been evolved by converse between the organism and its environment, are to be found the cause of all these manifestations; and that in the nature of things there have grown up these connexions between internal feelings and external manifestations. The production of sound by animals, is a necessary manifestation of the nervous and muscular force generated and expended by the impressions and expressions which constitute life. The intensity of sound demonstrates the strength of feelings involved, and the change and duration of sound indicate the variety of sentiments and passions aroused.

1 Herbert Spencer tells us that pleasures and pains are the incentives and restrictions by which life is prolonged and multiplied. No contemptuous title of pig-philosophy or the ascetic doctrines which strike at the root of human happiness (H. T. Bukle, *His. of Cir. in Eng.* Vol. III., p. 252) will alter the eternal truth that misery is the high way to death, while happiness is added life and the giver of life. It is an established induction of, and deduction from, the hypothesis of Evolution that pains are the correlatives of actions injurious to the organism, while pleasures are the correlatives of actions conducive to its welfare. "Chárvákas, the followers of the tenets of Brihaspati, an Indian philosopher, hold that nothing exists but the four elements, a kind of protoplasm, from which, when changed by evolution into organic body, intelligence is produced, just as the inebriating power is developed from the mixing of certain ingredients. The self is only the body qualified by intelligence, there being no evidence for a self without a body. The only means of knowledge is perception, the only object of man is the enjoyment."—*The Origin and Growth of Religion*, p. 140, Second Ed., Max Müller.

As regards perception Doctor J. W. Draper (*Conflict between Religion and Science*, p. 132) says:—"Two fundamental ideas are essentially attached to all our perceptions of external things: they are Space and Time, and for these provision is made in the nervous mechanism, while it is yet in almost rudimentary state. The eye is the organ of space, the ear of time, the perception of which by the elaborate mechanism of these two structures becomes infinitely more precise than would be possible if the sense of touch alone were resorted to."

increasing and varying conditions of the inconceivable mystery of the phenomena of life. This mystery forms the subject-matter of every school of philosophy, spiritual and materialistic.

The great Buddha-Gautama, the noblest religious reformer the world has ever seen (who lived six hundred years before Christ), says:—"Life is like the spark produced by the friction of wood. It is lighted and is extinguished—we know not whence it came or whither it goes. It is like the sound of a lyre (see pp. 231, 232-243), and the wise man asks in vain from whence it came and whither it goes."[1]

Herbert Spencer, the foremost thinker of the present century, philosophically concludes that all knowledge is relative and limited "and all that we know is only known as—won from the void and formless infinite."[2]

---

[1] *Chips from a German Workshop*, Vol. I., p. 217, Max Müller.

[2] *First Principles*, p. 75, Fifth Edition.

END.

INDEX.

The Oriental words are given in Italics.

A

A

B

C

E

F

H

I

Q

R

S

PAGE

T